ORIGINS AND THE ENLIGHTENMENT

ORIGINS AND THE ENLIGHTENMENT

Aesthetic Epistemology from Descartes to Kant

CATHERINE LABIO

CORNELL UNIVERSITY PRESS

ITHACA AND LONDON

This book has been published with the assistance of the Frederick W. Hilles
Publication Fund of Yale University.

First published 2004 by Cornell University Press

Printed in the United States of America

Library of Congress Cataloging-in-Publication Data

Labio, Catherine.
   Origins and the Enlightenment : aesthetic epistemology from Descartes to Kant /
Catherine Labio.
      p. cm.
   Includes bibliographical references (p.   ) and index.
   ISBN 0-8014-4275-3 (cloth : alk. paper)
   1. Aesthetics, Modern—18th century. 2. Origin (Philosophy)—History—18th
century. 3. Knowledge, Theory of—History—18th century. 4. Originality
(Aesthetics)—History—18th century. I. Title.
   BH181.L33   2004
   111'.85—DC22   2004007165

Cornell University Press strives to use environmentally responsible suppliers and materials to the fullest extent possible in the publishing of its books. Such materials include
vegetable-based, low-VOC inks and acid-free papers that are recycled, totally chlorine-
free, or partly composed of nonwood fibers. For further information, visit our website
at www.cornellpress.cornell.edu.

Cloth printing   10 9 8 7 6 5 4 3 2

For Yin Chin Tong

On ne sçauroit si bien conceuoir vne chose, & la rendre siene, lorsqu'on l'apprent de quelque autre, que lorsqu'on l'inuente soy mesme.

One cannot conceive something so well, and make it one's own, when one learns it from someone else as when one invents it oneself.

René Descartes, *Discours de la méthode*

Questo mondo civile egli certamente è stato fatto dagli uomini, onde se ne possono, perché se ne debbono, ritruovare i principi dentro le modificazioni della nostra medesima mente umana.

The world of civil society has certainly been made by men, and . . . its principles are therefore to be found within the modifications of our own human mind.

Giambattista Vico, *La Scienza Nuova*

Nur soviel sieht man vollständig ein, als man nach Begriffen selbst machen and zustande bringen kann.

We have complete insight only into what we can ourselves make and accomplish according to concepts.

Immanuel Kant, *Kritik der Urteilskraft*

CONTENTS

ACKNOWLEDGMENTS

This book has many origins and, along with them, many debts, which I am happy to have an opportunity to put on record here, even if that record is inevitably incomplete. Friends, family members, and colleagues in both the United States and Europe have given me much needed advice and support over a long period of time. I am thinking, in particular, of Agnès Bolton, Christos Cabolis, Marjorie Coeyman, Elizabeth Dillon, Raphael Falco, Cécile and Thomas Ferenczi, Mary Floyd-Wilson, Ann Gaylin, Maria Georgopoulou, Sondra and Gary Haller, Amy Hungerford, Nathalia King, Françoise Labio, Pericles Lewis, Juliette Loncour, Giuseppe Mazzotta, Marianne Mead, Chantal Snellings, Lisa Steinman, and Scott Wilcox.

I began thinking about questions of Enlightenment and origins while I was a Fulbright scholar and a graduate student at New York University, where I was fortunate enough to benefit from the insights of John Chioles, Pellegrino D'Acierno, Daniel Javitch, Perry Meisel, Philippe Roger, and Barbara Vinken. I completed this project during my tenure as a Morse Fellow at Yale University. I thank Edwin M. Duval, Michael Holquist, Christopher L. Miller, David Quint, and the members of the committee chaired by Richard H. Brodhead for giving me this crucial opportunity. I also thank Sandra Rudnick Luft and Tracy B. Strong, who read the manuscript for Cornell University Press, for their insightful and generous comments, and I express my gratitude to Bernhard Kendler for having taken an interest in my manuscript and having shepherded its publication. Many thanks are also due to Karen Hwa for her excellent work as manuscript editor, Jane Marie Todd for her helpful copy-editing, and Susan Barnett for her diligent marketing. I also wish to thank an anonymous reader who read a much earlier version of this manuscript. Finally and most importantly, I am indebted more than I can say to Timothy J. Reiss, who has supported and encouraged me at every turn and whose own work and commitment to it are a constant source of inspiration.

I presented a version of the Descartes chapter in the Open Forum Lecture Series organized by the Department of Comparative Literature at Yale University. I am grateful to Patricio Boyer for his invitation and to the participants for their wide-ranging comments.

Parts of the fourth and fifth chapters have appeared in "The Aesthetics of Adam Smith's Labor Theory of Value," *Eighteenth Century: Theory and Interpretation* 38, no. 2 (1997): 134–49. I gratefully acknowledge permission to reprint.

Translations are mine unless otherwise noted.

ORIGINS AND THE ENLIGHTENMENT

Introduction

We search for origins the way some cats chase their tails. After brief bursts of frenetic spinning, we think we have a grasp of our topic, but our hold is elusive. The Freudian primal scene, the big bang theory, and the discoveries of "Lucy" and the so-called First Family are cases in point. So are some of the most influential inquiries of the late twentieth century into the origins of its episteme, Hans-Georg Gadamer's *Truth and Method,* Jacques Derrida's *Grammatology,* and Michel Foucault's *Order of Things,* all of which focus, quite fittingly, on the eighteenth century, the period arguably more obsessed than any other with the notion of origins—of ideas, languages, nations, wealth, the universe, and so on.

The list does indeed go on, but I am not as interested in these individual topics as in the epistemological foundations that made eighteenth-century inquiries into origins possible and in the ways that these foundations are both similar to and different from our own. Origins are epistemologically porous, and their treatment tells us much about shifting assumptions regarding what can and cannot be known and how.

In 1989 Victor Brombert, in his presidential address to the Modern Language Association, noted in passing that contemporary literary criticism was marked by a "blurring of the notion of origins."[1] I take exception to any suggestion that genetic epistemology, or the

---

[1] Victor Brombert, "Mediating the Work: Or, The Legitimate Aims of Criticism," *PMLA* 105 (1990): 393.

privileging of origins as primary sources or modalities of knowledge, has ever been a straightforward affair or that origins have ever consisted of clear and distinct ideas. And yet the twentieth-century fascination with origins has often seemed to confine itself to a fairly narrow linear-historicist model in which origins can be defined only as beginnings or moments in time about which nothing will be truly known until an answer has been found to the problem of infinite regress. At the end of the day this is quite possibly the single most intractable challenge posed by both psychoanalysis and postmodernism, whose answers have clustered around the key notions of *Nachträglichkeit* (deferred action, *après-coup*) and difference. Indeed, for all their sophistication—or blurring—these concepts rest on a somewhat monochromatic view of origins and reveal (somewhat paradoxically since this is precisely what they are trying to overcome) an almost fetishistic clinging to the idea that there is such a thing as "the" (singular) origin, believed, implicitly or explicitly, to be the epistemological equivalent of the proverbial smoking gun. Hence the search for a time when origins were clear and accessible.

Needless to say, the eighteenth century was not such a time. The Enlightenment is nonetheless a good place to start, not only because of its compulsive attention to origins but also because its epistemological breadth can make our own period appear epistemologically challenged by comparison. Whereas the "blurring of the notion of origins" Brombert rightly identified as a key indicator of twentieth-century criticism betrayed a desire to topple a monolithic episteme, or at least one perceived as such, eighteenth-century inquiries into origins remind us instead that Enlightenment thinkers confronted a very different situation. They were faced with the daunting task of having to draw the implications of the tectonic shifts that had rocked seventeenth-century thought. That task involved formulating a wide and fluctuating range of epistemological options, which gave birth to an intellectual environment still quite familiar to us in many respects but also rather difficult for us to map, in spite, and in part because, of that familiarity.

Because of their ubiquity, versatility, and suitability for experimenting with new ways of knowing, eighteenth-century genetic speculations illustrate this difficulty well and can be relied on to isolate some of the most dominant features of Enlightenment epistemology and its organization. Foremost among these is a renewed interest in history and in the construction of new models of historical knowledge that do not quite match our own, but are instead still closely tied to an idealization of synchronic modes of understanding, especially geometry. I am thinking here, for instance, of John Locke's "historical method," which does not deal with the past in any way of Giambattista Vico's insistence on an axiomatic presentation for his "new science" of history, or of Robert Wood's geographically based defense of Homer's priority. Conversely, diachronic models intrude where we least expect them. Consider, for example, the rather odd promotion, in Adam Smith's *Wealth of Nations*, of agriculture as the ideal occupation of man on the grounds that it came first. Indeed, my point here is not that one should replace our current emphasis on primitivism as a dominant feature of eighteenth-century thought with a "rediscovery" of rationality and geometry as equally crucial elements of Enlightenment epistemology, but that one should be wary of overemphasizing primitivism when discussing eighteenth-century patterns of historical understanding. If there is a typical eighteenth-century position on the matter, it can be found in the works of the comte de Buffon, who defended the abstract neoclassical notion of *la belle nature* in his discourse on style and anchored his *Histoire naturelle* firmly in the present, yet did not hesitate to historicize nature itself in *Les époques de la nature*.

Eighteenth-century speculations on origins highlight another critical characteristic of Enlightenment epistemology: the growing reliance on psychological explanations, that is, on an increasingly complex definition of the human subject as the source of all possible knowledge. That is why I concentrate on a body of works framed by the publication of Locke's *Essay concerning Human Understanding* in 1690 and that of Immanuel Kant's *Critique of Judgment* in 1790. This phenomenon cut across what we would now think of as distinct disciplines and made it possible to think about individual, social, and natural history and their beginnings all in similar terms.

One of the most obvious sources for this new development can undoubtedly be found in the works of René Descartes. Nothing is indeed easier than to trace a line of descent from the *Discourse on Method* to the *Critique of Pure Reason*. One should nevertheless not take away too much from such a history. Eighteenth-century thought departed from its Cartesian roots in significant respects, including in its willingness to archeologize the human mind, to entertain the notion that certainty comes in different guises, and to turn to the senses as sources of knowledge. It did so, however, without necessarily refraining from appealing in the same breath to the categories of reason and nature and without discarding the older belief in mathematics as the royal road to knowledge. Instead, it created a new intellectual map in which greater preeminence was accorded to memory, language, the imagination, and the body, but which could only be read using the newly refurbished instruments of history and psychology, not to mention anthropology, alongside the more traditional tools of rationalism.[2]

In my view, the most significant consequence of these changes in the intellectual landscape of the eighteenth century is the emergence and increasing prominence of aesthetics as a master discourse, which reformulated and brought together under one conceptual roof the various elements we have just discussed with respect to the make up of Enlightenment epistemology, including the transformations of history and psychology. Aesthetics is not just a narrowly defined poetics for the visual arts, a body of disquisitions on taste, or a branch of philosophy devoted exclusively to the study of the beautiful, christened by Alexander Baumgarten in either 1735 or 1750 (depending on whether one chooses the *Meditationes* or the *Aesthetica* as the birthplace of aesthetics). As Terry Eagleton has remarked, "Anyone who inspects the history of European philosophy since the Enlightenment must be struck by the curiously high priority assigned by it to aesthetic questions." His explanation for the success of aesthetics stems from its ideological resilience and its ability to speak of politics, law, and economics through art. In the process, aesthetics both reflects and challenges what Eagleton calls the "middle class's struggle for political hegemony."[3] Needless to say, Eagleton is not alone in examining the interplay between developments in aesthetic theories and political discourse. The authors of a number of works devoted to eighteenth-century aesthetics in particular have underscored the connections between the emergence of aesthetics and the reorganization of civil society, a trend exemplified by the following: "The aesthetic sphere emerges as an alternative site for a harmony perceived to be slipping away in other areas of life, notably the political. An aesthetic paradigm of perception thus becomes a cultural means toward

[2] Michèle Duchet has analyzed the eighteenth-century recasting of anthropology as the study of the human condition as a whole rather than anatomy alone, as well as the ties that bound anthropology and history, in *Anthropologie et histoire au siècle des Lumières* (Paris: Maspero, 1971).

[3] Terry Eagleton, *The Ideology of the Aesthetic* (Cambridge, Mass.: Basil Blackwell, 1990), 1, 3.

the ultimately political end of homogeneity and solidarity among England's governing classes."[4]

My own claim is equally ambitious with respect to the importance of this emerging discipline, but I consider it from the point of view of epistemology rather than politics. Indeed, the central contention of this book is that inquiries into origins both reflected and shaped key eighteenth-century propositions regarding the nature of human knowledge. Inquiries into origins helped to formulate and cultivate the belief that knowing is a distinctly human activity grounded in the senses and the understanding and that to be human is to be "original," or to "derive one's origin from oneself rather than from something one imitates."[5] In other words, inquiries into origins made it possible for aesthetics, and one of its core constituents, the discourse of originality, to emerge. Not initially concerned exclusively with art, aesthetics in turn allowed art, that most human of activities, to be seen as giving the rule to knowledge.

In making this argument, I return to Baumgarten's own definition of aesthetics as a form of knowledge, an *epistēmē aisthētikē*. He conceded that aesthetics is epistemologically inferior to logic. However, he also believed that logic had become barren and saw aesthetics as a science that would build instead on what he characterized as the sound principles newly offered by psychology, which he believed presented a viable alternative to logic.[6] Foremost among these principles is "the law of the imagination" ("lex imaginationis") or "association of ideas" ("associatio idearum"), formulated in the following statement: "The partial perception of an idea brings back its totality" ("percepta idea partiali recurrit eius totalis").[7]

---

4 Elizabeth A. Bohls, "Disinterestedness and Denial of the Particular: Locke, Adam Smith, and the Subject of Aesthetics," in *Eighteenth-Century Aesthetics and the Reconstruction of Art*, ed. Paul Mattick Jr. (Cambridge: Cambridge University Press, 1993), 18. Also see John Barrell, *The Political Theory of Painting from Reynolds to Hazlitt: "The Body of the Public"* (New Haven: Yale University Press, 1986); Peter de Bolla, *The Discourse of the Sublime: Readings in History, Aesthetics, and the Subject* (Oxford: Basil Blackwell, 1989); Howard Caygill, *Art of Judgement* (Cambridge, Mass.: Basil Blackwell, 1989); and the other essays in Mattick, ed., *Eighteenth-Century Aesthetics*.

5 Adolphe Hatzfeld and Arsène Darmesteter, *Dictionnaire général de la langue française du commencement du XVIIe siècle jusqu'à nos jours* (Paris: Librairie Ch. Delagrave, [1895–1900]), s.v. "Original, -ale."

6 Alexander Gottlieb Baumgarten, *Meditationes philosophicae de nonnullis ad poema pertinentibus/Philosophische Betrachtungen über einige Bedingungen des Gedichtes*, trans. into German and ed. Heinz Paetzold (Hamburg: Felix Meiner Verlag, 1983), §§115–16.

7 Alexander Gottlieb Baumgarten, *Metaphysica*, part 3 ("Psychologia"), in *Texte zur Grundlegung der Aesthetik*, trans. into German and ed. Hans Rudolf Schweizer (Hamburg: Felix Meiner Verlag, 1983), §561.

Baumgarten's principles are of absolutely crucial importance for our understanding of what aesthetics was—and, to a limited extent, what it still is—and of the crucial role it played in shaping eighteenth-century epistemology. Basically, these principles not only put human beings at the center of the universe they identified humans as the source of any knowledge we may have of it. And they do so by giving equal weight to the intellect and to the senses. Thanks to the faculty of the imagination, which enable us to project the human body into time and place, we can actually summon the universe and stand in for it. Baumgarten makes this clear in a remarkable passage from the *Metaphysica:* "I am conscious of my past state, and therefore also of the past state of the world. The representation of the past state of the world, and therefore of my own past as well, is an imaginary form of representation (imagination, sight, vision). I therefore form images, i.e., I imagine, which is something I am able to do thanks to the power of my soul to model the universe for itself based on the position of my body."[8]

These dramatic claims go a long way toward explaining the epistemological importance of the eighteenth-century fascination with origins and its concurrent conceptualization of originality. Once they were defined as being in us, as being us even, origins could be thought of as completely accessible to the subject that had created—and was still creating—them. The upshot was that originality came to be seen as a guarantee, and even a condition, of certain knowledge. By predicating knowledge on creativity and fiction, aesthetics temporarily resolved the ambivalence manifested toward probability, whose truths were never more than true enough for proponents of Cartesian certainty, and made way for what Baumgarten called "aesthetico-logical probability" ("probabilitas aestheticologica").[9]

---

[8] "Conscius sum status mei, hinc status mundi, praeteriti. Repraesentatio status mundi praeteriti, hinc status mei praeteriti, est PHANTASMA (imaginatio, visum, visio). Ergo phantasmata formo seu imaginor, idque per vim animae repraesentativam universi pro positu corporis mei" (Baumgarten, *Metaphysica*, §557). This particular passage illustrates, as well as any other, Karsten Harries's claim that Baumgarten's aesthetics revolves around the twin notions of "self-sufficiency and completeness." See "Metaphor and Transcendence," in *On Metaphor*, ed. Sheldon Sacks (Chicago: University of Chicago Press, 1979), 88.

[9] Alexander Gottlieb Baumgarten, *Theoretische Ästhetik: Die grundlegenden Abschnitte aus der "Aesthetica" (1750/58)*, trans. into German and ed. Hans Rudolf Schweizer (Hamburg: Felix Meiner Verlag, 1983), §485. The German critic also uses the term "aesthetic truth" ("veritas aesthetica"; *Aesthetica*, §483), speaks of a poetic or clear (*lucidus*) method (*Meditationes*, §70), and argues that narration constitutes a form of order (*Meditationes*, §70), all of which echoes Vico's concepts of "true narration" and "poetic wisdom."

No wonder modern aesthetics can be said, without exaggeration, to have depended for its very existence on the conceptualization of originality, both as a subjective faculty and as its manifestations in the thing made.[10]

We should perhaps not be surprised to find a close connection between the eighteenth-century fascination with origins and the concurrent emergence of aesthetics as a new branch of philosophy. Aristotle had already reflected on the kinship between art (*technē*) and genealogy when he argued, in the *Nicomachean Ethics*, that "all art is concerned with coming into being, i.e., with contriving and considering how something may come into being which is capable of either being or not being, and whose origin is in the maker and not in the thing made; for art is concerned neither with things that are, or come into being, by necessity, nor with things that do so in accordance with nature (since these have their origin in themselves)."[11] Eighteenth-century thought focused on this coming into being by developing a series of genetic speculations that centered on the maker's relationship to the thing made, what Louis Dumont calls "artificialism" in his pathbreaking book on the emergence and triumph of *homo oeconomicus*.[12]

To do justice to both the breadth and the depth of these speculations I have included two different kinds of chapters in this book. The first, second, and fifth chapters are devoted to contributions made by key

[10] Classic studies of originality in the broader context of eighteenth-century literary criticism include M. H. Abrams, *The Mirror and the Lamp* (Oxford: Oxford University Press, 1971; Walter Jackson Bate, *From Classic to Romantic: Premises of Taste in Eighteenth-Century England* (New York: Harper and Row, 1961); Roland Mortier, *L'originalité: Une nouvelle catégorie esthétique au siècle des Lumières* (Geneva: Droz, 1982); Thomas McFarland, *Originality and Imagination* (Baltimore: Johns Hopkins University Press, 1985); John D. Boyd, *The Function of Mimesis and Its Decline* (Cambridge, Mass.: Harvard University Press, 1968; New York: Fordham University Press, 1980); Martin Kallich, *The Association of Ideas and Critical Theory in Eighteenth-Century England: A History of Psychological Method in English Criticism* (The Hague: Mouton, 1970); John O. Lyons, *The Invention of the Self: The Hinge of Consciousness in the Eighteenth Century* (Carbondale: Southern Illinois University Press, 1978); John L. Mahoney, *The Whole Internal Universe: Imitation and the New Defense of Poetry in British Criticism, 1660–1830* (New York: Fordham University Press, 1985); and Patricia Phillips, *The Adventurous Muse: Theories of Originality in English Poetics: 1650–1760*, Studia Anglistica Upsaliensia 53 (Uppsala: Acta Universitatis Upsaliensis, 1984), distributed by Almqvist and Wiksell International, Stockholm).
[11] Aristotle, *The Nicomachean Ethics*, trans. W. D. Ross, rev. J. O. Urmson, in *The Complete Works of Aristotle, The Revised Oxford Translation*, ed. Jonathan Barnes, Bollingen Series 71 (Princeton: Princeton University Press, 1984), 2:1140a.
[12] Louis Dumont, *From Mandeville to Marx: The Genesis and Triumph of Economic Ideology* (Chicago: University of Chicago Press, 1977).

individual thinkers, namely, Descartes, Vico, and Kant, while the third and fourth chapters are structured as a series of shorter inquiries into works by a broader range of writers and texts that cut across a variety of disciplines, including philosophy, literary criticism, and political economy.[13] In the opening chapter, I contrast Descartes's lack of interest in the study of origins as historical facts or singular events, along with his reliance on mechanistic explanations, to the fabulous nature of his account of the genesis of the universe. In particular, I interpret his use of the fable and the tableau in *Le monde* in terms of his broader claims regarding the human ability to conceive and envision, and as an expression of his ambivalence regarding the role of memory and of series in the acquisition of knowledge. There are a number of reasons for starting with Descartes. First, it is difficult to imagine that the eighteenth-century focus on the maker as source and the elaboration of an explicitly aesthetic model of understanding could have been possible without the heroic claims the French thinker had made for the thinking subject. Second, it underscores that, *pace* the tendency to present Enlightenment thought as dismissive of Cartesianism, eighteenth-century calls for a poetic reason or *epistēmē aisthētikē* were greatly indebted to Descartes and rationalism.[14] One could even say that aesthetics emerged in great measure as a response to and elaboration of the Cartesian position that conception and invention are a condition of knowledge. Finally,

---

[13] I hope thereby to avoid some of the "jump[ing] from mountain peak to mountain peak" Peter Hanns Reill has cautioned against in the preface to his own study of some of the lesser known figures of the German Enlightenment. See *The German Enlightenment and the Rise of Historicism* (Berkeley and Los Angeles: University of California Press, 1975), ix. More importantly, my goal is to give a sense of the luxuriance of eighteenth-century epistemology and to underscore the recurrence of a number of philosophemes and arguments across a broad spectrum of inquiries and disciplines.

[14] As noted by Annie Becq, not only does the birth of aesthetics not represent a break from rationalism, "it might be more correct to associate the genesis of modern aesthetics with a change in the meaning of the word *reason*." Annie Becq, *Genèse de l'esthétique française: De la raison classique à l'imagination créatrice, 1680–1814* (Pisa: Pacini Editore, 1984), 1:13. Ernst Cassirer made a related point some fifty years ago when he argued that "systematic aesthetics sprang from this conception of the interdependence and unity of philosophy and criticism," and went on to argue that "it is as if logic and aesthetics, as if pure knowledge and artistic intuition, had to be tested in terms of one another before either of them could find its own inner standard and understand itself in the light of its own relational complex." Ernst Cassirer, *The Philosophy of the Enlightenment*, trans. Fritz C. A. Koelln and James P. Pettegrove (Princeton, N.J.: Princeton University Press, 1951), 275, 277. My own point, of course, is somewhat different. I argue that neither logic nor aesthetics found separate standards but that the Enlightenment was marked by the temporary—though by no means brief—triumph of an aesthetic logic, or by the subsuming of logic under the category of the aesthetic.

the works of Descartes allow us to appreciate the continued yet often neglected emphasis on demonstrability and certainty in eighteenth-century works devoted to the study of origins and originality.

Nowhere is this more in evidence, perhaps, than in the third edition of Vico's *New Science* (1744), the focus of my second chapter. In that work, the Italian philosopher proposed a secular hermeneutics of history that revolved around a "genetic principle," which he hoped would allow him to balance the sometimes conflicting demands of what he called "philology" and "philosophy," and to merge the "credible impossibility" of a logic that was at once poetic, historical, and rhetorical with seventeenth-century criteria of demonstrable scientific truth. Unlike Descartes, Vico was interested in history and in individual facts. The Italian philosopher got around Descartes's objections by limiting his field of inquiry to what he called "the world of nations," namely the world of history, the only world we can know because it is the only world we have actually made, and by thinking of the origin as something other than a unique event. In the *New Science* he proffers a series of axioms or principles that add up to a hermeneutics of history grounded in an understanding of what he called "the modifications of the human mind" and in a process of autoarcheology that allows each person to recapitulate history and have immediate access to origins, henceforth characterized as both past and present.

Vico's obsessive attention to the minutiae of history notwithstanding, the Vichian origin is primarily a psychological necessity that is repeatable—not just a unique moment in time. In this respect, it parallels the special nature of the primacy of Homeric poetry, which is always already belated and forever internalized and reinvented on the basis of the traces it has left. My chapter on Vico accordingly begins with a discussion of Vico's historicization of Homer and its importance in the elaboration of Vico's hermeneutics. Indeed, Vico's views on Homer are the key to his claim that any hermeneutics that pertains to secular origins must be internalized. I then consider how this yielded an episteme dominated by a genetic principle.

Debated ad nauseam, origins functioned throughout the eighteenth century within the epistemological parameters set by Vico. The origin could be defined as cause, that is, as something that required a scientific or synchronic model of explanation, or it could be defined as that which came first chronologically, in which case it seemed to call for a historical model. This dual pattern is crucial to our understanding of eighteenth-century epistemology, beginning with Enlightenment views on the origins of ideas. The third chapter therefore opens with an exploration of Locke's treatise concerning the origins of human knowledge, while the fourth chapter begins with Etienne Bonnot de Condillac's treatise on the same subject. These represent two methodological options between which genetic epistemology constantly wavered: Locke's approach is almost exclusively synchronic—even in the context of what he himself calls a "historical method"—while Condillac's inquiries into the genesis of our ideas rest on the realization that ideas have a socio-historical component and on his somewhat reluctant conception of a "historicist" or archeological methodology.

This dichotomy manifested itself with particular acuteness in the conceptualization of originality. To the extent that it referred to the ability to create radically new works, originality could be conceived as hinging on the ability to sever one's ties to the past or at least to ignore them; conversely, it could be viewed as the mark of works belonging to early stages of human societies, that is, works that were defined, not unproblematically, as having no past. Depending on whether it was tied to primitivism or to the denial of one's ties to the past and its models, the conceptualization of originality either called for an archeological method or privileged an ahistorical present.

The two positions were not necessarily incompatible, however, as the recurring debates over Homeric poetry and temporal priority illustrate. Alexander Pope, for example, in his writings on Homer and Shakespeare, wrestled with whether authority was grounded in nature or in history. Pope was able to integrate nature and history, but, in eventually praising Shakespeare's genius over Homer's, he also paved the way for later theorizations of originality. In 1759 Edward Young equated originality with authenticity, which has little to do with inheritance and communicability and everything to do with an absolute right to the fruit of one's own labor. At this late stage in the continuing saga of the "Quarrel between the Ancients and the Moderns," Young squarely sided with the moderns. By contrast, though William Duff equated originality with spontaneity, he was also a proponent of primitivism. Moreover, one ought to note that not all Enlightenment thinkers chose to celebrate authenticity and spontaneity. The third chapter accordingly ends with a discussion of attempts by Alexander Gerard and Charles Batteux, among others, to refute those who did.

Primitivist explanations did not yield a consensus either. In the fourth chapter, beginning with Condillac's *Essay on the Origin of Human Knowledge,* I explore the setting in place of a historicist mode of knowledge and attempts at negating historicity, both of which could occur from within a primitivist discourse. Condillac's *Essay* maneuvers somewhat uneasily between the requirements of historicity and those of synchronicity, an unease Rousseau modeled with unequaled intensity. Believing that history stood between him and an origin that was utterly lost and could not be reclaimed, Rousseau made genetic epistemology dependent on internalization and idealized the static time that precedes the accelerated dynamic time of major civilizations. Simultaneously, he argued that one cannot actually wish for a return to stasis, since the new stasis one could summon would be only a negative version of the authentic and original state. Ultimately, the origin can be located only in those individuals who, like Jean-Jacques Rousseau, have retained traces of it.

As is well known, Rousseau had a profound influence on a number of German thinkers, including critics such as Heinrich Wilhelm Gerstenberg, Johann Georg Sulzer, and Johann Gottfried Herder, who radicalized the concept of *Originalgenie* in the 1760s and 1770s. Their combination of *Originalität* and *Eigentümlichkeit,* which also bore traces of Young's influence, was echoed in the classical economic theory elaborated by Adam Smith. Like the vast majority of his contemporaries, Smith analyzed economic wealth exclusively from the perspective of issues pertaining to the production process. But unlike some of his contemporaries—the physiocrats, for instance—Smith theorized that the root cause of national economic wealth lay in labor rather than in the land or other natural factors. Smith's labor theory of value paralleled developments in aesthetic theory, which focused less and less on nature and more and more on modes of production. In addition, in opposition to the received ideas of those who would read him two hundred years or more after the initial publication of the *Wealth of Nations,* Smith did not include a plea for growth but an idealization of stasis, which echoed Rousseau's own desire to eradicate history.

All these competing approaches to the question of origins and originality presented the Enlightenment with a major epistemological hurdle. It was exemplified in yet another theory on Homer's primacy, Robert Wood's defense of Homeric poetry on the grounds that the epic poet had been both a historian and a painter. For Wood, Homer's depictions of an immutable environment attest to his status as a historian. Through painting, the past is appropriated, both by Homer and by his modern readers.

Ultimately, throughout the eighteenth century, when it came to debating the origins of our ideas, our societies, and our art, the key question was essentially epistemological. Could the origin be known? And, if so, under what conditions? The overall consensus that emerged was ultimately that origins can be known only through a process of internalization and aestheticization. Whether the knowledge that this process generates belongs to the realm of the certain was debated endlessly but inconclusively.

The issue was taken up one more time by Immanuel Kant, whose writings bring together many of the threads I discuss in the early chapters, starting with the question of the origin of nature itself. The final chapter is therefore devoted to a study of the evolution of Kant's views on origins and originality in the *Universal Natural History*, the *Critique of Pure Reason*, the *Critique of Judgment*, and the *Anthropology*. Kant understood that certainty would not obtain so long as one continued to rely on a psychological model. Setting aside exclusively mechanistic as well as visionary models, he chose to limit the field of genetic inquiries and to study events in terms of both temporality and causality, underscoring that this knowledge depends on both permanence ("not something in me") and causality (a pure concept of the understanding that makes it possible for us to understand sequences or serialization). This holds true for both natural and human events. One significant distinction, however, is that though causality is at work in human events, its exact form cannot always be known; in human events, causality from freedom, as opposed to causality according to nature, is always possible. Kant elaborated on the notion of causality from freedom in the Third Critique, where he addressed the limitations of mechanistic and regressive analyses by introducing the notion of purposiveness, a concept without which one would be condemned to think of origins only in terms of infinite regress. His brief remarks on genius and originality play a crucial role in this respect. For Kant, genius is primarily "productive" rather than "eductive," while originality is nothing if not exemplary, that is, it is defined by what happens in the future rather than at the source, in the reception of the work rather than in the artist. Its purpose is set communally and must correspond to something other than itself, even when that something—in this case, nature—is actually in the artist. Purposiveness and originality freed Kant from both the constraints of referentiality and the perils of solipsism and tied together in an aesthetics of knowledge both the permanence of nature and the freedom of art, thereby bridging the gap between the understanding (*Verstand*), applicable to knowledge, and reason (*Vernunft*), applicable to ethics. By putting severe constraints on the study of origins, Kant freed them from the shackles of chronic time, infinite regress, and freewheeling associationism and anchored them in purposes or freedoms that are subject to the rules of communicability and all this implies, including a community and a tradition. One is almost tempted to argue that a critique of historical reason does exist; it can be found, albeit in embryonic form, in the Critique of Aesthetic Judgment.

CHAPTER ONE

Descartes's Fabulous World

Unique, miraculous even in the case of the Creation, origins are for that very reason one of the *laissés pour compte* of Cartesian natural philosophy, which focuses on what is subject to demonstration and, by extension, repetition. From a Cartesian perspective, origins are singular events or individual moments that can be apprehended only through the less than reliable work of history and memory. Any insight we might have into origins would only be probable and, as such, fruitless, since a natural fact can only be or not be; approximating it yields no useful, let alone certain, information. Descartes's resounding dismissal of the study of origins did not, however, prevent him from introducing a feigned genesis of the natural world in *Le monde*. In this chapter I intend to resolve the apparent conflict between Descartes's ban on the study of origins and his willingness to depict the birth of the natural world. In particular, I argue that Cartesian thought is less remarkable for Descartes's conspicuous excision of origins from the study of nature than for a feigned genesis that was not merely decorative but was grounded in the conviction that fiction creates its own truth and is therefore closer to geometry than to history.[1]

---

[1] The role of geometry as a master discourse in the seventeenth century has been the subject of numerous studies. The following references are of particular relevance for the present analysis: Jacques Roger, "The Cartesian Model and Its Role in Eighteenth-Century 'Theory of the Earth,'" in *Problems of Cartesianism*, ed. Thomas M. Lennon, John M. Nicholas, and John W. Davis (Kingston and Montreal: McGill-Queen's University Press, 1982), 95–112; Michel Fichant, "La géométrisation du regard: Réflexions

Unlike origins, a genesis consists of a hypothesis that has practical applications and explanatory power.[2] Furthermore, since it is a non-event, a genesis can be produced without any reference to a historical framework; unlike myth, it can be conceived independently of temporal considerations. We are, after all, talking about *a* genesis, not *the* Genesis. Better still, a genesis is true even when its particulars are known to be false, as in the case of the gradual and mechanical birth of the world provided by Descartes in *Le monde* and in part 5 of the *Discours de la méthode*, which contradicts the biblical account. Descartes makes this abundantly clear in part 3, §45 of the *Principles of Philosophy:*

> If we want to understand the nature of plants or of men, it is much better to consider how they can gradually grow from seeds than to consider how they were created by God at the very beginning of the world. Thus we may be able to think up certain very simple and easily known principles which can serve, as it were, as the seeds from which we can demonstrate that the stars, the earth and indeed everything we observe in this visible world could have sprung. For although we know for sure that they never did arise in this way, we shall be able to provide a much better explanation of their nature by

---

sur la *Dioptrique* de Descartes," *Philosophie* 34 (Spring 1992): 45–69; Timothy J. Reiss, *Knowledge, Discovery, and Imagination in Early Modern Europe: The Rise of Aesthetic Rationalism* (Cambridge: Cambridge University Press, 1997); and Jean-Pierre Cavaillé, *Descartes: La fable du monde* (Paris: Editions de l'Ecole des Hautes Etudes en Sciences Sociales and Librairie Philosophique J. Vrin, 1991). Michel Serres's discussion of the intrinsic differences between geometric and historical approaches is also worth consulting. See *Les origines de la géométrie: Tiers livre des fondations* (n.p.: Flammarion, 1993), esp. 26–27.
[2] See René Descartes, *Principles of Philosophy,* trans. John Cottingham, in vol. 1 of *The Philosophical Writings of Descartes* (Cambridge: Cambridge University Press, 1985), part 3, §44. Further references will be included parenthetically in the body of the text, preceded by the abbreviation CSMK (for the translators of *The Philosophical Writings:* John Cottingham, Robert Stoothoff, Dugald Murdoch, and Anthony Kenny). Translations of Descartes's other works will also be given in the text: *Meditations on First Philosophy,* trans. John Cottingham, in vol. 2 of *The Philosophical Writings of Descartes* (Cambridge: Cambridge University Press, 1984); and *Rules for the Direction of the Mind,* trans. Dugald Murdoch, in vol. 1 of *The Philosophical Writings.* References to Descartes' *Oeuvres,* ed. Charles Adam and Paul Tannery, 12 vols. (Paris: J. Vrin, in conjunction with the Centre National de la Recherche Scientifique, 1964–1976) will also be included, preceded by the abbreviation AT. When a work has appeared in AT in both Latin and French, both references will be included, with the Latin version given first. Unless otherwise noted, references to Descartes's other works will be to the AT edition.

this method than if we merely described them as they now are.
(CSMK 1:256; AT, vol. 8, bk. 1, 100; vol. 9, bk. 2, 124)

There is, then, something of a "genetic principle" at play in Descartes's philosophy. Unlike Vico's, however, it need not be tested against our knowledge of the past. Descartes's fables are contemporary fictions, not myths requiring a hermeneutics of history.

This chapter revolves around this basic yet potentially equivocal distinction in Descartes's natural philosophy, namely, that while origins should not be studied, this in no way argues against their being made up. On the contrary. More broadly, one should be wary of using the French thinker as a mere foil to Vichian and Enlightenment philosophy. Not only did eighteenth-century thinkers never entirely give up on the Cartesian dream of mathematical certainty, their insistent inquiries into origins and originality would not have been possible without Descartes's bold claims regarding the nature and possibilities of the human mind. I discuss, first, some of the key features of Descartes's rejection of the study of origins, including his belief that no certainty can obtain in the case of inquiries pertaining to individual facts, including the creation of the world. I argue in particular that Descartes's excision of the study of origins reflects a waning confidence in the ability of memory to contribute to the acquisition of knowledge as well as a preference for geometry and, more unexpectedly, fiction as royal roads to knowledge. To make this case, I distinguish between historical and fictional knowledge, using the work of one of his predecessors, Loys Le Roy, as partial justification for Descartes's desire to found a geometric rather than a historical method and to create an alternative world free of the vagaries of history, Scholastic pretensions, and theological limitations, that is, a world that could be known because it would be consonant with the rules set by Descartes himself. The French philosopher demonstrates this in *Le monde* when he invites his readers to imagine an initially chaotic world made of a finite quantity of matter that is subject to perpetual motion and extension, starting with the combination and recombination of extremely small particles. Subject to the same natural laws that govern the world his readers are familiar with, Descartes's fabulous world gradually becomes very similar to that world. God is responsible only for the creation of matter and an initial impulse (*conatus*). Descartes, as it were, conceives the rest.

The second part of this chapter is accordingly devoted to an account of Descartes's own genesis. Desmond M. Clarke has reminded us quite rightly of the hypothetical nature of Cartesian physics.[3] I shall underscore instead that Descartes's fable is also presented as true. It is not merely factual, hypothetical, or *vraisemblable*, though it is all these things as well, just as fiction is different from, yet not alien to, the study of physics, history, and belles lettres. Fiction is the truth the mind recognizes because it has made it, an epistemological stance made possible once each individual has been endowed with a unique and distinct ability to envision and conceive. Far from being a mere ornament, the fable is a primary mode of knowledge, whose demonstrability is guaranteed by two significant characteristics: it collapses the past into the present and it attests to the superiority of the visual over the narrative.

Finally, I argue in this chapter that though Descartes's insistence on the fable's ability to generate certain knowledge and thereby excise history and time from human inquiry is very much at odds with, among other later theories, Vico's hermeneutics of myth, the Cartesian fable (or tableau) links concepts and appearances in ways that will prove crucial to the aestheticization of knowledge in the eighteenth century.

ORIGINS: A REPUDIATION

Descartes's bold revision of the book of Genesis in *Le monde*, the *Discours de la méthode*, and the *Principles of Philosophy* made it increasingly clear that explanations concerning the origins of the world—and especially theologically based reports—are merely *vraisemblables*, or probable. However, before we can analyze the reasons Descartes gave for invalidating the study of cosmic origins, it is important to recognize that he did not dispute that there *was* a beginning. The origin is a fact for the French philosopher, but it is only a fact.[4] One could even say that this factuality is precisely what is wrong with origins, both in terms

---

[3] Desmond M. Clarke, "Descartes' Philosophy of Science and the Scientific Revolution," in *The Cambridge Companion to Descartes*, ed. John Cottingham (Cambridge: Cambridge University Press, 1992), esp. 264–72.

[4] For Descartes, the origin is neither a cause nor a primum mobile. See Annie Bitbol-Hespériès and Jean-Pierre Verdet, eds., *Le monde, L'homme*, by René Descartes (Paris: Seuil, 1996), 67n29. All further references to *Le monde* and all references to *L'homme* are to this edition and will be included parenthetically in the body of the text. Page numbers for the Adam and Tannery edition will also be given.

of principles and from a methodological point of view.[5] In addition, and not unproblematically, it is a fact at odds with a basic premise of organization in Descartes's world, namely, "that there is nothing anywhere that is not changing" (*Le monde* 12; AT 11:10).

Of course, if change is what matters to Descartes, there is no reason to privilege one particular moment or focus on or even believe in first causes. Hence the following dismissal: "I do not pause to seek the cause of their motions, for I only need to reason that they [the small particles of the world] began to move as soon as the world began to be" (*Le monde* 12; AT 11:11). For Descartes, the study of origins, like the study of other facts, must follow the study of the laws or principles that guide the series they belong to and must condition the movements that animate them.

It is true that Descartes's argument fails to address the question of the coexistence of the Creation and of infinity. It does, however, have the merit of separating the study of causation from that of motion and, as a result, of not conflating cause and origin, a distinction often ignored by later thinkers of the origin, who were unable to escape the trap of infinite regress.[6] In addition, his dismissal of the study of origins and, more broadly, of singular, that is, historical, facts, allowed him to address more immediate methodological concerns. In particular, it both reflected and justified his narrowing of the field of memory, on whose proper functioning the knowledge of individual moments and facts depends.

---

[5] Note that I am not using the word *fact* in any strict sense. For two very recent discussions of the importance of the modern fact in the development of natural and social sciences, see Barbara J. Shapiro, *A Culture of Fact: England, 1550–1720* (Ithaca, N.Y.: Cornell University Press, 2000); and Mary Poovey, *A History of the Modern Fact: Problems of Knowledge in the Sciences of Wealth and Society* (Chicago: University of Chicago Press, 1998).

[6] Jacopo Zabarella had defined regress as "a relation between cause and effect, when they interact mutually [*quando reciprocantur*], and the effect is better known to us than the cause." *Liber de regressu*, in *Opera Logica*, preface by Ludovici Havvenrevteri (Frankfurt, 1608), col. 481; quoted by Timothy J. Reiss, "Neo-Aristotle and Method: Between Zabarella and Descartes," in *Descartes' Natural Philosophy*, ed. Stephen Gaukroger, John Schuster, and John Sutton (London: Routledge, 2000), 207. Descartes makes explicit references to the question of infinite regress in the Third Meditation, devoted to demonstrating the existence of God. His answer to the dilemma of infinite regress consists in claiming "that there must be at least as much in the cause as in the effect" (*Meditations*; CSMK 2:34; AT 7:49; vol. 9, bk. 1, 39) and the effect never outruns, as it were, its cause. If God is Descartes's cause, "it is clear enough that an infinite regress is impossible here, especially since I am dealing not just with the cause that produced me in the past, but also and most importantly with the cause that preserves me at the present moment" (*Meditations*; CSMK 2:34; AT 7:50; vol. 9, bk. 1, 40). Note that the French version mentions "progrez à l'infiny," which suggests that Descartes is no more interested in a purposive defense of origins than in a regressive one.

In the *Rules for the Direction of the Mind*, Descartes initially makes room for memory as one of four cognitive faculties, the others being the understanding (*l'entendement*), the imagination, and the senses. Descartes's division of epistemological labor, however, is fraught with ambiguity. On the one hand, deduction—the only way of knowing considered to be certain—relies on memory to do its work. On the other, there is no particular reason why this should be so. As defined in the *Rules*, deduction presupposes the existence of "a continuous and uninterrupted movement of thought" that is a necessary condition of knowability for anything not directly in evidence (CSMK 1:15; AT 10:369).[7] Thought's movement in turn is a corollary of the notion that "all things can be arranged serially" (CSMK 1:21; AT 10:381). The series, appropriately called a kind of "cognitive linking of things" ("enchaînement cognitif des choses" as the Alquié edition translates Descartes's Latin phrase "rerum cognoscendarum series"; AT 10:383), is an important methodological principle authorized by thought's ability to function uninterruptedly, just as matter keeps going in accordance with the laws of nature.[8] The strength of this principle becomes clear once the series is compared to a syllogistic or dialectical approach.[9] Unlike syllogisms, series can function independently of a known and prescribed end. They are free of both forward and backward referentiality.

Memory's role consists in keeping the series together in an unbroken train of thought and thereby lending deduction its certainty. Unfortunately, Descartes is unclear as to exactly how deduction and memory conspire to achieve this result, which causes him to raise a question of method just as he makes his most forceful statement on the importance of memory: "Deduction *in a sense* gets its certainty from memory" (*Rules*; CSMK1:15; AT 10:370, emphasis added). This qualification, "in a sense" ("quodammodo"), reiterated later in the text—"its certainty *in a sense* depends on memory"—puts the certainty of deductions in question.[10]

---

[7] Jean-Marie Beyssade has dealt with this question in *La philosophie première de Descartes: Le temps et la cohérence de la métaphysique* (n.p.: Flammarion, 1979), 143–54.

[8] René Descartes, *Règles pour la direction de l'esprit*, trans. Jacques Brunschwig, in *Oeuvres philosophiques*, vol. 1 (1618–1637), ed. Ferdinand Alquié (Paris: Garnier, 1963), 104. This edition will henceforth be referred to as "Alquié" and page references will be included in the body of the text. Note that in this respect at least, Descartes's philosophy is not so different from that of Kant, for whom the knowledge of events in the natural world depends on serialization.

[9] See notes to Rule 8 in the Alquié edition (1:128–30).

[10] CSMK 1:37, emphasis added. The Latin reads: "ejus certitudo *quodammodo* à memoriâ dependent" (AT 10:408, emphasis added).

Descartes never explains how memory lends deduction its certainty, which raises some doubt about how certain that certainty is. Brunschwig's translation ("pour la déduction, . . . c'est à la mémoire qu'elle emprunte, d'une certaine manière [quodammodo], sa certitude" [Alquié, 1:89]) is correct: "une certaine manière" is not une manière certaine.

Memory is at once crucial and unreliable, a kind of necessary evil that Descartes rapidly attempts to dispense with. His initial way around the problem is to hope for deductions so rapid that "memory is left with practically no role to play" (Rules; CSMK 1:38; AT 10:409). Since this hope has little chance of ever being realized, Descartes also urges the reader of the Rules to turn to the study of geometry. Geometric figures, as is clear from the argument presented in rules 14 to 18, make it possible to bypass the problems presented by memory. This argument represents an intermediary step in what will amount to a summary dismissal of memory from the Meditations on the grounds that it is deceitful: "I will believe that my memory tells me lies, and that none of the things that it reports ever happened" (CSMK 2:16; AT 7:24; vol. 9. bk. 1, 19).[11]

Descartes's marginalization of memory reflects a growing desire to free his method from the shackles of temporality and a need to refer either to a past motive or a putative purpose. Logically enough, it is accompanied by a radical ahistoricism that represents not only an explicit answer to Scholastic philosophy but is also a significant departure from earlier philosophies of history.[12] I am thinking, of course, of two extremely successful works, Jean Bodin's Method (1566) and especially, Loys Le Roy's De la vicissitude ou variété des choses en l'univers (1575), which will be the primary focus of the following discussion.[13] At first glance, such references may seem out of place. If anything, cyclical and evolutionary universal histories appear to be at odds with Descartes's expulsion of history from science and to herald instead eighteenth- and nineteenth-century brands of historicism. A brief incursion into the state

[11] In the treatise L'homme, memory is portrayed as a prelude to photographic impressions, not an invitation to develop an archeological method or to focus on the past. It is a mechanical, even glandular, process by which ideas imprint themselves on the brain where they leave a physical trace, which can then be accessed by the imagination (L'homme, 153–54; AT 11:177–79).

[12] See Clarke, "Descartes' Philosophy of Science," esp. 259–60; and Reiss, "Neo-Aristotle and Method," on Descartes and Scholastic philosophy.

[13] Le Roy's work quickly become popular, with five French reprints in ten years as well as translations into Italian (1585) and English (1594).

of historical discourse inherited by Descartes is nevertheless worth making at this point, if only to identify some of the reasons for and characteristics of Descartes's ahistoricism and to set the stage for future discussions of eighteenth-century thinkers' recourse to history as a valuable source of answers to the question of origins.

Although Bodin may seem to have anticipated the notion of periodization in Vico's sense, he, unlike eighteenth-century philosophers, was not interested in establishing a set of principles guiding human history. This explains in part why he rejected the idea of degenerescence and did not share Vico's belief that enlightened forms of barbarism are worse than more primitive ones. Bodin provided a sense of directionality and periodization, but no theory of change. In his view, "human history is mostly the product of the will of men, and this will is never the same."[14] Here, of course, Bodin and Descartes meet in the notion that human history is marked by randomness or by what Le Roy would call *vicissitude*, or variety.

Le Roy's concept of vicissitude relies not only on a principle of cyclical repetition and alternation but also on a principle of outwardly random permutation, which, in the hands of Divine Providence, introduces the possibility of incrementation and addition, or progress (and decline) over time. This double-edged principle creates a number of unresolved tensions. On the one hand, Le Roy develops a whole system of correspondences: between nations; between nations and stars; between nations and the four elements; and between nations and the earth. On the other hand, by turning vicissitudes into a universal principle (what holds true for the earth holds true for its elements, the nations that live on it, and the heavens it mirrors), Le Roy invalidates a strictly linear or cyclical model because vicissitudes are inherently chaotic— or at least do not subscribe to the traditional dicta of temporality. This forces (or allows) him to introduce nontemporal factors into the scheme of history—both natural and social. Time rules but can be overruled by Divine Providence, which is then not only a condition of temporal order but also the denial of its authority. In addition, this theological causality is not only the condition of progress and linearity, it is also a guarantee of the world's eventual return to chaos in that the accretion over time afforded by Providence is both positive and negative.

[14] Jean Bodin, *Methodus ad facilem historiarum cognitionem* (Paris, 1566) in *Oeuvres philosophiques*, ed. Pierre Mesnard (Paris, 1951, 115), quoted and translated in George Huppert, "The Renaissance Background of Historicism," *History and Theory* 5 (1966): 57.

It is worth noting that Le Roy was not particularly interested in origins because they are not truly determinant. What counts are the possibility of *accroissement* and the goals that a modern society has to set for itself. The truth of the ending is more important than the limited and superseded reality of beginnings. To be concerned with origins would be to fall into the following trap: "When shall we cease to mistake grass for wheat, the flower for the fruit, the bark for the wood— merely translating, correcting, commenting on, annotating, or abridging the books written by the ancients?"[15]

Their best efforts notwithstanding, Bodin's and Le Roy's works were riddled with inconsistencies that no philosophy of history managed to resolve. Both philosophers acquiesced to randomness and Le Roy's decision to subsume his historical model under a theological order that conflicted with the observations he made at the level of civil history would do little to recommend the study of history to Descartes. For his assault on skepticism and the formulation of a science that, as concisely noted by Jean-Pierre Cavaillé, "spurns the logic of verisimilitude," Descartes found a stronger ally in fiction.[16] It is only superficially paradoxical that Descartes preferred the conception of an outright fiction or *feinte* to the poorly contrasted drama of the merely *vraisemblable*. Unlike history, fiction does not attempt to unearth something hidden whose organization could well be random and therefore has little or no explanatory or even rhetorical merit. By contrast, the Cartesian fable exposes truth by creating it.

DESCARTES'S (FICTIONAL) GENESIS

Descartes's decision to "clothe" his science in fables has long puzzled commentators, who have struggled to reconcile this with his lapidary dismissal of the study of history and belles lettres in the *Discours de la méthode*.[17] This difficulty is genuine. To some extent, Descartes's fables

---

[15] [Loys] Leroy, *De la vicissitude ou variété des choses en l'univers* (n.p.: Fayard, 1988), 433.

[16] Cavaillé, *Descartes*, 132.

[17] Fables have an unstable status in Descartes's work. In the *Discours de la méthode*, he proposes to represent his life as an *histoire* and a *fable* (AT 6:4), but also dismisses fables on the grounds that they "make us imagine several events as possible, even when they are not" (AT 6:6–7). On the basis of the *Discours* alone, where the reliance on fables is accompanied by a concurrent rejection of history and letters as sound epistemological

are just another weapon in the regrettable necessity that is Descartes's formidable rhetorical arsenal. Adopting a Vichian perspective, one might even say that Descartes's recourse to such tools reveals the limits of Cartesian thought. Such an acknowledgement, however, would sidestep the unique status of the Cartesian fable, which performs specific demonstrative functions.[18] Indeed, Descartes's fables or *feintes* are not to be confused with stories, understood as a succession of facts. They are products of the human mind that bring to light the distinction between the true and the false and as such belong to the order of geometry rather than history or literature (as we understand that term today). The *Discours de la méthode* makes this abundantly clear: *la feinte* enables Descartes to demonstrate that even if the world itself turned out not to exist, this would not affect the (Cartesian) principles—arrived at by means of conceptual fictions and visions—according to which we know it could have existed.

The theologically determined belief in a finite time span of about six thousand years made claims about the history of the world particularly improbable and forced Descartes to make potentially controversial moves. These included a radical fictional leap and the conception of a natural history of the world that demonstrated most vividly the need to free human knowledge from the crippling and ineffective demands of finitude and historicity. As we have already seen, any history, theological accounts included, is made up of singular events that could in and of themselves well be random. Descartes's fable, by contrast, is an attempt to get at the truth by setting the histories of Scholastic philosophers aside and providing an account that could be mechanistically duplicated, even in the absence of God: "My objective is not to account, as they do, for the things that are actually in the real world, but only to feign one as I please, a world in which there will be nothing that the coarsest minds will not be able to conceive and which could nonetheless be created just as I shall have made it up" (*Le monde* 24; AT 11:36).

Descartes's first grand move accordingly rests on a deliberate ignorance, in the strongest sense of the term, of God's unique creation. Like

---

tools, one might be tempted to think of Descartes's recourse to fables as "merely" rhetorical. This would leave his method open to allegations of inconsistency, as Vico and others have charged. Incorporating his use of fiction in *Le monde* into the analysis complicates the issue in a useful way.

[18] I use the term *demonstrative* in a fairly generic manner, that is, interchangeably with *conclusive*. For a discussion of the demonstrability of hypotheses in Descartes's physics, see Clarke, "Descartes' Philosophy of Science," 264.

an actor on a stage, he invites his readers to step into a world truer than the Mosaic world of limited explanatory value that they are familiar with: "Allow therefore your thinking to leave this world for a little while in order to come and see another brand new world that I shall bring into existence in your mind's presence in the imaginary spaces" (*Le monde* 22; AT 11:31). This invitation is tempered by a quick word of caution: "Let us enter only as far as we need to in order to lose sight of all the creatures God made some five or six thousand years ago" (*Le monde* 22; AT 11:32). Descartes's fabulous world is, contrary to what one might expect and to the claims of Scholastic philosophy concerning the infinity of "espaces imaginaires," quite small. Therein lies its usefulness. By setting limits to his object of study, Descartes accomplishes several things. First, he creates a world that is knowable. Infinity, by contrast, is a hindrance to knowledge. Second, he turns Scholastic philosophy against itself by relying on the imagination, as Scholastic philosophers had done in their discussion of infinite spaces, and which, as Annie Bitbol-Hespériès and Jean-Pierre Verdet have observed, ironically authorized Descartes's own fabulous discourse (*Le monde* 75n69). Third, he distances himself from any theological rebuke by pointing out that "we are far better able to prescribe limits to our thinking ["l'action de notre pensée"] than to the works of God" (*Le monde* 22; AT 11:33). Finally, the fable's inescapable need for exogenous corroboration from the world of God, as demonstrated by the slippery references to God's creation and laws, forces Descartes to challenge the intrinsic validity of any claim of infinity, even for imaginary spaces.[19] This he does ever so subtly by preferring to speak of indefinite distances rather than infinite spaces.

The fact remains that if Descartes's fable is true, its specifics will be valid for any point outside Mosaic time, which at the very least reopens the question of the accepted chronology of cosmic history and should, one might think, reintroduce infinity as a possibility. Yet Descartes refused to pursue this question and insisted that we can know, because we can set them, only the limits of our mind, not God's creation. By doing so, Descartes did more than sidestep a potentially controversial issue; he made a value judgment about what he considered valid

[19] As noted by Judith Butler, Descartes's "conjecturing and supposing have to be understood as fictional exercises that are nevertheless not devoid of referentiality." I would, however, be loath to go so far as to agree that his attempt "to falsify false belief involves a positing or fictionalizing that, homeopathically, recontracts the very illness it seeks to cure." I find it more significant that Descartes's *feintes* enable him to reach conclusions that are radically different from those of his predecessors. Judith Butler, " 'How Can I Deny That These Hands and This Body Are Mine?' " *Qui Parle* 11 (1997): 14.

fields of inquiry.[20] By speaking of "indefinity," as it were, as opposed to infinity, he posited that inquiring about infinity is as useless an exercise as privileging beginnings and endings or wondering about origins. He peremptorily removed time and history from the field of scientific or certain knowledge. It remains to be seen what he replaced them with and on what authority.

Le monde begins, somewhat unexpectedly, with considerations on light, the first of which is a warning that "there may be some difference between the sensation we have of it, i.e., between the idea of light that takes shape in our imagination by the intervention of our eyes, and what is in the objects that generates this sensation in us, i.e., what is in the flame or the Sun that is called by the name light" (*Le monde* 9; AT 11:3). This statement warrants close scrutiny. First, it impresses on the reader the notion that the world must be grasped in human terms. It must be envisioned. The source of the sensation—light, the sun—is secondary, our idea of it and our name for it primary. Vision must here be understood as a product of the senses whose operation depends on the thinking mind. In other words, the world is immediately portrayed as revolving around the human mind. The emphasis on light should not distract us into thinking that actual phenomena or our sense of sight are paramount. The eyes are but go-betweens. Descartes at once removes any ambiguity by proposing a semantic model of human knowledge. Contrary to a commonly held impression, he immediately argues, ideas do not fully resemble the objects that give rise to them ("there may be some difference . . ."). Arguing analogically from what we now call the arbitrariness of the linguistic sign, he asks "why nature might not have been able to establish as well some sign that would make us have the sensation of light though this sign may have nothing in it that resembles this sensation" (*Le monde* 9; AT 11:4). Of course, for Descartes, nature itself is still responsible for these signs, just as, he then argues, it is responsible for the laughter and tears that enable us to "read" joy and sadness. By contrast, words are a distinctly human institution and it is this institution that gives its model to nature. In the end, nature can be conceived only in reference to a different—and more fundamental—semantic model.

[20] Ferdinand Alquié and Annie Bitbol-Hespériès have made a convincing case against overestimating the fear of Church censorship in accounting for Descartes's turn to fables in *Le monde*. See Ferdinand Alquié, *La découverte métaphysique de l'homme chez Descartes*, 2nd ed. (Paris: Presses Universitaires de France, 1966), 118; and Bitbol-Hespériès's introduction to *Le monde, L'homme*, xxx.

Nature, and with it, sources and origins, plays a secondary role in the Cartesian model of conception. All are signs of human institution and, as such, are always already mediated—are in medias res. More specifically still, they are the product of Descartes's own mind. As Timothy J. Reiss notes, "It is not for nothing that this text [Le monde] is followed by the Discours de la méthode, in which the I-discourse (of 'autobiography') is constituted as the origin and certification of all certain knowledge."[21] We see traces of this genealogy in Descartes's theory of elements, which he prefaces by saying: "I must describe them to you in my own way" (Le monde 18; AT 11:24). More pointedly, he argues that description precedes discovery—"it is not possible that I should find any such form in the world except for the three I have described"—and hinges on conceptualization rather than observation (19; AT 11:26). This accounts for the presence of what Reiss has called the "concevoir motif" and for Descartes's reliance on his own authority as ultimate source of knowledge, as, for example, in the case of his axiomatic declaration that "the forms of the elements must be simple" (19; AT 11:26).[22]

The autobiographical references included in the Discours de la méthode are a direct consequence of Descartes's privileging of subjective authority. At the same time, however, they seem to have opened the Cartesian method to charges of incoherence. Vico, for instance, thought that Descartes's reliance on narrative was at odds with some of his most famous pronouncements, including his marginalization of belles lettres. I would argue instead that the memorable scene of the birth of Descartes's method in a stove-heated room is not out of place in a work devoted in part to making distinctions between orders of knowledge and levels of certainty.

In part 3 of the Discours the French thinker allows explicitly that in the realm of morality, where it is necessary to act on the basis of incomplete information, one ought to rely on probable knowledge. This need was compounded by his belief that "because of the corruption of our mores

[21] Timothy J. Reiss, "The 'Concevoir' Motif in Descartes," in La cohérence intérieure: Etudes sur la littérature française du XVIIe siècle présentées en hommage à Judd D. Hubert, ed. Jacqueline van Baelen and David Lee Rubin (Paris: Jean-Michel Place, 1977), 210.

[22] Playing on two meanings of the word concevoir, that is, perception (of natural signs) and cognition (of ideas), Reiss defines the concevoir motif as an operator, in the mathematical sense, that allows Descartes to separate "natural signs from their (natural) referent" and to assimilate them instead into an existing discursive or conceptual practice ("The 'Concevoir' Motif," 212). Of course, I am tossing a third meaning into the mix: conception as generation or beginning.

there are few people willing to say all that they believe" (*Discours;* AT 6:23), a belief shared by many of his contemporaries. *La princesse de Clèves* (1678), for instance, to use a well-worn example, is undeniably devoted to the question of the corruption of appearances. Such a parallel should not, however, make us confuse Descartes's fable with what we have come to define as works of fiction. Not only is the *fable du monde* different from the histories of a Bodin or a Le Roy, it bears only a superficial resemblance to the works of playwrights and novelists. As his critique of *vraisemblance* demonstrates, Descartes wanted his fable to be judged by different criteria than plays, *romans,* and *nouvelles.* All narratives are not created equal as far as Descartes is concerned, and distinctions between the Cartesian fable and what we usually think of as fiction need to be made. Indeed, Descartes's skepticism vis-à-vis appearances may have prompted him to turn to narrative in his autobiography and in his fable, but this decision was not accompanied by a desire to tease out the literary possibilities of the category of the *vraisemblable.*[23] Instead, he chose to maintain restrictions on its range of application and to subordinate his fable to "the necessary order" ("l'ordre qu'il faut"; *Discours;* AT 6:19), that is, the order of mathematics, especially geometry and algebra. A fable was to be judged by its closeness to scientific or certain knowledge.

This explains, of course, why Descartes's first precept—"never to receive anything as true that I did not know to be so on the basis of evidence" (*Discours;* AT 6:18)—presupposes a methodical purge of verisimilitude as a form of knowledge. As indicated in Etienne Gilson's footnote in his edition of the *Discours:* "The opposite of that which is evident is: 1) that which is false; 2) that which is merely probable. The rule of evidence therefore rules verisimilitude as a whole out of the realm of philosophy."[24] Of course, if Gilson is correct—and I see no reason to believe he is not—then some of the statements made in part 5 of the *Discours de la méthode* concerning the theological account of the birth of the world are even more radical than anything to be found in *Le monde.*

After summarizing the arguments made in his yet unpublished treatise, Descartes makes the following observation: "However, I did not want to infer from all these things that this world had been created the

[23] I have studied the relationship between Descartes's rejection of *vraisemblance* and the history of the novel in "Epistolarité et épistémologie: La Fayette, Descartes, Graffigny et Rousseau," *SVEC* (2002) 06: 79–91.

[24] René Descartes, *Discours de la méthode,* ed. Etienne Gilson (Paris: Librairie Philosophique J. Vrin, 1989), 69n1.

way I was proposing; for *it is far more likely that, from the beginning, God made it as it was supposed to be.*"[25] Ostensibly, we are dealing here with a hedging of the potentially controversial aspects of his theories, including his earlier assertion that "even if God had created several worlds, not one could possibly exist in which they [the Laws of Nature] would fail to obtain" (*Discours*; AT 6:43), which suggests that our knowledge of God could eventually be subordinated to an understanding of the laws of nature.[26] On close examination, however, Descartes's hedging is remarkably sibylline since he has otherwise defined the *vraisemblable* as that which is doubtful. This in turn calls into question all theological histories and, possibly, theology itself as a way of knowing.

This is precisely Descartes's next move. His concession that "it is far more likely that, from the beginning, God made it [this world] as it was supposed to be" is immediately followed by a statement ultimately equivalent to a claim that the moment of creation, that is, the moment of God's active involvement with the world, is less significant than the conception of the laws of nature, made knowable and conceivable to the human mind by their very immutability. "However, it is certain . . . that even if he [God] had in the beginning given [the world] no other form than that of Chaos, one is entitled to believe, without prejudice to the miracle of creation, that as long as he had established the Laws of Nature and assisted it so that it [Nature] would operate as it customarily does, this alone would have made it possible for all things that are purely material to become what we now see" (*Discours*; AT 6:45). Again, Descartes's caveat notwithstanding, it is difficult to refrain from reading into this statement the possibility that God's role was not, in the end, or rather, at the beginning, indispensable. This accounts for Paolo Rossi's decision to ignore the distinction between fictional and actual geneses, or between the beginning of *a* world and that of *the* world: "What else had Descartes done in the fifth part of his *Discourse*

---

[25] "Toutefois ie ne voulois pas inferer de toutes ces choses, que ce monde ait esté creé en la façon que ie proposois; car *il est bien plus vraysemblable que, dés le commencement, Dieu l'a rendu tel qu'il deuoit estre*" (*Discours*; AT 6:45, emphasis added).

[26] Descartes does underscore that his reasoning has been founded throughout on "no other principle than the infinite perfections of God" (*Discours*; AT 6:43). I do not dismiss this statement as disingenuous, but interpret it instead as a step taken to deal with what I see, perhaps naively, as Descartes's increasingly daunting realization that the views he had espoused in *Le monde* involved a quasi-Copernican shift in the respective roles and importance of the creating force of God and the thinking human mind in making the world intelligible and, possibly, present.

on *Method* (1637), in his *Principia* (1644), in his short treatise, *Le Monde ou le traité de la lumière* (finished in 1633, but published only in 1664 and 1677), if not present an alternative account to that of Genesis? If not describe the birth of the physical world?"[27]

And yet, Descartes's *feinte* remains indispensable as a rhetorical as well as a conceptual or constitutive epistemological tool. Without fiction, Descartes would have been limited to the study of actual origins, which can only be "known" through inferior modes of knowledge that rely on substandard tools of understanding, such as memory and verisimilitude. Even in the case of God's creation, this is unacceptable to Descartes, who turned to fiction in part to be able to reinforce the traditional division of epistemological labor between certain and probable knowledge.[28] That such certainty was rarely achieved did not deter him. The world cannot be presented bare, any more than numbers can, if the human mind is to make sense of it.[29] In any case, a fictional world may well be all we have access to. As Ferdinand Alquié remarked some time ago, "removing the World from the realm of reality . . . makes its analysis possible" ("la déréalisation du Monde est . . . la condition de son explication").[30] More bluntly put, truth is a work of fiction, or rather, fiction is the only truth we can know. Indeed, Jean-Luc Nancy was absolutely justified in claiming that "the question of the fable of the Discourse, of the Fable-Discourse, must not be tackled by way of the distinction between truth and fiction."[31]

[27] Paolo Rossi, *The Dark Abyss of Time: The History of the Earth and the History of Nations from Hooke to Vico*, trans. Lydia G. Cochrane (Chicago: University of Chicago Press, 1984), 45.

[28] This division remained in place as long as probability was above all a criterion used to judge the reliability of witnesses. See Douglas Lane Patey, *Probability and Literary Form: Philosophic Theory and Literary Practice in the Augustan Age* (Cambridge: Cambridge University Press, 1984), 7–9. The history of probability has been the focus of several other excellent works: Ian Hacking, *The Emergence of Probability: A Philosophical Study of Early Ideas about Probability, Induction, and Statistical Inference* (London: Cambridge University Press, 1975); Barbara J. Shapiro, *Probability and Certainty in Seventeenth-Century England: A Study of the Relationships between Natural Science, Religion, History, Law, and Literature* (Princeton, N.J.: Princeton University Press, 1983); Lorraine Daston, *Classical Probability in the Enlightenment* (Princeton, N.J.: Princeton University Press, 1988); and Thomas M. Kavanagh, *Enlightenment and the Shadows of Chance: The Novel and the Culture of Gambling in Eighteenth-Century France* (Baltimore: Johns Hopkins University Press, 1993).

[29] "I have spoken of its 'outer garment,' not because I wish to conceal this science and shroud it from the gaze of the public; I wish rather to clothe and adorn it so as to make it easier to present to the human mind" (*Rules;* CSMK 1:17; AT 10:374).

[30] Alquié, *Découverte métaphysique*, 115.

[31] Jean-Luc Nancy, *Ego sum* (Paris: Flammarion, 1979), 107.

⁓

How does fiction become a primary source of knowledge whose success does not depend on its ability to imitate or approximate the real? Not by virtue of its narrative components or external or factual corroboration, at least not primarily. The certainty of a fable depends on a writer's ability to create a vision that can, on being observed, be internalized by the reader/observer who will conceive it in turn.[32] Because he or she has conceived it, the observer will know it to be true. Additionally, only fiction can provide the contrasts that comprehension requires and that make it possible for the world to become visible.

It was of particular interest to Descartes, of course, that such a truth or vision be experienced at any time and not be tied to any particular historical context. The use value of fiction, as it were, lies in its ability to work analogically and visually.[33] It is true that Descartes understood only too well the link between birth and conception and the human fascination with creation myths and primal scenes. His autobiographical incursions attest to this. At the same time, Descartes's narratives also have a definite static, or synchronic, as well as visual quality. To be sure, Descartes's fiction is, to use Jacques Chouillet's carefully chosen words, "susceptible d'historicité."[34] "Historicity," however, was the option not taken by Descartes, who, if anything, was intent on disabling it. Even when he writes of the gradual birth of material things, he makes no claim to historical knowledge. Instead, he take pains to mention that he is referring to events best understood when conceived in our presence and in the present moment: "And *their nature can be conceived far more easily when we see them being born* gradually in this manner than when we look at them

[32] Although the context of his remark is different, Bernard Williams's introduction to Cottingham's translation of the *Meditations* is worth quoting at this point: "Although we are conscious, in reading the *Meditations*, that they were written by a particular person, René Descartes, and at a particular time, about 1640, the 'I' that appears throughout them from the first sentence on does not specifically represent that person: it represents anyone who will step into the position it marks" ("Introductory Essay," in *Meditations on First Philosophy: With Selections from the Objections and Replies*, by René Descartes, trans. and ed. John Cottingham, rev. ed. (Cambridge: Cambridge University Press, 1996), vii.

[33] Pierre-Alain Cahné has demonstrated the importance of analogies (*comparants*) in Descartes's scientific writings. See *Un autre Descartes: Le philosophe et son langage* (Paris: J. Vrin, 1980), esp. 67–73.

[34] Jacques Chouillet, "Descartes et le problème de l'origine des langues au 18e siècle," *Dix-huitième Siècle* 4 (1972): 48.

already made" (*Discours;* AT 6:45, emphasis added). Descartes wants his genesis to be of the present, not in the past.

We can now understand why Descartes's *fable du monde* is a tableau as much as it is a story. This is yet another way of ensuring that his fictional genesis will not fall victim to the inadequacies of the historical and the *vraisemblable.* Yet it is important to note that Descartes never argues that the visual is superior to the historical on the grounds that it is more complete or detailed, or, to use the terminology anachronistically, realistic. Instead we are given to believe that the success of Descartes's tableau/fable hinges on the lack of completion and clarity of his own design. It must contain gaps and shadows if it is to leave room for the viewer/reader's own projections: "I do not promise to include exact demonstrations of all my statements in this work; it will suffice for me to open the way that will enable you to come up with them on your own, should you decide to take the trouble to look for them. . . . Also, in order to make a tableau that will be agreeable to you, I need to use shadows as well as light colors. I shall then be content to continue the description I have already begun, as though my only objective was to tell you a fable" (*Le monde* 29; AT 11:48). One perfect example of the mutual dependency between shadows and visibility can, of course, be found in Descartes's dreams. Although the images of the melon, the church, and the dictionary are vivid enough, their meaning is unstable, a quandary dealt with in the dreams themselves.[35] For Descartes as for contemporary Dutch painters, the visual is not more transparent than the historical.

INTERLUDE: DESCARTES IN THE EIGHTEENTH CENTURY

The known past expanded from six thousand years to millions of years between the time of Matthew Hale, Robert Hooke, Nicholas Steno, and Thomas Burnet, who clung to the accepted chronology even as they provided mounting evidence to the contrary, and that of Kant.[36] Needless to say, this development had serious implications for the conceptualization of origins in the eighteenth century. Clearly, our ability to think of origins as present and what is meant by that will vary,

[35] See AT 10:180–88.
[36] See Rossi, *Dark Abyss;* Shapiro, *Probability and Certainty;* as well as Stephen Toulmin and June Goodfield, *The Discovery of Time* (Chicago: University of Chicago Press, 1982).

depending on whether beginnings exist within an apprehensible point in time. Though Descartes's views played a role in opening up the debate about the age of the world and of mankind, the gradual inclusion of a probabilistic methodology into the "higher" episteme eventually gave a different shape to eighteenth-century inquiries about origins, including those of the universe.[37] Although Descartes may in some instances have anticipated Rousseau's summons in the Second Discourse—"Let us therefore begin by setting all the facts aside"[38]— the Cartesian mistrust of facts did not make him turn to the hypo-thetico-deductivist model of knowledge that would eventually be deemed ideally suited to the study of origins, increasingly thought of as infinitely recessive and inaccessible to demonstration. Unlike his successors, Descartes remained faithful to the notion that, if facts are unreliable, one needs to turn to the sciences in which facts are irrelevant, or try to approximate them as much as possible by relying, if necessary, on fictionalization: "Arithmetic, geometry, and other subjects of this kind, which deal only with the simplest and most general things, regardless of whether they really exist in nature or not, contain something certain and indubitable. For whether I am awake or asleep, two and three added together are five, and a square has no more than four sides" (*Meditations;* CSMK 2:14; AT 7:20; vol. 9, bk. 1, 16).

Descartes's insistent privileging of certain knowledge and his marginalization of history as object and method of study, became increasingly untenable as the eighteenth century unfolded. The question raised by Chouillet is absolutely valid: "How is it that philosophical thought, which in the classical period had seemed to be about the human present, was then [in the eighteenth century] transformed into a para-historical discourse in which the words 'foundations' and 'origins' appear to be completely interchangeable and necessarily linked? It is as though it became impossible for Enlightenment philosophy to gaze on a nearby object without resorting to that retrospective or lateral perspective made possible by either spatial or temporal distance."[39] Chouillet's tentative answer goes a long way toward explaining why eighteenth-century

<hr/>

[37] See Shapiro, *Probability and Certainty,* 97–98.

[38] Jean-Jacques Rousseau, *Discourse on the Origins of Inequality (Second Discourse); Polemics; and Political Economy,* ed. Roger D. Masters and Christopher Kelly, trans. Judith R. Bush, Roger D. Masters, Christopher Kelly, and Terence Marshall, in *The Collected Writings of Rousseau,* ed. Roger D. Masters and Christopher Kelly (Hanover, N.H.: Published for Dartmouth College by University Press of New England, 1992), 3:19.

[39] Chouillet, "Descartes," 46–47.

thinkers often took pains to distance themselves from their predecessor in the matter of origins. This was particularly true of Vico, who bracketed the world of nature in favor of the study of the world of nations on the grounds that we can know only what we have made, and who would recognize Descartes's own primal scene in part 2 of the *Discours* only as *vera narratio*. However, the French thinker's militant belief that we can conceive only what we make ourselves—"one cannot conceive something so well, and make it one's own, when one learns it from someone else as when one invents it oneself" (*Discours*; AT 6:69)—does seem to have made possible the emphasis on the self as a source of knowledge and on the equation between knowing and making that is so characteristic of eighteenth-century thought when it turned to the question of origins.[40] Indeed, though Descartes's portrayal of *l'homme* as a spectator, as demonstrated by his emphasis on the defining role of vision,[41] owes much, as Cavaillé has beautifully argued, to a baroque aesthetic, his semiotics of vision and conception also prefigures a number of important eighteenth-century inquiries. These include not only the Kantian turn to concepts as the only sound epistemological basis and even, paradoxically, Vico's insights into the etymological nature of historical and mental change, but also a modern aesthetic of knowledge grounded in the human body as primary site of knowledge, if only of the distance between world and thought, and in a conception of "man" as a visionary rather than a spectator or player on the world's stage. Although the historical nature of eighteenth-century genetic thought is indeed striking, it coexisted with an idealization of presence and synchronicity. Geometry—not to mention Cartesianism—did not go quietly. As Jean-Luc Nancy has noted, "the fable of the *Discourse* must not be mistaken for a literary envelope"; in the same way, Vico's axioms should not be dismissed as "geometrical affectations."[42]

[40] This idealizing of the subject as source of knowledge is particularly evident in the challenge to the existence of God issued in the *Meditations,* in which Descartes not only allows for the possibility that God might be a deceiver, but also that he, Descartes, might be God. That he eventually dismisses this possibility takes nothing away from the supposition.

[41] See Descartes, *L'homme* 137; AT 11:151.

[42] "La fable du *Discours* ne peut pas être traitée comme enveloppe littéraire" (Nancy, *Ego sum*, 107). See also Donald R. Kelley, "Vico's Road: From Philosophy to Jurisprudence and Back," in *Giambattista Vico's Science of Humanity*, ed. Giorgio Tagliacozzo and Donald Phillip Verene (Baltimore: Johns Hopkins University Press, 1976), 27.

Vico's Genetic Principle

What Descartes had looked askance at, Vico embraced, when he founded his *New Science* on a genetic principle and maintained that ignorance is an inescapable condition of human knowledge. This distinction should not, however, be mistaken for a blanket dismissal by the Italian writer of all things Cartesian. The relationship between the two thinkers is far more complex. Nowhere is this more in evidence than in their common yet markedly different acknowledgment of the importance of fiction in generating and communicating knowledge. Whereas Descartes had turned to his own fable-making abilities to picture and stage in the present moment the creation of the world, Vico insisted on the continued presence of the past in all human endeavors and authored a hermeneutics of myth and history. Yet, remarkably, Vico also argued that historical knowledge can rise to the level of geometric certainty and made a concerted effort to make history and mathematics interdependent. In the process he gave birth to an epistemological model that attempted to yield both credible impossibilities and axiomatic truths. The primary goal of this chapter is to analyze Vico's epistemological model and the genetic principle that sustained it.[1]

In view of the fragmented and labyrinthine exposition of the *New Science,* it is only fitting that many roads should lead to Vico's epistemology. At the same time, there is perhaps no better starting point than

---

[1] Vico's thoughts on the origins of nations and languages are discussed in chapter 4, where his views are contrasted to Rousseau's.

the "Discovery of the True Homer," since it deals with the beginning, or, to be more accurate, the beginning of record, of poetic wisdom. Additionally, the "Discovery" offers a perfect example of Vico's methodology and of his ability to weave particulars and generalities so tightly that the reader has trouble conceiving them separately. I shall nevertheless attempt to do so. More specifically, I shall discuss the particulars of Vico's "Discovery"—and the ways it represents a departure from earlier treatments of Homeric poetry—before moving on to an examination of the hermeneutics of the *New Science* and of Vichian epistemology. In the process I shall rely primarily on the third edition of the *New Science* (1744), drawing on the *Autobiography* (1725 and 1731), the earlier treatises *On the Most Ancient Wisdom of the Italians* (1710) and *On the Study Methods of Our Time* (1709), as well as on the six inaugural orations (1699–1707) on an ad hoc basis.[2]

THE "DISCOVERY" AND HOMERIC SCHOLARSHIP

The "Discovery of the True Homer" has long been recognized to be intimately linked to what Vico has called the master key of his *New Science*, namely, that "the first gentile peoples, by a demonstrated necessity of nature, were poets who spoke in poetic characters."[3] This notion, which, Vico notes in the same paragraph, "has cost us the persistent research of almost all our literary life," was introduced in the *second* edition of the *New Science*, written between December 25, 1729, and April 9, 1730.

Vico's "discovery" signaled a remarkable departure from earlier manifestations of interest in Homeric poetry, which has not always occupied a secure place in the literary pantheon. His reception in mid-seventeenth-century France, for instance, was so unenthusiastic that Noémi Hepp, in her wonderfully detailed investigation of what

---

[2] My goal is not to trace the evolution of Vico's thought or settle the debate as to the extent to which the *New Science* represents a significant departure from his earlier work. Readers interested in Vico's entire corpus will want to read Giuseppe Mazzotta's *The New Map of the World: The Poetic Philosophy of Giambattista Vico* (Princeton, N.J.: Princeton University Press, 1999).

[3] *The New Science of Giambattista Vico: Unabridged Translation of the Third Edition (1744) with the Addition of "Practic of the New Science,"* trans. Thomas Goddard Bergin and Max Harold Fisch (Ithaca, N.Y.: Cornell University Press, 1984), §34. Future references to paragraphs in the Bergin and Fisch translation will be included parenthetically in the body of the text, preceded, whenever necessary, by the initials *NS*.

amounted to an absence, could justifiably write that "if Aristotle had not praised Homer, it is probable that nobody would have been concerned with him."[4] Critics did recognize Homer's temporal primacy, originality (to use a noun that made its first appearance in French in 1699), and genius, but these were not, after all, essential criteria of evaluation for neoclassicists.[5]

This ambivalence was hardly unique. Homeric poetry had been found wanting since at least the fifteenth century, a situation often thought to have been caused by the absence of good translations. However, neither the publication, in 1544–1550, of Eustathius's twelfth-century commentaries nor the translations that appeared around the same time swayed critics such as J. C. Scaliger, who retained his abiding preference for a Virgilian sense of decorum. Additionally, those who did take the trouble to study Homer generally relied on the kind of moralizing allegorical interpretations that featured prominently in Eustathius's criticism. As a result, for at least another two hundred years, Homer was studied primarily as an important source of esoteric wisdom. Vico was to distance himself from this allegorical reading, which not only affected his interpretation of Homer as the father of poetry but shaped his entire hermeneutics as well.[6]

[4] Noémi Hepp, *Homère en France au XVIIeme siècle* (Paris: C. Klincksieck, 1968), 335. Hepp's work has been the object of a recent sequel: *Homère en France après la Querelle (1715–1900)*, ed. Françoise Létoublon and Catherine Volpilhac-Auger (Paris: Honoré Champion, 1999).

[5] The word *originalité* had already made an appearance in the late fourteenth century, when it was used to refer to lineage or extraction. It was only in the late seventeenth century, however, that the word was first used to refer to the original quality of a work, with the first mention of record dating to 1699, in Roger de Piles's *Abrégé de la vie des peintres*. The word quickly came to denote singularity or oddity as well, with a first occurrence recorded for 1722. Adolphe Hatzfeld and Arsène Darmesteter, *Dictionnaire général de la langue française du commencement du XVIIe siècle jusqu'à nos jours* (Paris: Librairie Ch. Delagrave, 1895–1900), s.v. "Original, -ale,"; and Alain Rey, ed., *Dictionnaire historique de la langue française* (Paris: Dictionnaires le Robert, 1993), s.v. "Origine." The first occurrence of the English noun *originality* dates to 1742. *OED Online*, http://dictionary.oed.com/cgi/entry/00164869.

[6] For detailed theoretical and historical discussions of allegory as they relate to Homeric poetry, see, in order of publication, Félix Buffière, *Les mythes d'Homère et la pensée grecque* (Paris: Les Belles Lettres, 1973); Philip Rollinson, *Classical Theories of Allegory and Christian Culture* (Pittsburgh: Duquesne University Press, 1981); Howard Clarke, *Homer's Readers: A Historical Introduction to the "Iliad" and the "Odyssey"* (Newark: University of Delaware Press, 1981); Jon Whitman, *Allegory: The Dynamics of an Ancient and Medieval Technique* (Cambridge, Mass.: Harvard University Press, 1987); and Anthony Grafton, "Renaissance Readers of Homer's Ancient Readers," in *Homer's Ancient Readers: The Hermeneutics of Greek Epic's [sic] Earliest Exegetes*, ed. Robert Lamberton and John J. Keaney (Princeton, N.J.: Princeton University Press, 1992), 149–72.

Vico's position was fostered in part by the critical lull that settled in during the second half of the seventeenth century until, of course, the start of the Quarrel between the Ancients and the Moderns. According to Hepp, there were fewer commentaries between 1644, the year of Louis XIII's death, and 1686 than in the previous forty and the following thirty years.[7] This pause seems to have made possible the contextualization of Homeric poetry from a more historical perspective, an approach that owed much to Renaissance historicism and the tradition of biblical scholarship. Just as Homer had sometimes come under attack, so did moral allegorism, as some critics began to turn to history and ethics for their valorization of the *Iliad* and the *Odyssey*, and as competing approaches to myth emerged.

One such critic was Francis Bacon, who in his preface to the *Wisdom of the Ancients* remarked that ancient parables "must absolutely be receiued, as a thing graue and sober, . . . and exceeding profitable and necessary to all sciences." Fables, he claimed, were not deliberate moral allegories but repositories of knowledge belonging to a prerationalistic era, to "the first ages," when "all things were full of Fables, enigmaes, parables, and similies of all sortes: by which they sought to teach and lay open, not to hide and conceale knowledge, especially, seeing the understandings of men were in those times rude and impatient, and almost incapable of any subtilties, such things onely excepted, as were the obiects of sense: for as *Hieroglyphicks* preceded letters, so parables were more ancient then Arguments." According to Bacon, fables like the ones written down in the *Iliad* and the *Odyssey* were modified historical narrations, "sacred reliques or abstracted ayres of better times, which by tradition from more ancient Nations fell into the Trumpets and Flutes of the Graecians."[8]

It is true that Bacon did not object to the moral allegorization of these "sacred reliques." In a fairly typical commentary on the Sirens, for instance, he interpreted Ulysses's wax trick as a method by which inconstant and baser people can avoid succumbing to debauchery. Nevertheless, he did help to define the new hermeneutic avenues that would eventually make it possible to conceptualize Homeric poetry as a source of historical knowledge rather than esoteric wisdom.[9] This task was

---

[7] Hepp, *Homère en France*, 318.

[8] Francis Bacon, *The Wisedome of the Ancients*, trans. Arthur Gorges Knight (London, 1619), unpaginated.

[9] One finds references to Bacon's *De sapientia veterum* in NS §§80, 384, and 654.

taken up most notably by Abbé d'Aubignac in his *Conjectures académiques ou dissertation sur l'Iliade* (published in 1715 but written between 1664 and 1670 and mentioned by other critics prior to its publication). D'Aubignac claimed that Homer never existed and that the *Iliad* and the *Odyssey* were actually compilations of shorter poems, an insight similar to Vico's description of "Homer as a binder or compiler of fables" (*NS* §852).[10] Finally, at about the same time, Fontenelle also rejected the notion that Homer was a source of esoteric wisdom and, in his *Nouveaux dialogues des morts* (1683), refused to accredit the old equation between Homeric poetry and philosophy:

AESOP: What! Did you not intend to hide important mysteries in your works?

HOMER: Alas! Not at all.

AESOP: And yet all the scholars of my era said so; there was nothing in the *Iliad* or the *Odyssey* to which they did not attribute the most beautiful allegories in the world.[11]

This historicization of Homer conformed with the increasing interest in primitivism, or the idealization of early versus late phases of societal development and the attendant interest in society's beginnings, which was to be one of the hallmarks of eighteenth-century thought.[12] Vico had several immediate precursors in this area, both in Italy and abroad, including Gian Vincenzo Gravina (1664–1718), author of *Della ragione poetica* (1708) and Thomas Blackwell (1701–1757), whose *Enquiry into the Life and Writings of Homer* (1735) rested on the claim that Homer's

---

[10] I am not claiming that Vico read D'Aubignac, even though, as Donald Phillip Verene has persuasively argued, the Italian philosopher was "certainly not as ignorant [of French] as he claims in the *Autobiography*." *The New Art of Autobiography: An Essay on the "Life of Giambattista Vico Written by Himself"* (Oxford: Clarendon Press, 1991), 113. For more information on Vico's sources, see Fausto Nicolini, *La giovinezza di Giambattista Vico, 1688–1700*, 2nd ed. (Bari: Gius. Laterza, 1932); Fisch's introduction to Vico's *Autobiography*, trans. Max Harold Fisch and Thomas Goddard Bergin (Ithaca, N.Y.: Cornell University Press, 1975); Karl-Otto Apel, *Die Idee der Sprache in der Tradition des Humanismus von Dante bis Vico*, 2nd ed. (Bonn: Bouvier, 1975); Paul D. L. Avis, *Foundations of Modern Historical Thought* (London: Croom Helm, 1986); Peter Burke, *Vico* (Oxford: Oxford University Press, 1986); and Giorgio Tagliacozzo and Donald Phillip Verene, eds., *Giambattista Vico's Science of Humanity* (Baltimore: Johns Hopkins University Press, 1976), especially Donald R. Kelley, "Vico's Road: From Philology to Jurisprudence and Back" (15–29), and Nancy S. Struever, "Vico, Valla, and the Logic of Humanist Inquiry" (173–85).

[11] Bernard le Bovier de Fontenelle, *Nouveaux dialogues des morts*, ed. Donald Schier (Chapel Hill: University of North Carolina Press, 1965), 47.

[12] The issue of primitivism is discussed in greater detail in chapter 4.

poems had not been works of the imagination or instances of any unfettered primitive genius—but were rather faithful copies of Homeric society.[13] The *Enquiry* also echoed the claim made by Hobbes in 1675 that one of the virtues of an epic poem is that it "belongeth as well to History as to Poetry. For both the Poet and the Historian writeth only (or should do) matter of Fact."[14]

Such a broad historical turn—also noticeable in the vogue for movements such as euhemerism and antiquarianism—cannot be ascribed solely to a growing dissatisfaction with moral allegorism.[15] Vico's reliance on historical modes of explanation also helped him draw analogies between the customs of early peoples and other areas of inquiry, especially the study of childhood and, above all, the study of contemporary "primitives."[16] More generally, it enabled him to break away from the tyranny of the more exclusive or restricted species of seventeenth- and eighteenth-century scientific discourses and to celebrate a form of cognition that had been discredited by Descartes and ignored by another of his *maîtres à penser*, Isaac Newton.

Neglected by French critics for decades, Homer found himself back in the thick of intellectual debate as a pawn in the Quarrel between the Ancients and the Moderns. In a first phase, his poetry was casually

[13] On Gravina and Homeric poetry, see Kirsti Simonsuuri, *Homer's Original Genius: Eighteenth-Century Notions of the Early Greek Epic (1688–1798)* (Cambridge: Cambridge University Press, 1979), 87–89. For a discussion of the different conclusions drawn by Gravina and Vico, see Mazzotta, *New Map*, 152–55. On Blackwell's *Enquiry*, see Simonsuuri, *Homer's Original Genius*, 99–107, and Duane Coltharp, "History and the Primitive: Homer, Blackwell, and the Scottish Enlightenment," *Eighteenth-Century Life* 19 (1995): 57–69.

[14] Tho: Hobbes of Malmsbury, "Preface Concerning the Vertues of an Heroique Poem," in *The Iliads and Odysses of Homer*, trans. Tho: Hobbes of Malmsbury, 2nd ed. (London, 1677), A7.

[15] The cornerstone of the euhemerist doctrine was that myths stood for actual events whose historical existence could be established. See Frank Manuel, *The Eighteenth Century Confronts the Gods* (Cambridge, Mass.: Harvard University Press, 1959), 85 and 103–4. On the essential difference between the *New Science* and euhemerism, see Gianfranco Cantelli, "Myth and Language in Vico," and Donald Phillip Verene, "Vico's Science of Imaginative Universals and the Philosophy of Symbolic Forms," both in Tagliacozzo and Verene, *Giambattista Vico's Science of Humanity*, 47–63 and 295–317.

[16] *NS* §§186–87, 206–17, 375, and 552 deal with the question of childhood, while *NS* §§375, 435, 437, 470, 486, 542, 658, 841, and 1095 focus on primitivism. In this connection, let me mention the parallel—recognized by both Friedrich Meinecke and Peter Burke—between Vico's method and that of Jean-François Lafitau's *Customs of the American Savages, Compared to the Customs of Early Times* (1724). See Friedrich Meinecke, *Historism: The Rise of a New Historical Outlook*, trans. J. E. Anderson (London: Routledge and Kegan Paul, 1972), 37–53, and Burke, *Vico*, 52.

used as an example of primitive and backward expression by a number of critics, most notably Charles Perrault in his *Parallèle des anciens et des modernes* (1688–1697).[17] After a weak reaction on the part of André Dacier and Boileau, among others, in the early 1690s, a twenty-year lull settled in. The Quarrel flared up again in 1714–1716, when it focused exclusively on Homer.[18] This time, the chief protagonists were Anne Dacier, whose translation of the *Iliad* appeared in 1711, and Antoine Houdar de la Motte, whose adaptation of the *Iliad* (1701–1714) Anne Dacier found particularly offensive. In 1714 she accordingly published *Des causes de la corruption du goust*. Somewhat surprisingly in view of the comparatively late date, this staunch supporter of Homer tried to discredit her opponents by stressing the fablelike or allegorical quality of Homeric poetry. Even the *Iliad*, she claimed, the poem that lends itself the least to allegorical interpretations, "is indeed a fable," if only by virtue of being an epic poem: "A poem could very well resemble neither the *Iliad* nor the *Odyssey* and still be an Epic Poem, so long as it were similarly constituted, i.e., that its subject was a fable, words invented to influence mores through instruction disguised as allegorical action."[19]

Allegory remained Dacier's principal weapon in her battle against those who had been trying to discredit Homer. To those who criticized, for instance, the gods' apparent lack of wisdom, she objected that "everything that seems most contrary to Divinity in the works of Homer, redeems itself by means of Allegories." What other line of defense could be adopted by a critic who saw belles lettres as "the source of good taste, Politesse, and all good Government?" If literature is to be defended on moral grounds, then a good poem is necessarily a moral poem. The premises of her interpretation were therefore that "the Subject of the Poem is a great instruction, since it is a Fable . . . and no Fable exists that does not have Morality at its foundation, since it is a point of Morality disguised as the Allegory of an action." If the *Iliad* and the *Odyssey* were *contraires aux bonnes moeurs*, then Homer could not be defended. He therefore had to be allegorized, turned into a pagan version of La Fontaine.

[17] On the impact of the Quarrel on eighteenth-century criticism, including Wolf's *Prolegomena*, see Anthony Grafton, Glenn W. Most, and James E. G. Zetzel's introduction to F. A. Wolf, *Prolegomena to Homer, 1795*, trans. Anthony Grafton, Glenn W. Most, and James E. G. Zetzel (Princeton, N.J.: Princeton University Press, 1985), esp. 8–12.

[18] Joan DeJean has taken up the question of this second phase of the Quarrel in *Ancients against Moderns: Culture Wars and the Making of a Fin de Siècle* (Chicago: University of Chicago Press, 1997), 94–108.

[19] Anne Dacier, *Des Causes de la corruption du goust* (Paris, 1714), 61, 68–69.

One is not surprised to find, then, that Dacier heeded the tradition that equated Homer's poetry with philosophy itself: "The *Iliad* has been liked, because not only is Morality far from being violated in this work, it is actually very good and very sensible, and because this Poem is more moral and more philosophical than Philosophy itself."[20]

A strict moralist, Anne Dacier rejected the interpretations of critics who, like Houdar de la Motte, argued that Homer's epic poems are actually historical repositories or archeological documents, even when such critics were trying to defend the *Iliad* and the *Odyssey*. Vico, by contrast, wished to account for Homer's "base sentences, vulgar customs, crude comparisons, local idioms, licenses in meter, variations in dialect, and his having made men of gods and gods of men" (§§883–89) without relying on "the props of philosophical allegories" (§890). He also wished to discredit the esoteric wisdom attributed to Homer as the product of a belated, postheroic consciousness. He therefore distinguished between philosophical allegories on the one hand, which depend on a deductive and analogical principle inaccessible to the poetic mind and which yield a multiplicity of interpretations, and "true poetic allegories" on the other, which came on the heels of the fables and myths of the first, or theological, poets and "gave the fables univocal, not analogical, meanings" (§210). As he described it in the *New Science*, the early fables of the Greeks had been "certain imaginative genera (images for the most part of animate substances, of gods or heroes, formed by their imagination) to which they reduced all the species or all the particulars appertaining to each genus. . . . These divine or heroic characters were true fables or myths, and their allegories are found to contain meanings not analogical but univocal, not philosophical but historical, of the peoples of Greece of those times" (§34). These "imaginative genera" or "imaginative universals" illustrate the primary distinction between poetic and philosophical thought. Where the latter has rested at least since Plato on a process of division or *ratio*, the former is characterized primarily by what Donald Phillip Verene has aptly called "its power to assert *identities*, not *similarities*."[21]

[20] Ibid., 106, 9–10, 260, 278.

[21] Donald Phillip Verene, *Vico's Science of Imagination* (Ithaca, N.Y.: Cornell University Press, 1991), 76. See also John D. Schaeffer, *Sensus Communis: Vico, Rhetoric, and the Limits of Relativism* (Durham, N.C.: Duke University Press, 1990), 86–92, for further remarks on imaginative universals; and David Rapport Lachterman, *The Ethics of Geometry: A Genealogy of Modernity* (New York: Routledge, 1989), 29–33, for an analysis of the link between *logos*, *ratio*, and *analogia*.

With regard to Homeric scholarship, the first crucial consequence of this poetics is that Homer, who appeared, according to Vico's calculations, "eighteen hundred years after the institution of marriage had laid the first foundations of Greek civility" (§901), was neither "the founder of Greek polity or civility" (§899) nor "the father of all other poets" (§900) nor "the source of all Greek philosophies" (§901), but was instead "the first historian of the entire gentile world who has come down to us" (§903). His poems should not be valued for their moral worth but "should henceforth be highly prized as being two great treasure stores of the customs of early Greece" (§904).

This theory of early poetic wisdom allowed Vico to dismiss the attack launched against Homer by those who thought his sense of decorum left much to be desired. If the *Iliad* upsets modern literary expectations, if its heroes are unreasonably vindictive, its gods petty, and its customs crude and savage, it is because Homer "had to conform to the quite vulgar feelings and hence the vulgar customs of the barbarous Greece of his day" (§781). In addition, "the ineptitudes and indecencies are effects of the awkwardness with which the Greek peoples had labored to express themselves in the extreme poverty of their language in its formative period" (§830). Vico's summation is that the *Iliad* demonstrates that Homer was "unrivaled in creating poetic characters, the greatest of which are so discordant with this civil human nature of ours, yet perfectly decorous in relation to the punctilious heroic nature" (§783). Their properties can pertain only to a heroic age when men "are like children in the weakness of their minds, like women in the vigor of their imaginations, and like violent youths in the turbulence of their passions; whence we must deny to Homer any kind of esoteric wisdom" (§787).

Vico's historical and philological reading of the *Iliad* and the *Odyssey*, as well as the comparisons he drew between these works and the fabulous beginnings of other nations, eventually led him to conclude that "the two poems were composed and compiled by various hands through successive ages" (§804). They were originally "true and severe narrations" (§814) made of poetic characters that "were imaginative universals . . . to which the peoples of Greece attached all the various particulars belonging to each genus. To Achilles, for example, who is the subject of the *Iliad*, they attached all the properties of heroic valor, and all the feelings and customs arising from these natural properties, such as those of quick temper, punctiliousness, wrathfulness, implacability, violence, the arrogation of all right to might" (§809). With time these fables "gradually lost their original meanings" (§814) and "were received by Homer in this corrupt and distorted form" (§815). As such, they nevertheless "contain historical significations referring only to the earliest times of Greece" (§818) when imagination and memory were one.

THE "DISCOVERY" AND VICHIAN HERMENEUTICS

Vico's historicization of Homer served a variety of purposes: it allowed him to provide a quasi-sociological reading of the customs described in the *Iliad* and the *Odyssey*; it both reinforced and refined the adequation of poetry and custom and, by extension, of literature and memory expostulated in book 2 of the *New Science*; and it strengthened his emphasis on the relationship between language, law, and history. We can therefore appreciate the stated importance of the "Discovery" in the conceptualization of the second *New Science*: "By 'The Discovery of the True Homer' all the institutions that make up this world of nations are clarified, proceeding from their origins according to the order in which the hieroglyphs come forth into the light of the true Homer" (§41). Not surprisingly, then, a close analysis of Vico's methodology in the unveiling of his "discovery" in the third book of his magnum opus is bound to yield valuable insight into Vico's hermeneutics, including his problematization of origins. Let us therefore take a closer look at the precise manner in which the historicization of Homer proceeds in book 3 of the *New Science*.

True heir to the humanist tradition, Vico begins by investigating a variety of anachronisms. He notes, first of all, that one can easily see, especially in the *Iliad*, that more refined customs exist alongside the barbarism manifested by some of the Homeric heroes. He then goes on to argue that such anachronisms denote a time lag between the events referred to and the time of composition. He reinforces this theory by agreeing with the accepted notion that "the interval runs to as much as 460 years" (§803). At this point in the text, however, he departs from tradition. In a move that is not at first accounted for, instead of focusing on Homer's belatedness vis-à-vis the Trojan War, Vico unexpectedly claims—as though it were self-evident that a necessary cause-and-effect relationship obtains between anachronism and multiple authorship—that "lest barbarous acts be confounded with gentle ones . . . we must suppose that the two poems were composed and compiled by various hands through successive ages" (§804).

Rhetorical motivations such as a desire to keep the best arguments for last and to depart from tradition only one cautious step at a time so as not to lose his readers certainly account for the construction of Vico's argument. Yet the fact remains that the "discovery" unfolds in a logically unstable fashion. It is indeed on the strength of a shakily grounded premise that Vico feels entitled to affirm that Homer's poetry is characterized by a "complete absence of philosophy" (§806), an obvious attempt to corroborate one of the main elements of his theory of poetic wisdom, namely, that such wisdom is not philosophical or esoteric but historical. Vico then goes on to write that "inasmuch as the poets came certainly before the vulgar historians, the first history must have been poetic" (§813), a point whose logical necessity does not depend on the presence of anachronisms in Homeric poetry but rather on the axiom laid down earlier, that "men are naturally impelled to preserve the memories of the laws and institutions that bind them in their societies" (§201).

Up to this point in the text, the reader cannot discern whether theory depends on praxis (or Vico's theory of poetic wisdom on his "Discovery," as he often claimed) or the reverse. The argument is largely circular well into the third book of the *New Science*. The hard evidence for the discovery comes late. Contrary to Vico's own methodological claims, the discovery is introduced in deductive terms: since the first poets were historians, and since Homer is our first known poet, Homer must also be our first historian. Homer—"the father of poetry"— therefore did not come first in absolute terms. And, since Homer himself came late, he must have received original heroic fables in a corrupt form. As a result, instead of reading into Homer the philosophy of a more polite age, we must read into Homer the original meanings of the fables. This indeed fits into the larger goal of the *New Science*, which is to provide a hermeneutic theory grounded in the notion that "the fables in their origin were true and severe narrations, whence *mythos*, fable, was defined as *vera narratio*" (§814).

After laying the groundwork for his discovery, Vico finally catalogs the particulars that have convinced him that Homer is "a binder or compiler of fables" (§852):

1) The rhapsodes who "went about the cities of Greece singing the books of Homer at the fairs and festivals . . . were stitchers-together of songs, and these songs they must certainly have collected from none other than their own peoples. Similarly [the common noun] *homēros* is said to come from *homou*, together, and *eirein*, to link" (§§851–52).
2) The poems "still retain a great variety of dialects" (§860).
3) "The fatherland of Homer is not known" (§861).
4) "Almost all the cities of Greece laid claim to him" (§862).
5) "The Homer of the *Odyssey* was from the west of Greece and toward the south, and . . . the Homer of the *Iliad* was from the east and toward the north" (§863).
6) "Not even Homer's age is known" (§864).

Vico's only certain conclusion from this array of general and particular justifications "is that the Greek peoples were themselves Homer" (§875) and "that the reason why opinions as to his age vary so much is that our Homer truly lived on the lips and in the memories of the peoples of Greece throughout the whole period from the Trojan War down to the time of Numa, a span of 460 years" (§876). As for the rhapsodes, his ultimate conclusion is that "they were the authors of these poems inasmuch as they were a part of these peoples who had composed their histories in the poems" (§878).

Finally, Vico feels free to state his thesis fully: "Thus Homer composed the *Iliad* in his youth, that is, when Greece was young and consequently seething with sublime passions, such as pride, wrath, and lust for vengeance, passions which do not tolerate dissimulation but which love magnanimity; and hence this Greece admired Achilles, the hero of violence. But he wrote the *Odyssey* in his old age, that is, when the spirits of Greece had been somewhat cooled by reflection, which is the mother of prudence, so that it admired Ulysses, the hero of wisdom" (§879).

Vico's unveiling of his discovery prompts several observations that are of relevance to the epistemological—and, by extension, at least in this instance, genetic—principles of the *New Science*. First and foremost is an arresting pattern of inversion of traditional categories. Allegorism is a case in point. As traditionally conceived, allegory proceeds from the abstract to the particular. Conversely, Vico's true or poetic "allegories" inflate particulars into universals. Vico thus subverts the traditional meaning, which then allows him to dismiss another commonplace of philosophy: "The philosophers did not discover their philosophies in the Homeric fables but rather inserted them therein" (§901).

At the same time, it is important to note that, in spite of Vico's dismissal of philosophical readings of Homer, it is not clear whether it is philology (one element in a group that also comprises history, poetry, and rhetoric) or philosophy (associated with the natural sciences and mathematics) that has allowed him to develop a method leading to his "Discovery." Clearly, neither can stand on its own. And each is to a degree redefined by the other. Philology is undoubtedly the preferred method— the *New Science* does after all revolve around an analysis of poetic wisdom that excludes philosophy as inherited by Vico. Yet one cannot ignore that the historicization of Homer is grounded in a series of philosophical principles lined up in the form of geometric arguments, of "axioms, both philosophical and philological, including a few reasonable and proper postulates and some clarified definitions" (§119).[22] As described in the "Idea of the Work," Vico's goal is not to exclude philosophy:

> In the present work, . . . philosophy undertakes to examine philology
> (that is, the doctrine of all the institutions that depend on human
> choice; for example, all histories of the languages, customs, and
> deeds of peoples in war and peace), of which, because of the
> deplorable obscurity of causes and almost infinite variety of effects,
> philosophy has had almost a horror of treating; and reduces it to the
> form of a science by discovering in it the design of an ideal eternal
> history traversed in time by the histories of all nations; so that on
> account of this its second principal aspect, our Science may be con-
> sidered a philosophy of authority. (§7)

[22] The matter of the scientific status of history in Vico's *New Science* has been dealt with in a number of works, including R. G. Collingwood, *The Idea of History* (Oxford: Clarendon Press, 1946); Leon Pompa, *Vico: A Study of the "New Science,"* 2nd ed. (Cambridge: Cambridge University Press, 1990); Lionel Rubinoff, "Vico and the Verification of Historical Interpretation," *Social Research* 43 (1976): 484–511; James C. Morrison, "Vico's Principle of *Verum* Is *Factum* and the Problem of Historicism," *Journal of the History of Ideas* 39 (1978): 579–95; and Perez Zagorin, "Vico's Theory of Knowledge: A Critique," *Philosophical Quarterly* 34 (1984): 15–30. Of these authors only Pompa and Collingwood do not find Vico's geometric method to be incompatible with his focus on history. Others have either dismissed the mathematical framework of Vico's philosophy of history as fanciful or peripheral or have labeled the combination an epistemological failure. The latter charge is made not only by Morrison (see esp. 579 and 588), but also by Benedetto Croce in *The Philosophy of Giambattista Vico*, trans. R. G. Collingwood (New York: Russell and Russell, 1964) and A. Robert Caponigri in *Time and Idea: The Theory of History in Giambattista Vico* (Notre Dame: University of Notre Dame Press, 1968).

There is, needless to say, nothing simple about this enterprise. In particular, one must note that if it can be construed as a desire to overcome the disciplinary schism between philosophy and history, it does not do so without casualties to both sides. Philosophy must archeologize its hermeneutics and history must be conceptualized into "an ideal eternal history traversed in time by the history of every nation in its rise, development, maturity, decline and fall. Indeed, we make bold to affirm that he who meditates this Science narrates to himself this ideal eternal history so far as he himself makes it for himself by that proof 'it had, has, and will have to be.' For the first indubitable principle . . . is that this world of nations has certainly been made by men, and its guise must therefore be found within the modifications of our own human mind" (§349).

The "master key" to this immanent metaphysics is the discovery that "the first gentile peoples, by a demonstrated necessity of nature, were poets who spoke in poetic characters" (§34). To understand the first institutions, Vico therefore did not look for a convention or pact but for poetic representations or myths that he decoded etymologically. In an effort to understand how legal institutions, for example, came into being, Vico claimed that the term *ius* is derived from *Jove*, and it is this insight into the reciprocal determination of language and institutions that constitutes one of Vico's most original contributions. His theories on language are therefore of crucial importance to the principles of the *New Science*, where *history* and *philology* are often interchangeable terms. According to Vico himself, he had erred in the first edition of the *New Science* (1725) in that he had "treated the origins of ideas apart from the origins of languages, whereas they were by nature united."[23] Vico's genetic principle is indeed a linguistic principle that manifests itself in his description of the origins of languages.

Vico also rewrites the categories of poetry and history. He develops a detailed theory of poetic wisdom that culminates in a discovery of the arch-poet of the Western tradition "only" to reach the conclusion that this poet was not what would traditionally be thought of as poet but was rather a historian. Vico values the *Iliad* and the *Odyssey* primarily as repositories of history. Yet Vico's poetics, the master key of his *New Science*, rests on his analysis of Homer the historian, so that his theory of poetry can only be understood as a critique of historical judgment.

---

[23] Vico, *Autobiography*, 194.

In §§890–98, he accordingly makes fun of those who have praised Homer's greatness as a poet. He ridicules the usual causes for praise by noting these were not Homer's but "were properties of the heroic age of the Greeks, in which and throughout which Homer was an incomparable poet, just because, in the age of vigorous memory, robust imagination, and sublime invention, he was in no sense a philosopher" (§896). A later comment leaves some doubt, however, as to what "Homer" means: "Neither philosophies, arts of poetry, nor arts of criticism, which came later, could create a poet who could come anywhere near to rivaling Homer" (§897). Here again, we have an alternative use of a common vocabulary. Just as Vico's uses of allegory undermine tradition, so do his uses of the name "Homer." The passage seems to imply that Homer is a poet, since what else would a(nother) poet want to rival? Yet Homer, as we have seen, did not "make" anything but functioned as a repository of history. And indeed, for every statement supporting Homer's poetic status, there is another that undermines it. This is one of the essential aspects of Vichian hermeneutics.

What, then, is poetry? Is there such a thing as poetry that is not history? And, if not, why do we need both terms? Also, is Homer a poet at all? These questions are left dangling and the two categories become hybridized, just as the opposition between philology and philosophy redefined both terms, a pattern that also applies to the concept of "first." The first men, we are told, were poets (§376), but Homer was not among them. What, then, does "being first" mean?

The question is important because one of Vico's uses of Homer, traditionally acclaimed as the first poet, is to defer primacy indefinitely. As we have already noted, the only primacy left Homer is that of the historian, an occupation marked by secondariness. As a matter of principle, then, Vico turns to beginnings as the locus of poetic wisdom. Yet he also implies that these cannot be apprehended regressively or with any degree of immediacy. This illustrates, of course, the difficulty inherent in any chronologically based genetic claim, and Vico's own solution is particularly apt. By not making Homer's originality dependent on temporal primacy—the primitivist urge—Vico is eventually able to free genetic epistemology from chronometric considerations. Instead, the Italian philosopher introduced the notion that origins are not just past but also present. They remain encoded in our mind, which retains the traces of its modifications and where they are always, as it were, in the making. History, then, is indeed poetry. Moreover, while relying on philology, Vico also undermines it, by methodologically acknowledging the need to rely on what could almost be called its alter ego, philosophy, even though he axiomatically contends, in the "Establishment of Principles," that "philosophy considers man as he should be and so can be of service to but very few" (§131).

The writing of the *New Science* parallels these issues. Its recursive and spiraling structure delays the stating of elements crucial to the reader's understanding.[24] In addition, mutual territorial concessions are made by the traditionally disengaged or warring realms of poetry and geometry. In both spheres, something is being constructed or made. That explains why this critique of historical judgment, clearly conceived as an attack on philosophy in general and on some of the excesses of Cartesianism in particular, rests on a series of "elements" or axioms. In true Vichian fashion, however, this incorporation of a geometric vocabulary problematizes rather than supports Cartesian methodology—as well as history. History surpasses other forms of scientific discourses when it comes to "the world of nations," but it nevertheless also seeks to reach a degree of certainty determined by scientific methods: "And history cannot be more certain than when he who creates the things also narrates them. Now, as geometry, when it constructs the world of quantity out of its elements, or contemplates that world, is creating it for itself, just so does our Science [create for itself the world of nations], but with a reality greater by just so much as the institutions having to do with human affairs are more real than points, lines, surfaces, and figures are" (§349). This scientific approach echoes the idealization of geometry characteristic of seventeenth-century thought and exemplified in the parallel drawn by Thomas Hobbes, in the epistle dedicatory of *Six Lessons to the Professors of the Mathematics* (1656), between geometry and "civil philosophy," on the basis of their common demonstrability: "Geometry therefore is demonstrable, for the lines and figures from which we reason are drawn and described by ourselves; and civil philosophy is demonstrable, because we make the commonwealth ourselves."[25]

---

[24] The fragmentation and repetitions of the *New Science*, as well as the delayed introduction of its primal scene (practically a third of the way into the work) are reminiscent of the various introductions and prefaces that delay access to Rousseau's *Discourse on the Origins of Inequality*—what Starobinski has aptly described as "the endless *mesure pour rien* that precedes the beginning." Jean Starobinski, "Rousseau et la recherche des origines," in *Jean-Jacques Rousseau: La transparence et l'obstacle, suivi de sept essais sur Rousseau*, Tel 6 (Paris: Gallimard, 1971), 324.

[25] Thomas Hobbes, *The English Works of Thomas Hobbes of Malmsbury*, ed. William Molesworth (London: J. Bohn, 1837–1845), 7:184.

Vico's new science is, in its application to a hermeneutics of history, nevertheless unlike any scientific theory developed in the seventeenth century. Additionally, some of his most fundamental assumptions are unlike anything found in Cartesian philosophy. Consider, for instance, that the first axiom to open the section on elements (§119–329) in the "Establishment of Principles" postulates the *indefiniteness* of the human mind and grounds knowledge in ignorance: "Because of the indefinite nature of the human mind, wherever it is lost in ignorance man makes himself the measure of all things" (§120). We can begin to understand another essential trait of Vichian hermeneutics. As elaborated in the explanation that supports the first axiom, ignorance is undoubtedly the epistemological condition of primitive and civilized man:

> It is noteworthy that in all languages the greater part of the expressions relating to inanimate things are formed by metaphor from the human body and its parts and from the human senses and passions. . . . All of which is a consequence of our axiom that man in his ignorance makes himself the rule of the universe. . . . So that, as rational metaphysics teaches that man becomes all things by understanding them (*homo intelligendo fit omnia*), this imaginative metaphysics shows that man becomes all things by *not* understanding them (*homo non intelligendo fit omnia*); and perhaps the latter proposition is truer than the former, for when man understands he extends his mind and takes in the things, but when he does not understand he makes the things out of himself and becomes them by transforming himself into them. (§405)

This ignorance has few limits. Although Vico recognizes "that rumor is deflated by presence" (§121), he nevertheless makes clear that presence is indefinitely deferred. This he does in the course of a series of pregnant or providential misunderstandings, or "Vichian slips," as I heard Pellegrino D'Acierno call them in a memorable seminar on the works of Giambattista Vico.[26]

One such slip is made daily by modern thinkers who misinterpret early forms of expression just as surely as giants misinterpreted the

---

[26] In the same line of thought, it is not irrelevant to be reminded by Kelley ("Vico's Road," 16) that, as described in the opening paragraph of the *Autobiography*, Vico's first meaningful act is to fall "head first from the top of a ladder" (*Autobiography*, 111). This first "Vichian slip" also has pride of place in Verene, *New Art*, 161–74, and in Mazzotta, *New Map*, 22–34.

primal scene by giving thunder religious significance and thereby making possible the foundation of gentile society. One element at least, then, links the modern scholar to primitive man. This yields the next "axiom" or "element," namely, that "it is another property of the human mind that whenever men can form no idea of distant and unknown things, they judge them by what is familiar and at hand" (§122). This accounts for what Vico calls the "conceit of scholars," "who will have it that what they know is as old as the world" (§127).

Vico saw the recent reception of Homer as a prime example of this conceit and this allowed him to enter the Quarrel between the Ancients and the Moderns and to redefine its terms: "This axiom disposes of all the opinions of the scholars concerning the matchless wisdom of the ancients. . . . It further condemns as impertinent all the mystic meanings with which the Egyptian hieroglyphs are endowed by the scholars, and the philosophical allegories which they have read into the Greek fables" (§128). Vico does not tackle the issue at any great length in the *New Science*, however. It is referred to in only one other instance, in connection with one of his "four authors" (Plato, Tacitus, Bacon, and Grotius): "This discovery of the origins of poetry does away with the opinion of the matchless wisdom of the ancients, so ardently sought after from Plato to Bacon's *De sapientia veterum*. For the wisdom of the ancients was the vulgar wisdom of the lawgivers who founded the human race, not the esoteric wisdom of great and rare philosophers" (§384). These references—no matter how brief in the context of the *New Science*—are important, because they extend the parameters of the Quarrel in that the question of the conceit of scholars (and its obvious implications for the Quarrel) becomes intertwined with the issue of competing contemporary methodologies.[27] Vico's axioms do not simply support or refute the superiority of the ancients versus the moderns. They link this issue to the debate about the dominance of scientific discourse inherited from the seventeenth century. As the passage cited above already reveals, Vico is at least as interested in trying to prevail over Bacon as in settling the debate over the respective validity of ancient and modern wisdom. For Vico, ancient versus modern also means rhetoric versus science.

---

[27] On the role of the Quarrel in the genesis of Vico's thought, see B. A. Haddock, "Vico's 'Discovery of the True Homer': A Case-Study in Historical Reconstruction," *Journal of the History of Ideas* 40 (1979): 583–602; and Joseph M. Levine, "Giambattista Vico and the Quarrel between the Ancients and the Moderns," *Journal of the History of Ideas* 52 (1991): 55–79.

To appreciate this fully, one needs to turn to *On the Study Methods of Our Time*, an oration delivered in 1708 at the beginning of the school year and expanded and published in 1709. In this address Vico's basic and conventional position is that the ancients are superior in poetry and the moderns in the sciences. This position allows Vico to emphasize the link between the Quarrel and seventeenth-century science. The Italian philosopher understood that what was at stake was not who is better than who over time but who is better than who here and now: Descartes or Vico, for example.[28] He saw rightly that the Quarrel was about the control of the contemporary mind and the validity of certain forms of knowledge, including the notions of scientific probability and certainty.

The main purpose of the oration is accordingly to set up dams to control the dominance of scientific discourse in general and, as the indirect references to the *Discours de la méthode* underlined below indicate, of Cartesianism in particular:

> In conclusion: whosoever intends to devote his efforts, not to physics or mechanics, but to a political career, whether as a civil servant or as a member of the legal profession or of the judiciary, a political speaker or a pulpit orator, *should not waste too much time, in his adolescence, on those subjects which are taught by abstract geometry.* Let him, instead, cultivate his mind with an ingenious method; let him study

[28] This is nowhere more in evidence nor more succinctly put than in the Second Response included in the Disputation that followed the publication of the *De antiquissima*: "We are certainly in debt to Descartes, . . . but that only his judgement must be employed and only the geometrical method—that is too much." *On the Most Ancient Wisdom of the Italians Unearthed from the Origins of the Latin Language, including the Disputation with the "Giornale de' letterati d'Italia,"* trans. L. M. Palmer (Ithaca, N.Y.: Cornell University Press, 1988), 184. This statement is also significant in that it underscores that Vichian criticism is sometimes too quick to turn Vico's opposition to Descartes into a simple binarism (though Cartesianism as such is indeed fair game). Certainly, Vico's philosophy can be read profitably (indeed, must be read) as signaling an important departure from Cartesian philosophy, but even in the Inaugural Orations, Vico finds no incompatibility between praise of Descartes and of ancient poets or between urging the study both of science and of literature. *On Humanistic Education: (Six Inaugural Orations, 1699–1707)*, trans. Giorgio A. Pinton and Arthur W. Shippee (Ithaca, N.Y.: Cornell University Press, 1993), esp. 78–89. Also, it is worth noting that Descartes is mentioned only once in the *New Science*, in §706, where Vico writes approvingly of Descartes's description of vision in the *Dioptrics*. Distancing himself from his great predecessor is simply no longer so important. Note also that, as Harold Samuel Stone has recently pointed out, Vico's public criticism of Descartes and his influence abated in the 1720s, even though an attack on the French thinker and on Cartesianism would actually have been politically expedient at that particular juncture. *Vico's Cultural History: The Production and Transmission of Ideas in Naples, 1685–1750* (Leiden: E. J. Brill, 1997), 214–16.

topics, and defend both sides of a controversy, be it on nature, man, or politics, in a freer and brighter style of expression. *Let him not spurn reasons that wear a semblance of probability and verisimilitude.* Let our efforts not be directed towards achieving superiority over the Ancients merely in the field of science, while they surpass us in wisdom; let us not be merely more exact and more true than the Ancients, while allowing them to be more eloquent than we are; let us equal the Ancients in the fields of wisdom and eloquence as we excel them in the domain of science.[29]

As we have seen, the importance of the "Discovery" extends beyond the strict confines of Homeric scholarship. It not only offers an alternative to the moral and euhemerist allegorizations of myths, it also paves the way for the realization that scientific rationalism is not suitable for the study of origins. As such, its relationship to the larger context of the *New Science* is similar to that of Vico's study of the various developments of Greek and Roman history, which interested him because they were instances of "an ideal eternal history, traversed in time by the history of every nation in its rise, development, maturity, decline and fall" (§349). In a telling detail, for example, Vico stresses that "Homer" never went to Egypt or Phoenicia (§89). Although of importance in itself and in the context of the "Discovery," that fact also emphasizes one of the main tenets of the *New Science*, namely, the rejection of the diffusionist cultural theories popular at the time in favor of a "science" of autochthonous development, of which we also find traces in Vico's study of feudalism and its independence from Roman law.[30] Proceeding in much the same way, we have gradually moved from the relative concreteness of the "Discovery" to the larger context of Vico's hermeneutics. We now need to turn our attention to Vico's theoretical elaboration of an episteme grounded in the concept of origins—or, to adopt a specifically Vichian terminology—of principles.

We can already discern some of the facets of the problem at hand. Origins are characterized by as much indeterminacy as the identity of the "first" poet. Methodologically, we now need to ask how the *New Science* provides the tools with which we can hope to apprehend ori-

---

[29] Giambattista Vico, *On the Study Methods of Our Time*, trans. Elio Gianturco (Ithaca, N.Y.: Cornell University Press, 1990), 41, emphasis added.

[30] See Kelley, "Vico's Road," 24–25.

gins. It is indeed quite possible that the *New Science,* grounded as it is in a principle of indeterminacy, may well be a most apt expression of the problematic surrounding any theory of origins.

Whatever the case may be, we can henceforth appreciate why Vico included a statue of Homer in the frontispiece to the *New Science*—an appropriate form of introduction for a philosopher who claimed writing came before speech (even if its subject is generally considered the exemplary representative of an oral culture). In this picture, the ray of Divine Providence "is reflected from the breast of metaphysic onto the statue of Homer, the first gentile author who has come down to us" (§6). This image, Vico is quick to point out in his introduction, supports not the conventional notion of Homer as a source of esoteric wisdom but rather Homer as a source of insight "into the crude minds of the first founders of the gentile nations" (§6). Even more significantly, however, the base of the statue shows a noticeable crack, which, Vico cryptically points out to the still unsuspecting reader, "signifies the discovery of the true Homer" (§6).

GENESIS AS EPISTEMOLOGICAL PRINCIPLE

In an age when history was by and large looked on as an inferior source of knowledge, how did it become the linchpin of the *New Science?* Our discussion of the "Discovery of the True Homer" has already given us several clues. We now need to see how this hermeneutic theory yields an episteme dominated by a genetic principle and how this approach makes it possible to conceptualize in more general terms the relationship between origins and epistemological models.

For Vico the study of history constitutes the only conceivable hermeneutic field because human beings cannot apprehend anything but their own production. In the *New Science* he therefore sets aside both sacred history (in which Jews are in a direct relationship with God) and the world of nature (which has been made by God and can therefore not be deciphered by man) and focuses on gentile or secular history, in which humanity has fallen away from the relationship with God and has had to create its own history, its own institutions—the "world of nations"—as it left the world of giants behind. This world of nations is something we can know because we have made it ourselves, no matter how blindly, ignorantly, or providentially.

This distinction made, Vico distances himself from Cartesian discourse and from the rationalism of natural law philosophers. Unlike Descartes, Vico privileges history because mathematics and physics are at best asymptotic, human codes that try to decode the world of nature. Vico argues further that the cogito is a product of history, the result of what he calls a "modification of the human mind," which cannot be apprehended in exclusively synchronic terms. If philosophy wants to ascertain the truth of a belated concept like *cogito*, it needs to account for the modifications of the human mind that made the position of consciousness possible. Contrary to what Cartesians would like to believe, the human mind is, in Vichian terms, of an "indefinite nature" (§120) and has to be accounted for genetically.

Similarly, natural law theorists erred in their use of belated concepts such as *contract* and *common good*, which were not available to primitive people and cannot account for "the natural law of the gentes," which is that "of utility and force" (§1084). According to Vico, "the nature of institutions is nothing but their coming into being (*nascimento*) at certain times and in certain guises. Whenever the time and guise are thus and so, such and not otherwise are the institutions that come into being" (§147). Needless to say, Vichian nature is not to be confused with a state of nature; it does not exist outside history and must always be accounted for genetically. In fact, to speak of a "genetic principle" is, from a Vichian perspective, a tautology. As noted by Max Harold Fisch in his introduction to the *New Science*, the abstract connotations of the key words *principle, nature,* and *nations* are not to be considered independent of their respective etymologies, namely, *beginning* and *birth*. As he rightly emphasizes, "it is the genetic meaning that is emphatic, and the technical meaning is either explicitly redefined genetically or, without redefinition, undergoes a displacement in that direction" (§A3).

That displacement is nowhere more apparent than in the following axiom: "The order of ideas must follow the order of institutions" (§238). Institutions clearly engender ideas, as Vico explains in the following two paragraphs. These are worth quoting at some length for they are exemplary of Vico's genetic method:

> This was the order of human institutions: first the forests, after that the huts, then the villages, next the cities, and finally the academies.

This axiom is a great principle of etymology, for this sequence of human institutions sets the pattern for the histories of words in the various native languages. Thus we observe in the Latin language that almost the whole corpus of its words had sylvan or rustic origins. For example, *lex*. First it must have meant a collection of acorns. Thence we believe it derived *ilex*, as it were *illex*, the oak. . . . *Lex* was next a collection of vegetables, from which the latter were called *legumina*. Later on, at a time when vulgar letters had not yet been invented for writing down the laws, *lex* by a necessity of civil nature must have meant a collection of citizens, or the public parliament; so that the presence of the people was the *lex*, or "law," that solemnized the wills that were made *calatis comitiis*, in the presence of the assembled *comitia*. Finally, collecting letters, and making, as it were, a sheaf of them for each word, was called *legere*, reading. (§239–40)

As can be seen from this example, language is first "instituted" by the things themselves, which it then reinstitutes in turn. To observe this pattern of reciprocal determination, one has to go back to the original constitutive moments or things. This procedure will eventually yield the following axiom: "Doctrines must take their beginning from that of the matters of which they treat" (§314). The choice of the word "institutions" as a translation for *cose* is therefore conceptually appropriate. It is even warranted within the context of a Vichian etymology because of the euphonic affinity between the Italian cose and the Latin *causae*.[31]

Just as constitutive moments are multiple, so are natures. Vico had already insisted in the *Study Methods* that mutability is an essential property of nature.[32] In the *New Science* nature becomes plural, and Erich Auerbach was right to suggest that "there are many passages in the *Scienza Nuova* where the word *natura* should best be translated by 'historical development' or 'stage of historical development.'"[33] There are three essentially different kinds of natures, which correspond to three different forms of government, three different kinds of reason, three different kinds of languages and natural law, as well as three "sects of time" (theological, heroic, and human).

[31] For an excellent theoretical discussion of the *rétromotivation* of things by language through etymology, see Pierre Guiraud, "Etymologie et ethymologia (motivation et rétromotivation)," *Poétique* 3 (1972): 405–13.

[32] Vico, *Study Methods*, 35.

[33] Erich Auerbach, "Vico and Aesthetic Historism," *Journal of Aesthetics and Art Criticism* 8 (1949): 118.

This plurality of natures was not accompanied by a privileging of the study of historical facts. Although Rousseau's "Let us therefore begin by setting all the facts aside" would have given Vico pause, the interest of the *New Science* does not reside in the compilation of singular facts.[34] Vico's aim is to describe "an ideal eternal history," and the *New Science* therefore does not depend on a total conformity between empirical facts and the principles it develops. Of course, the question remains: What, in the final analysis, gives credence to these principles?

According to the *Autobiography*, the *New Science* describes "a metaphysics of the human race" that tries to recapture the principles of its genesis.[35] In this endeavor, Vico was guided by one "truth beyond all question: that the world of civil society has certainly been made by men, and that its principles are therefore to be found within the modifications of our own human mind" (*NS* §331). Since institutions and the modifications of the human mind are reciprocally determinative, any archeological endeavor must be based on a philological hermeneutics, that is, a hermeneutics grounded in memory (including imagination and invention) as much as in reason. In this context, it is clear that etymology became the key to the *New Science*, since every word has a retrosignification that includes the history of nations, which is in turn determined by the modifications of the human mind. Accordingly, one finds in Vico's late work "a real ontological connection between the individual mind and the historical process."[36] And, since consciousness (*coscienza*) and institutions (*cose*) are not autonomous, Vico's approach had to include an autoarcheology. According to the logic of the *New Science*, any approach limited to the sphere of the cogito could not hope to account for the history of the human mind. Any hermeneutics that pertains to secular history must be internalized. It is then clear why, in the *Autobiography*, Vico chose to reproduce the thesis he had submitted to his university in 1699: " 'That the knowledge of oneself is

<hr />

[34] Jean-Jacques Rousseau, *Discourse on the Origins of Inequality (Second Discourse); Polemics; and Political Economy*, ed. Roger D. Masters and Christopher Kelly, trans. Judith R. Bush, Roger D. Masters, Christopher Kelly, and Terence Marshall, in *The Collected Writings of Rousseau*, ed. Roger D. Masters and Christopher Kelly (Hanover, N.H.: Published for Dartmouth College by University Press of New England, 1992), 3:19.

[35] Vico, *Autobiography*, 167.

[36] Avis, *Foundations*, 154.

for each of us the greatest incentive to the compendious study of every branch of learning.' "[37]

In view of all this, it is difficult to agree with Friedrich Meinecke's contention that "Vico did to some extent manage to achieve the ideal expressed later on by Ranke, the ideal of a complete eclipse of self in order to become a vehicle for the overpowering might of historical phenomena," when such an ideal clearly runs counter to the foundation of Vichian epistemology. Like many others, of course, Meinecke subscribed to the notion that Vico had been a colorful figure on the fringes of "European" thought: "At this point there appeared, like the vision of some miraculous oasis, Giambattista Vico (1668–1744)." The problem with this "myth," encouraged by Vico himself, is that it made it easy for Meinecke to marginalize Vico and to comment, for instance, that the Italian philosopher had "none of the joy of the Enlightenment in analysing and decomposing facts," a misreading that any consideration of Vico's etymologies, for instance, would easily dispel. As a result, Meinecke was unable to develop the implications of one of his own remarks. Indeed, he noted that Vico's "sense of stratification was important, the survival of remnants of ancient constitutions and customs embedded in more recent material—what was later called *survivals*, which are to the historian what leading fossils are to the geologist." Yet he could not see that beyond history and science, another parallel could be drawn, this time to the human mind: *Survivals* could also be said to be to the historian what memory traces are to psychoanalytic theory, a link that offers some enlightening parallels to the Vichian theory concerning the constitutive moment(s) of society and the mind.[38]

The initial movement of consciousness was generated, as we have already mentioned, by a first instance of the "Vichian slip," a first slip of the mind that consisted of the providential but erroneous adequation of the first postdiluvian roll of thunder and flash of lightning with

[37] Vico, *Autobiography*, 140. In his study of the *New Science*, Pompa convincingly argues that "to be *found* within the modifications of our own human mind" should read "to be '*rediscovered*,'" which "corresponds more closely with Vico's use of the verb *ritruovare*" (*Vico*, 155n1, emphasis added). Nevertheless, I do not agree with Pompa that "this formulation is so vague, however, that it might well be nothing more than a restatement of the purely metaphysical principle that history, being a human product, must be explained by certain aspects of human nature, rather than a claim about knowledge of these" (Pompa, *Vico*, 156). Although it could conceivably be interpreted from a variety of perspectives, it seems to me that Vico's phrase crystallizes a specific feature of his epistemology rather than a general metaphysical principle.
[38] Meinecke, *Historism*, 45, 37, 48, 46.

divinity, which accounts for the decidedly human beginnings of gentile civility from the feral nature of the giants who roamed the earth after the flood.

> Thereupon a few giants, who must have been the most robust, and who were dispersed through the forests on the mountain heights where the strongest beasts have their dens, were frightened and astonished by the great effect whose cause they did not know, and raised their eyes and became aware of the sky. And because in such a case the nature of the human mind leads it to attribute its own nature to the effect, and because in that state their nature was that of men all robust bodily strength, who expressed their very violent passions by shouting and grumbling, they pictured the sky to themselves as a great animated body, which in that aspect they called Jove, the first god of the so-called greater gentes. (§377)

As with Homer, one finds no esoteric encoding of this primal scene in Vico's *New Science*. Conation is grounded in fear, ignorance, and an imaginative acculturation of a suddenly human body.[39] Contrary to what Cantelli would like us to believe, gentile language is in no way "born divine." It is not "a copy, an imitation (a picture) of this divine language."[40] How could postlapsarian men imitate what they by definition could not have access to?

Similarly, poetic physics and its portrayal of chaos as an actual monster need not be understood as a metaphorical rendering of later scientific theories of primeval matter: "But the scholars thus made sublime

[39] It is tempting to think of Vico's giants as metaphors, but Stam, Rossi, and Cristofolini are right to insist on the literal aspect of this gigantism. See James H. Stam, *Inquiries into the Origin of Language: The Fate of a Question* (New York: Harper and Row, 1976), 14; Paolo Rossi, *The Dark Abyss of Time: The History of the Earth and the History of Nations from Hooke to Vico*, trans. Lydia G. Cochrane (Chicago: University of Chicago Press, 1984), 177–78; and Paolo Cristofolini, *Vico et l'histoire* (Paris: Presses Universitaires de France, 1995), 47–51. Unlike Rousseau's giants in the third chapter of the *Essay on the Origin of Languages*, in which Rousseau claims that the name *giants* first came up as the result of a wild man's initial and therefore frightening encounter with other members of his species, whom he mistakenly thought were bigger than he was and identified as belonging to a different species, Vico's giants are not human at all. They exist in what Rossi aptly calls "a sort of no-man's-land" (*Dark Abyss*, 180) between Hebrew humanity and gentile history. They are presented as ontologically different from Hebrews and are prehistoric and therefore nonhuman in the context of gentile history, which is characterized by the twin birth of humanity and history.

[40] Cantelli, "Myth," 53.

learning out of what was doltishness and simplicity on the part of the first men, who (just as children, looking in a mirror, will try to seize their own reflections) thought from the various modifications of their own shapes and gestures that there must be a man in the water, forever changing into different shapes" (§688). The world is the imaginary mirror of the giant during the constitution of its humanity and the emergence of the consciousness of the ego (and, of course, of the other).

To use more contemporary imagery, the feral/human institution of the first imaginative genera parallels the formation of the *I* in the Lacanian mirror stage, described in terms strikingly appropriate for the Vichian primal scene, of which it could also be said that it is "a drama whose internal thrust is precipitated from insufficiency to anticipation." The analogy can be taken further in that the giants' first semiotic act, their first inscription, is marked by a *"specific prematurity of birth"* insofar as they are clearly prehuman in their awareness. In addition, for both Vico and Lacan, the primal constitutive moment of history (social or personal) occurs via an asymptotic imaginative identification. According to Lacan, "the important point is that this form [the Ideal-I] situates the agency of the *ego*, before its social determination, in a fictional direction, which will always remain irreducible for the individual alone, or rather, which will only rejoin the coming-in-being *(le devenir)* of the subject asymptotically, whatever the success of the dialectical syntheses by which he must resolve as *I* his discordance with his own reality."[41] In Vico's system, such a moment can, however, be recuperated thanks to the remanence of modifications of the human mind, which are to Vichian epistemology what *Erinnerungsspuren* (memory traces) are to psychoanalytic theory.

Is Vico's recourse to interiority surprising, then, or should we not rather think of it as the correlate of any genetic historiography? Indeed, how can one hope to apprehend empirically a precultural reality? On the contrary, it must be admitted that the production of any primal scene *must* be organized in accordance with a mode that is neither empirical nor grounded in the cogito but is rather immanent. As a result, not only does the problematic of origins "oscillate," as Sylvain Auroux has written, "between the abstraction of a genesis and

[41] Jacques Lacan, "The Mirror Stage as Formative of the Function of the I as Revealed in Psychoanalytic Experience," in *Ecrits: A Selection*, trans. Alan Sheridan (New York: W. W. Norton, 1977), 4, 2. I am indebted to Pellegrino D'Acierno for having drawn my attention to this parallel.

the reality of a history," it also oscillates, in the *New Science*, between phylogeny and what could be called "autogeny."[42] Let us remember Vico's claim: "He who meditates this Science narrates to himself this ideal eternal history so far as he himself makes it for himself" (§349).

We have recognized autogeny as essential to Vico's genetic principle and have described its manifestations, but that is not the end of the story. By calling his theory a science, Vico implied that its validity is subject to criteria of verifiability that are not solipsistic. Nevertheless, we still need to examine the theoretical foundations of Vico's truth claims. Within the confines of the *New Science*, does Vico still subscribe to the proposition that "man is neither nothing nor everything," the epistemological principle of *De antiquissima*?[43] Now that we have seen that the *New Science* helps apprehend origins by developing an immanent metaphysics or a science grounded in human consciousness, it is time to account for Vico's emphasis on history as science and hence for genetic epistemology as a scientific proposition.

The verifiability of Vico's truth claims is an important issue. After all, if one restricts the object of the *New Science* to the world of nations or human history, the result is often remarkably circular arguments (as though it were not enough that human knowledge is the child of indeterminacy and ignorance). For instance, it is not enough to say that nature has a genetic meaning and then assume that the study of genesis will give us the tools necessary to define nature. After all, nature has two meanings in Vichian thought. Not only is it essentially historical and genetic in its definition and hence very much the topic of the *New Science;* it is also what is excluded from that science because made by God. Hence the possible topos of inquiry is not really nature itself—regardless of its definition—but rather the human reflection on nature. The aboriginal giant, for example, is not the subject of the *New Science*, which studies only what has an origin, in this case humanity, which has given birth to itself by severing itself from its aboriginal nature through that first flash of consciousness that marks it as secondary and asymptotic. Whereas giants were "sons of the Earth" (§531), human beings are always already historians.

The primal scene was grounded in fear, ignorance, and consciousness and gave birth to a non-Adamic form of discourse. To stay within

---

[42] Sylvain Auroux, *La sémiotique des Encyclopédistes: Essai d'épistémologie historique des sciences du langage* (Paris: Payot, 1979), 54.

[43] Vico, *Most Ancient Wisdom*, 63.

the limits of our knowledge and its birth, Vico had to conclude that the "proper material" of poetry "is the credible impossibility" (§383) of our constitutive misreadings: "It is impossible that bodies should be minds, yet it was believed that the thundering sky was Jove" (§383). In such a context, the nature of the world of nations can be evoked only from within a theory of "poetic wisdom." Of course, this conclusion reflects Vico's intimate familiarity with the rhetorical tradition, which he had already discussed in *On the Study Methods of Our Time*, where he observed, without any claim to originality, that "it frequently occurs, in fact, that orators in a law court have greater difficulty with a case which is based on truth, but does not seem so, than with a case that is false but plausible."[44] The claims made for the *New Science* are not limited to questions of poetic credibility and forensic oratory, however.

For Giambattista Vico, our knowledge of origins oscillates between two requirements that appear to be mutually exclusive: the "credible impossibility" of poetry on the one hand and the axiomatic truth of geometry on the other. As David Lachterman has remarked, the second half of this proposition is often set aside in contemporary Vichian criticism, which prefers to emphasize Vico's anti-Cartesianism and to downplay the mathematical framework of his philosophy of history.[45] This neglect is understandable in that the historico-philological dimension of Vico's project is undoubtedly its most compelling feature. And yet, to appreciate Vico's method, one must also acknowledge his desire to make mathematics and history—or, to use his preferred terminology, philosophy and philology—interdependent and to redefine both branches of learning in the process. This is particularly the case since his decision to play on both a mathematical and a historicist register and his continued aspiration to the certainty associated with geometric constructs are characteristic features of genetic epistemology from Vico to Kant, as will become increasingly clear.

First, it is worth noting that, in spite of Vico's inclusion of Bacon among his "four authors," his method is far more Cartesian than Bacon-

---

[44] Vico, *Study Methods*, 13.

[45] "Vico's role in the history of post-Cartesian thinking is of considerable interest here, not least because of contemporary efforts to make of him a genuinely *alternative* starting-point for modern philosophy, attempts in which his rhetorical-topical style of understanding the history of human institutions is contrasted with the analytical and mathematical method of Descartes. These efforts are, in the main, misguided inasmuch as they overlook the essentially mathematical roots and orientation of Vico's conception of human knowing" (Lachterman, *Ethics*, 7).

ian. Not only is Vico's position not inductive, it is clear that the success of the *New Science* is not contingent on the verifiability of the myriad "facts" that make up its intricate texture. It need not be tested against empirical data or experiments but only against consciousness.[46] This also explains why Vico did not turn to hypothetical or probabilistic models of explanation. For the Italian philosopher, certain knowledge is a definite possibility since origins are not just past but are also present. They remain encoded in our minds and are reenacted at various stages of our individual and social histories. The *New Science* therefore cannot be said to deal with hypothetical knowledge. Like early poetry, it is a true narration.

The *New Science* is the science of that truth and the study of origins is its cornerstone. Its goal is to yield mathematical certainty (which can itself be historicized) by means of a science devoted to the study of the reciprocal determination of poetry and institutions. On the one hand, Vico grounds historical certainty by drawing a parallel between sociability and mathematics. To the extent that "the world of civil society has certainly been made by men" (§331), it is very similar to the world of mathematical propositions, which Vico's axioms are meant to underscore. On the other hand, origins introduce the temporal and conceptual divisions, ruptures, and breaks that rational thought depends on, as Vico had explicitly recognized in *De antiquissima*.[47] Yet their authority also rests on the possibility of integrating ontologically unrelated elements, as in the case of metaphors, which function outside the rational realm. Vico's science, in short, aims to ground history in mathematical certainty while emphasizing the poetic nature of rational thought, and to redefine both orders of knowledge in the process.

This explains, of course, why Vico, like so many of his seventeenth-century predecessors, tended to idealize geometry. As Hobbes had noted in chapter 5 of the *Leviathan*, geometry is more than addition or subtraction. Geometry, like poetry, is able to incorporate both a rational and a nonrational dimension. It has, I would argue, an aesthetic quality that is related to geometry in the same way that poetic figures are

---

[46] In this respect, it is interesting to note that Vico chose to write his "periautography" in the third person. As Fisch notes, this decision "is a reaction from the ubiquitous 'I' of [Descartes's] *Discourse*" (introduction to Vico's *Autobiography*, 7). It also underscores Vico's dual reliance on the claims of mathematics and of the individual consciousness. The "I" becomes objectivized.

[47] Vico, *Most Ancient Wisdom*, 48.

related to the logos and rational thought. It is this same quality that brings the past into a present that can be conceived and known.

In the end, geometry did help Vico to merge the requirements of philosophy and philology. "Philosophy contemplates reason, whence comes knowledge of the true; philology observes that of which human choice is author, whence comes consciousness of the certain" (§138). One cannot reduce his axioms to aphorisms or " 'geometrical affectations' " or claim, as Mark Lilla does, that they are merely idiomatic tools destined to promote an "anti-modern 'teaching.' "[48] As Peter Burke notes, "he did claim, unlike Bacon, to be deductive. 'We will demonstrate,' he wrote on more than one occasion, *dimostreremo*. He also referred to his 'proofs' and his 'corollaries.' "[49] Philosophy may be "of service to but very few" (§131) but these few included Vico.

[48] Kelley, "Vico's Road," 27; and Mark Lilla, *G. B. Vico: The Making of an Anti-Modern* (Cambridge, Mass.: Harvard University Press, 1993), 155. James Robert Goetsch Jr. has also dismissed Vico's axioms as aphorisms, affectations, and ritualistic bows to Euclidean geometry. See *Vico's Axioms: The Geometry of the Human World* (New Haven: Yale University Press, 1995), esp. 88–92 and 114–5. On the other side of this particular divide, Leon Pompa, whose interpretation of the *New Science* rests on his acceptance of "Vico's claim to have produced a science, in some fairly rigorous sense" (*Vico,* xiv) and, more recently, David Lachterman have insisted, as I do, on the need to take seriously Vico's decision to integrate his work into the discourse of science.

[49] Burke, *Vico,* 82.

CHAPTER THREE

Origins Here and Now

Vico redefined epistemological certainty by denouncing the urge to think of science as arhetorical and by insisting that mathematics needs to be thought of as a product of history, or, more precisely, of a history of the human mind and institutions. Accordingly, his science revolved around a genetic principle grounded in the human will and the ability to remember and create. It was the result of a series of ongoing negotiations between a number of related binarisms, including temporality and atemporality, diachrony and synchrony, institutions and nature, memory and invention.

Vico's genetic turn, his belief in the explanatory powers of origins, is an essential feature of Enlightenment thought. Although they focused on topics as varied as the conditions of human knowledge, the configuration of the ideal society, and the nature of wealth, Condillac, Rousseau, and Smith, along with many other eighteenth-century thinkers, all found it necessary to turn to origins to make their respective cases. And they did so largely within the parameters of Vico's science. Indeed, the eighteenth-century study of origins navigated between two epistemological possibilities: on the one hand, origins were defined as what came first, which raised a host of methodological questions pertaining to historical knowledge; on the other, origins derived their authority from their ability to introduce a radical rupture from the past or to provide causal explanations independent of temporal considerations, in which cases they had to be understood in psychological rather than historical terms. Additionally, Enlightenment inquiries into origins brought to the fore the speculative nature of human knowledge and the need to restrict the field of knowledge to human creations, be they institutions, concepts, or works of art.

This epistemological framework accounts in great measure for the emergence of a new discipline dedicated to the study of the human ability to perceive and produce and for the foundational role played by originality in the construction of the new science of aesthetics. The role of this chapter and the next is to convey the crucial role played by aesthetics in the elaboration of an epistemology proper to the Enlightenment and to highlight the ways that the discourse of originality can be used as a touchstone against which other inquiries into origins can be made sense of, including inquiries into the origins of ideas, languages, societies, and commerce. This chapter is devoted to an analysis of the synchronic nature of Locke's "historical method" and of the controversial rise of originality as a defining feature of eighteenth-century epistemology in works by Pope, Young, William Duff, Alexander Gerard, Charles Batteux, and others. In the following chapter, I explore the debates on originality and original genius that dominated the intellectual landscape of the second half of the eighteenth century and their discursive ties to a wide range of inquiries into the nature of historical knowledge and the foundations of property. I start by contrasting Condillac's epistemology to Locke's, and Rousseau's origins to Vico's genetic principle, before moving on to the 1770s conceptualization of *Eigentümlichkeit*, Adam Smith's idealization of early over late modes of production, and Robert Wood's rediscovery of Homer.

Although I have elected to devote this chapter to synchronic approaches to questions of origins and originality and the next to diachronic approaches, I also want to underscore that this division does not reflect a correspondingly strict polarization in the works under discussion. As already mentioned, eighteenth-century debates oscillated between two urges: to proceed ahistorically (as in the case of Locke, for instance, his "historical method" notwithstanding) *and* to develop a historical method for thinking about the evolution of groups and individuals. Although the historical method may be more closely associated with the eighteenth century, the boundaries between these two approaches were hardly impermeable and the ahistorical model endured in a number of guises throughout the period.

Additionally, the split between synchronic and diachronic approaches was not necessarily accompanied by an agreement on a number of key issues. Thinkers who tended to favor an ahistorical method, for instance, were split on the question of the source of human knowledge. Some, including Batteux, Buffon, and Jean Le Rond d'Alembert, turned to a more objective model, claiming quite consistently that only "Nature" can truly be "Original." Locke and Young, by contrast, focused on the mind's ability to generate ideas. Similarly, not all those who favored a historical method adopted a primitivist posture, deeming it necessary to hypothesize about the beginnings of civilization (as did Condillac, Smith, Johann Joachim Wincklemann, and Wood) or believing that earlier is better.

In short, though concepts such as *synchrony* and *diachrony* are useful when mapping the intellectual landscape of the eighteenth century, one must be wary of trying to force individual thinkers into a binary straitjacket. Buffon, for instance, defender of *la belle nature* when it came to style, was also the author of *Les époques de la nature,* an inquiry into the past ages of the natural world, which included an investigation of its most ancient origins. In addition, these distinctions were continually being undermined from within, as the unavoidably frequent redefinitions of concepts such as history, primacy, and immediacy will give ample proof. Historical approaches are often coupled with a strong urge to systematize and to proceed synchronically. In his multivolume *Histoire naturelle, générale et particuliere,* for instance, Buffon warns against the adoption of a single system of classification and favors comparative descriptions based on direct observation over speculations regarding the history of the earth and of species, which, in this case, he is notably reluctant to enter into. The true villain in our story is neither history nor science but rather the possibility of a gap in our knowledge or an absence of boundaries. This concern is very much in evidence, for instance, in applications of Locke's associationism to the study of history. On the one hand, the association of ideas is a comforting notion because it rests on an assumption of unbroken continuity, which in turn suggests that complete knowledge may indeed be possible. On the other hand, it also raises the specter of infinite and uncontrollable free association, which is a form of madness.

The above-mentioned categories, then, must not be taken as separate elements in a dialectic. If anything, the so-called dialectic of the Enlightenment is a myth. Eighteenth-century thinkers were not particularly interested in a system of binary oppositions but in a discourse of closeness versus distance, and in distinctions of degree rather than kind. This is nowhere clearer than in the dialectic dissolution prevalent in Rousseau's writing. When issues are discussed in Manichaean terms, entropy follows. In that sense too, to focus on *originalité*, the distinction "which is meant both positively and negatively" is particularly appropriate.[1]

What counts above all is closeness to the truth. The desire to know origins signals a desire to eradicate distance, defined as the opposite of light. We find evidence of this in the rules of admissibility of English law, which were premised, as noted by Locke, on the belief that the difference between true and probable knowledge is only one of degree, or rather, distance: "Any Testimony, the farther off it is from the original Truth, the less force and proof it has."[2] The farther away, the darker. True Enlightenment, then, is an exercise in the appropriation of the original. This could be accomplished in a number of ways that were sometimes at odds but were not mutually exclusive.

This emphasis on closeness and appropriation is echoed in the frequent references to painting as the ideal form of art and communication. Overwhelmingly, it is painting rather than sculpture that is the art of reference in eighteenth-century aesthetics (not to mention linguistics). Sculpture would seem to be closer to nature in that it is three-dimensional. Yet painting wins out, as it were, because it presupposes distance more than sculpture does. This distance exists not only between the viewer and the painting but also between the artist and the canvas and makes it possible to master and dominate the painting's subject matter. In that sense, painting is more deliberately artistic—in the sense of "artificial" and "controlled"—than sculpture.

The distance necessary to painting is not to be understood as an objectification—though the two concepts are generally connected in Western thought (what could be both more distant and "objective" than the work of a camera, we may ask)—but rather as a recognition, spelled out in late eighteenth-century theories of the *Originalgenie*, of the artist's mastery and creative force and control. To know the origins (of our

---

[1] *Encyclopédie ou dictionnaire raisonné des sciences, des arts et des métiers* (1751–1772), s.v. "Originalité." http://www.lib.uchicago.edu/efts/ARTFL/projects/encyc/.

[2] John Locke, *An Essay concerning Human Understanding*, ed. Peter H. Nidditch (Oxford: Clarendon Press, 1985), 663–64. Further page references to Locke's *Essay* will be included parenthetically in the body of the text. Douglas Lane Patey quotes this passage and discusses probability and Lockean thought in *Probability and Literary Form: Philosophic Theory and Literary Practice in the Augustan Age* (Cambridge: Cambridge University Press, 1984), 27–34.

ideas, of our institutions, of our artistic ability) is to appropriate the past and cancel the distance between the past and the present. Hence the synchronic quality of much eighteenth-century historiography and its historicization of the present in ongoing swings of the epistemological pendulum.

LOCKE'S SYNCHRONIC GENERATION

The roots of this synchronic quality are nowhere more in evidence than in Locke's *Essay concerning Human Understanding,* which opens with a "true *History of the first beginnings of Humane Knowledge*" (162), since Locke's goal is "to enquire into the Original, Certainty, and Extent of humane Knowledge" (43). As Joel C. Weinsheimer has argued, Locke's epistemology supposes that there be a first, a beginning.[3] From a post-nineteenth-century perspective, however, this genetic epistemology rests on a paradox: though Locke discussed the origins of human understanding on the basis of a "historical method," he did not feel compelled to do so diachronically.

This is particularly true for the fundamental notion that there are no innate ideas or principles of the mind. The mind has to be impressed and to perceive itself to be impressed. This presupposes a beginning and, to that extent, a historical method. However, this historical method is severely limited in that ideas are not generated by the human mind but by objects external to it. This is particularly true of "simple *Ideas,* which since the Mind, as has been shewed, can by no means make to it self, must necessarily be the product of Things operating on the Mind in a natural way" (563–64). If this is the case, then what does it mean to "enquire into the Original . . . of humane Knowledge?" Negatively put, it means Locke is not concerned with origins as moments in time but with the kind of certainty that obtains outside history. According to Locke, the sources of our understanding are therefore not to be found in children or savages, whom he lumps together with the mentally retarded and the grossly illiterate. Unlike Condillac, who will turn to childhood as one locus of origins, Locke refuses "to argue from the thoughts of Infants, which are unknown to us" (62), though he grants that we have our first ideas in the womb (144).

3 Joel C. Weinsheimer, *Eighteenth-Century Hermeneutics: Philosophy of Interpretation in England from Locke to Burke* (New Haven: Yale University Press, 1993), 39–40.

For Locke, the genealogical method is not going to yield the original, which can only be arrived at synchronically. God, "the divine Original" (706), excepted, there can be only two "Originals": "External, Material things, as the Objects of SENSATION; and the Operations of our own Minds within, as the Objects of REFLECTION, are, to me, the only Originals, from whence all our *Ideas* take their beginnings" (105).

The synchronic dimension of Locke's experimental method accounts for his lack of interest in the origins of languages, an issue he set aside at the beginning of book 3: "God having designed Man for a sociable Creature . . . furnished him also with Language" (402). Similarly, it is symptomatic that he was virtually alone among English intellectuals in having no interest in constitutional history.[4] For Locke, history still belongs to the realm of opinion. It merely illustrates the relativity of ethics (or practical principles).

The limits of this synchronic historical method become apparent once one tries to understand the role of memory in Locke's epistemology. Locke defines memory as the ability to perceive again and considers it to be determinant in our ability to make general propositions. It is as such a primary operation of the mind. The problem is that memory is not necessarily coeval with ideas, which are coeval with sensations. Indeed, Locke never makes clear when or why memory begins or when the understanding stops being passive: "For, methinks, the *Understanding* is not much unlike a Closet, wholly shut from light, with only some little openings left, to let in external visible Resemblances, or *Ideas* of things without; would the Pictures coming into such a dark Room but stay there, and lie so orderly as to be found upon occasion, it would very much resemble the Understanding of a Man, in reference to all Objects of sight, and the *Ideas* of them" (163).

On the one hand, Locke denies dreams the status of ideas because he does not believe that memory is involved in dreaming. On the other, he claims that ideas exist before words and are independent of them. Some ideas imprint themselves before memory. The process happens

[4] In *Ancient Constitution and the Feudal Law: A Study of English Historical Thought in the Seventeenth Century,* a reissue with a retrospect (Cambridge: Cambridge University Press, 1987), John G. A. Pocock briefly reflects on "how exceptional Locke was in omitting any discussion of English legal or constitutional history from the *Treatises of Civil Government*" (188). I would add that, in the First Treatise, Locke's rejection of Filmer and patriarchalism is also a rejection of historical modes of justification. See *Two Treatises of Government,* ed. Peter Laslett (Cambridge: Cambridge University Press, 1988), esp. 153–54.

"in time," however, and despite his denial, Locke often does refer to children and the evolution of their minds.

A further consequence of—or explanation for—Locke's distrust of diachrony or genealogy is that, unlike his follower Condillac, he has a deep mistrust of language. In coming after ideas, words introduce the possibility of confusion. Locke does not wish to state whether the "responsibility" for confused ideas rests with the ideas or the inadequacies inherent in names, but the fact nevertheless remains that confusion is always linguistic in nature. Simple ideas do not need language since the message behind simple ideas can be communicated through experiential repetition: "*Simple Ideas*, as has been shewn, *are only* to be *got by* those *impressions* Objects themselves make on our Minds, by the proper Inlets appointed to each sort. If they are not received this way, all the *Words* in the World, *made use of to explain, or define any of their Names, will never be able to produce in us the* Idea *it stands for*" (424). Language, by contrast, cannot communicate simple ideas since words are at two removes from the thing. They have no referent outside the mind: they are the signs of ideas, which are already approximations of particular things. To the simplicity and certainty of that knowledge, which constitutes real truth, Locke opposes the notion of verbal truth, which deals with propositions that "stand for *Ideas* in the Mind, that have not an agreement with the reality of Things" (577). He never even raises the question of how it is possible for the mind to produce ideas that are incompatible with nature.

There are some names that "are *not arbitrary at all*" (428). They stand for simple or "real ideas," defined as "such as have a Foundation in Nature; such as have a Conformity with the real Being, and Existence of Things, or with their Archetypes" (372).[5] These are rare, however, and Locke's discussion of words, "so slight a Subject" (437), is therefore presented as an afterthought. Nevertheless, for all the conventional assault on "Rhetorick, that powerful instrument of Error and Deceit" (508), Locke cannot help but suggest that one "should *use the same Word constantly in the same sense*" (523), a fantasy that Condillac was still to entertain despite the fact that Condillac's own theory can be used to demonstrate in great measure the practical impossibility of such an attempt. By contrast, Pope's view of the limits and possibilities of

---

[5] We find an echo of this longing for the "real idea" as late as Smith's discussion of real versus nominal price.

language as a tool of communication "owned" by a large group of people was far more complex.

"True *Genius* is but rare," wrote Alexander Pope, stating one of those patent facts that can apparently always bear repeating.[6] It accounts in part for a neoclassical absence of emphasis on the notion of genius and on one of its attendants, originality. In that respect, the "Essay on Criticism" is fairly typical in its exhortations to measure, restraint, method, and imitation of the ancients. Pope's topic, after all, is criticism, and not the "one *Science* only" that "will one *Genius* fit" (line 60). He prefers to emphasize instead, in a traditional triad that will remain unchallenged for many decades to come, the need to bring together memory, the understanding, and the imagination. On the subject of originality, he seems to favor the middle ground: "The *Vulgar* thus through *Imitation* err; / As oft the *Learn'd* by being *Singular*" (lines 424–25). Originality must be held in check by writers, who should strive to avoid the dangers of vulgar imitation and of the excessive singularity that would make "*Gen'rous Converse*" (line 641) impossible.

Pope's emphasis on rules and "the Critick's Law" (line 132) is nevertheless not one-sided. Some of his most biting sarcasm is directed at those who "mimick" (line 331) or "prey on" the ancients (line 112), and he stresses early on that

> Some Beauties yet, no Precepts can declare,
> For there's a *Happiness* as well as *Care*.
> *Musick* resembles *Poetry,* in each
> Are *nameless Graces* which no *Methods* teach,
> And which a *Master-Hand* alone can reach.
> If, where the *Rules* not far enough extend,
> (Since Rules were made but to promote their End)
> Some Lucky LICENSE answers to the full
> Th'Intent propos'd, *that Licence* is a *Rule.*
>
> (lines 141–49)

---

[6] "An Essay on Criticism," in *Poetry and Prose of Alexander Pope,* ed. Aubrey Williams (Boston: Houghton Mifflin, 1969), line 11. Further line references will be included in the body of the text.

This view was of course not new to the eighteenth century. Nicolas Boileau, for instance, had made a similar observation in "L'Art poétique" (1674):

> Sometimes in its course, a powerful mind,
> Hemmed in too tightly by art, breaks with prescribed rules,
> And learns to exceed the bounds of art itself.

> Quelquefois dans sa course un esprit vigoureux,
> Trop resserré par l'art, sort des règles prescrites,
> Et de l'art même apprend à franchir leurs limites.[7]

A century earlier, Lodovico Castelvetro had already noted that "the imitation the poet is expected to use not merely does not follow the example laid down by another, . . . but does something completely separate from what has been done, and sets before itself, so to speak, another example to follow."[8] It is only in the eighteenth century, however, that originality came to dominate discursive practices associated with judging works of art and literature, a change in focus that was in part an offshoot of the Quarrel between the Ancients and the Moderns. Indeed, the conceptualization of originality was closely tied to the critics' need to assess the achievements of earlier writers, particularly in the case of more immediate predecessors. The evolution of Pope's own critical vocabulary illustrates this trend and the problems attached to it.

In the *Essay* Pope betrays a pained sense of belatedness. Not only is he fearful of the rapid evolution of the English language (lines 474–87), he also urges the study of classics such as Homer whose rules, he claims, were one with nature. Reading Homer supposedly allows one to recapture origins and "trace the Muses *upward* to their *Spring*" (line 127). Homer's epic poetry represents the single instance of poetry that need be compared only to itself.

Pope perceives more clearly than Locke that words are part of his nature and that his predecessors have mediated his experience. The Lockean longing for immediacy, for that "*Something* . . . / That gives us back the Image of our Mind" (lines 299–300), though present, is then

---

[7] Nicolas Boileau-Despréaux, "L'Art poétique," in *Oeuvres*, ed. Sylvain Menant (Paris: Garnier-Flammarion, 1969), 2:85–115, canto 4, lines 78–80.

[8] Lodovico Castelvetro, *[Selections from] The Poetics of Aristotle Translated and Annotated*, trans. Allan H. Gilbert, in *Literary Criticism: Plato to Dryden*, ed. Allan H. Gilbert (1940; Detroit: Wayne State University Press, 1962), 312.

mediated by a host of paradoxical notions such as *"Nature Methodiz'd"* (line 89): "To copy *Nature* is to copy *Them* [ancient rules]" (line 140), and *"Licence is a Rule"* (line 149).

A similar problematic plays itself out in a letter to the *Guardian* published on September 28, 1713, in which Pope discusses "the origin of letters." On the one hand, the author of the letter clearly disagrees with Locke, for whom confusion is always linguistic in character. As we saw, the Lockean ideal of real and simple ideas is alinguistic ("For what need of a Sign, when the Thing signified is present and in view?"; Locke, *Essay*, 567) and he contrasts the notion of verbal truth to the real truth that has "a Foundation in Nature" (Locke, *Essay*, 372).

Although Pope recognizes that the relationship between letters and sounds is arbitrary and draws a parallel between this phenomenon and the arbitrariness that exists between "those Sounds and the Ideas of the Mind they immediately stand for," he also believes that letters and, by extension, language cancel the distance imposed by time and space. Taken as a whole, language generates a new nature that is actually superior to what we look at passively. Additionally, writing allows for a visual representation of this secondary—yet preferred and in that sense primary—reality. The role of letters is to represent images given to us by the mind, not by nature. The comparison to painting makes this clear: "Have any of any School of Painters, gotten themselves an Immortal Name, by drawing a Face, or Painting a Landskip, by laying down on a piece of Canvas a Representation only of what Nature had given them Originals? What Applauses will he merit, who first made his Ideas set to his Pencil, and drew to his Eye the Picture of his Mind!" Visual equivalents are still presented as partaking of an ideal form of knowledge. The distinction introduced here concerns the way they can be generated: from within rather than without. Letters, which make the visualization of sounds possible, then become conceptually primary (though not temporally, as had been the case for Vico, who thought that writing had come before speech).[9]

Moreover, even though they may be arbitrary denotations of sounds, letters represent a "universalizing" force: "Notwithstanding which Difficulty [the absence of 'connexion' between sounds and letters], and the Variety of Languages, the *Powers* of the Letters in each are very

---

[9] Alexander Pope, "[On the Origin of Letters]," in *The Earlier Works, 1711–1720*, vol. 1 of *The Prose Works of Alexander Pope*, ed. Norman Ault (Oxford: Basil Blackwell, 1936), 142–43. I am indebted to Perry Meisel for having alerted me to the existence of this short essay.

nearly the same, being in all Places about Twenty Four." Indeed, in addition to its aesthetic potential, writing also represents an inherently powerful agent of ideological domination. This, as Pope points out, is more indicative of "the *Powers* of the letters" than any artistic application: "But to drop the Comparison of this Art with any other, let us see the Benefit of it in itself. By it the *English* Trader may hold Commerce with the Inhabitants of the *East* or *West Indies*, without the Trouble of a Journey." Writing also benefits astronomers and philosophers. Its main benefit, however, consists in turning the world into a potential audience for English or Western modes of thought: "What is spoken and thought at one Pole, may be heard and understood at the other." The philosopher may "lay open his Heart to all the World." In hindsight, of course, it becomes clear that writing is praised in significant measure for its power to unify an empire. Thanks to letters, "converse" becomes very generous indeed.[10]

Such a perspective was not lost on other eighteenth-century thinkers, especially Condillac, for whom the concept of a "natural sign" is an oxymoron: "So you see commerce rescues mankind from that state wherein he only attended to the present object which affected him more. . . . But, you will ask me, are natural signs nothing? I answer that, until commerce, natural signs are not at all properly signs."[11] Note that defining commerce as both trade and conversation was a staple of eighteenth-century thought. In the *Essay on the Origins of Languages*, Rousseau claimed that alphabetic writing "must have been devised by commercial peoples who, traveling in several countries and having to speak several languages, were forced to invent characters that could be common to all of them." "This," Rousseau immediately adds, "is not precisely to depict speech, it is to analyze it."[12]

---

[10] Ibid., 142–43. Adam Smith would also note the importance of narrowing down the number of characters to twenty-four in his "Considerations concerning the First Formation of Languages," in vol. 4 of *The Glasgow Edition of the Works and Correspondence of Adam Smith*, ed. J. C. Bryce, gen. ed. A. S. Skinner (Oxford: Oxford University Press, 1983; Indianapolis: Liberty Fund, 1985), 217–18.

[11] Condillac, *Lettres inédites à Gabriel Cramer*, ed. Georges Le Roy (Paris: Presses Universitaires de France, 1953), 85, quoted in Jacques Derrida, *The Archeology of the Frivolous: Reading Condillac*, trans. John P. Leavey Jr. (Pittsburgh: Duquesne University Press, 1980), 111.

[12] Jean-Jacques Rousseau, *Essay on the Origin of Languages* and *Writings Related to Music*, trans. and ed. John T. Scott, in *The Collected Writings of Rousseau*, ed. Roger D. Masters and Christopher Kelly (Hanover, N.H.: Published for Dartmouth College by University Press of New England), 7:297.

Whether or not letters entail the painting of speech, it is, as noted earlier, by "the *Powers* of the letters" that "the *English* Trader may hold Commerce with the Inhabitants of the *East* or *West Indies*." This helps us to understand Pope's inclusion of the conventional contention that "the use of Letters, as significative of these Sounds, is such an additional Improvement to them, that I know not whether we ought not to attribute the Invention of them to the Assistance of a Power more than Human." However, since letters are undeniably human in origin, Pope's remark certainly suggests that man is, like God, able to initiate an origin.[13]

In the end, though Pope valued immediacy, he also believed it could be created. This contradicted Locke, for whom immediacy was something that needed to be preserved. Aesthetically, this epistemological choice was not yet clearly defined at the time Pope wrote the "Essay." It was formulated more explicitly, however, as Pope's writings on Homer evolved.

In the 1715 "Preface to the Iliad," Pope emphasizes Homer's "invention": "Homer is universally allow'd to have had the greatest Invention of any Writer whatever"; "His Invention remains yet unrival'd"; "It is to the Strength of this amazing Invention we are to attribute that unequal'd Fire and Rapture, which is so forcible in *Homer*, that no Man of a true Poetical Spirit is Master of himself while he reads him. What he writes is of the most animated Nature imaginable; every thing moves, every thing lives, and is put in Action." Pope also notes that Homer's greatness was at least in part a function of his chronological priority: "We acknowledge him the Father of Poetical Diction, the first who taught that *Language of the Gods* to Men. His Expression is like the colouring of some great Masters, which discovers itself to be laid on boldly, and executed with Rapidity. It is indeed the strongest and most glowing imaginable, and touch'd with the greatest Spirit."[14]

The course of Pope's own career came to give the lie to this belief, however. As long as he insisted that the *Iliad* had no antecedents, his own work could easily be charged with being derivative or secondary. He conceptualized it as such in his translations. Yet Pope also knew what possibilities his own belatedness offered and how to exploit them.

---

[13] Pope, "[On the Origin of Letters]," 142, 143, 141.
[14] "Preface to the Iliad," in *Poetry and Prose of Alexander Pope,* ed. Aubrey Williams (Boston: Houghton Mifflin, 1969), 439, 440, 445.

The "last son" had a keen sense of what it meant "to write in a public idiom."[15] This is why, as noted by John Paul Russo, "his verse protestations to Dr. Arbuthnot asserting the very naturalness of his coming to be a poet are in fact couched in language borrowed from Ovid."[16] Such borrowings add a new twist to his claim that "to copy *Nature* is to copy *Them*" ("Essay on Criticism," line 140).

Equally important, one of the most interesting features of the "Preface to the Iliad" is the absence of what he could write only ten years later in his "Preface to the Works of Shakespear," namely, that "*Homer* himself drew not his art so immediately from the fountains of Nature, it proceeded thro' Ægyptian strainers and channels, and came to him not without some tincture of the learning, or some cast of the models, of those before him."[17] Of course, the question here is not whether Homer had Egyptian sources, but why Pope chose in 1725 to emphasize a piece of information he had ignored in 1715, even though he must have had access to it after spending years on his translation of the *Iliad*. It is possible that the discrepancy arose because of the requirements of the genre. If a preface to the work of a great author requires high praise, Pope may indeed have risked contradicting himself when prefacing the works of Shakespeare and Homer, especially since the two prefaces are separated by an interval of ten years. It is hard to imagine, however, that Pope would have forgotten how highly he had praised an author he had so painstakingly translated. Moreover, such an explanation would fail to account for the noticeable shift in critical vocabulary that had taken place in the meantime. Indeed, we are dealing here with more than a simple contradiction. Pope defended his "Modern" on grounds that were intrinsically different from those he had used to praise Homer. His very choice of Shakespeare over Homer is significant in that his preface to Shakespeare allowed him to introduce a defense of originality as such, which had not been part of his earlier work. By 1725, Pope's critical values had changed and so had his terminology.

[15] Maynard Mack, *Alexander Pope, A Life* (New York: W. W. Norton; New Haven: Yale University Press, 1985), 87. The phrase "the last son" refers to line 196 of the "Essay on Criticism": "The last, the meanest of your sons inspire."

[16] John Paul Russo, *Alexander Pope: Tradition and Identity* (Cambridge, Mass.: Harvard University Press, 1972), 2. Russo also notes that "Johnson first noted the source in *The Rambler*, No. 143" (2n).

[17] Pope, "Preface to the Works of Shakespear," in *Poetry and Prose of Alexander Pope*, ed. Aubrey Williams (Boston: Houghton Mifflin, 1969), 460.

In the "Preface to the Works of Shakespear," the word *invention* is no longer mentioned. Instead, *originality*, not used in the *Essay on Criticism*, comes to the fore, if only in its adjectival form. After two introductory paragraphs, Pope takes an unequivocal plunge in a remarkably strong statement: "If ever any Author deserved the name of an *Original*, it was *Shakespear*." He then compares him favorably to Homer, who "drew not his art so immediately from the fountains of Nature. . . . The Poetry of *Shakespear* was Inspiration indeed; he is not so much an Imitator, as an Instrument, of Nature; and 'tis not so just to say that he speaks from her, as that she speaks thro' him." Pope then proceeds to give his definition of an original: "His *Characters* are so much Nature her self, that 'tis a sort of injury to call them by so distant a name as Copies of her. Those of other Poets have a constant resemblance, which shews that they receiv'd them from one another, and were but multiplyers of the same image: each picture like a mock-rainbow is but the reflexion of a reflexion. But every single character in *Shakespear* is as much an Individual, as those in Life itself." The original poet is then a maker, someone who, godlike, can generate new life forms without the need of Lockean "objects of sensation" or primary images to draw from. Unlike Homer's invention, which was derivative, Shakespeare's originality manifests itself in his ability to generate new images.[18]

The contrast—set up by Pope—now enables him to deal with the impossibility of "trac[ing] the Muses upward to their Spring." As an original author, Shakespeare is a possessed creature, inspired by a power that takes control. Being original entails being one with nature to the point that imitation is no longer an issue. This gives a new twist to Pope's earlier and much discussed remark that "*Nature* and *Homer* were, he found, the *same*," but his praise of Shakespeare seems far more romantic in tone. Shakespeare's work is apparently effortless and requires no preparation: "He seems to have known the world by Intuition" rather than formal education. In short, he appears "to be the only Author that gives ground for a very new opinion, That the Philosopher and even the Man of the world may be *Born*, as well as the poet." This "very new opinion" is not wholeheartedly embraced by Pope, who is loath to admit

---

[18] Pope, "Preface to the Works of Shakespear," 460–61. In "Preface to the Iliad," Shakespeare had not fared so well: "In *Shakespear*, it [Poetical *Fire*] strikes before we are aware, like an accidental Fire from Heaven: But in *Homer*, and in him only, it burns every where clearly, and every where irresistibly" (440).

that even the poet may be born. The neoclassicist in him resurfaces, for example, when he tries to discredit reports that Shakespeare "scarce ever *blotted a line*," hardly cause for praise in Pope's book. Nevertheless, he helped shape the "very new opinion" that was to gain increasing ascendancy in the following decades.[19]

The evolution of Pope's critical vocabulary between the early 1710s and 1725 was hardly solipsistic, as a comparison between Joseph Addison's eleven essays "on the pleasures of the imagination" (published in *The Spectator* in 1712) and Francis Hutcheson's *Inquiry into the Original of Our Ideas of Beauty and Virtue* (first published in 1725) will show.

Addison mentions novelty as one of three sources of pleasures. His praise of novelty is hardly extravagant, however. On the one hand, he acknowledges that "Every thing that is *new* or *uncommon* raises a Pleasure in the Imagination, because it fills the Soul with an agreeable Surprise, gratifies its Curiosity, and gives it an Idea of which it was not before possest." On the other hand, he cautions that what is new is often merely strange and fanciful. Fairy tales, a legitimate but not intrinsically praiseworthy genre, belong to that category: "The Ancients have not much of this Poetry among them, for, indeed, almost the whole Substance of it owes its Original to the Darkness and Superstition of later Ages." But even when agreeableness is not contaminated by strangeness, novelty is not presented as a particularly powerful tool of criticism. Describing a forerunner of motion pictures, Addison writes: "I must confess, the Novelty of such a sight may be one occasion of its Pleasantness to the Imagination, but certainly the chief Reason is its near Resemblance to Nature, as it does not only, like other Pictures, give the Colour and Figure, but the Motion of the Things it represents." Needless to say, Addison never uses the word *original* in a modern sense. Depending on the context, *original* is either an adjective referring to the model used for representation or a noun synonymous with the word *origin*.[20]

By the time Hutcheson wrote his *Inquiry*, however, the word *original* had acquired an additional meaning. In an influential distinction between "Original" or "Absolute" and "Comparative" or

---

[19] Pope, "Essay on Criticism," lines 127, 135; "Preface to the Works of Shakespear," 461, 463.

[20] [Joseph] Addison, ["On the Pleasures of the Imagination"], in *The Spectator*, ed. Donald F. Bond (Oxford: Clarendon Press, 1965), no. 412 (3:541); no. 419 (3:572); no. 414 (3:551).

"Relative" beauty, Hutcheson defined original beauty as "that Beauty which we perceive in Objects without *Comparison* to any thing external, of which the Object is suppos'd an Imitation, or Picture." Hutcheson did not see how this distinction could affect literary criticism. According to him, absolute beauty is a category applicable mainly to *"Works of Nature, artificial Forms, Figures,"* while *"relative Beauty* is what they [the Poets] should principally endeavour to obtain, as the peculiar *Beauty* of their Works." The English philosopher did not challenge the time-honored tradition that poetry is an imitative art, but other thinkers, drawing in part on the epistemological implications of Hutcheson's aesthetics, which David Paxman has recently brought to light so convincingly, eventually did give us the tools necessary for a change in emphasis.[21]

Foremost among these are Young's defense of originality in his "Conjectures on Original Composition" (1759) and Duff's *Essay on Original Genius* (1767). Before I discuss these two works, however, I would like to note that Pope had already put his finger on the core problem associated with the modern conceptualization of originality. Of the author who "deserved the name of an *Original,"* Pope warned, we have no "originals" but only *"Original Copies."* This paradox exceeds the bounds of Pope's interest in Shakespeare's status and underscores more broadly the logical problems associated with trying to frame originality in terms of temporal primacy. This conceptual difficulty explains why, after the introductory praise of Shakespeare, the preface focuses exclusively on the textual corruption of the so-called originals of Shakespeare's text.[22]

YOUNG'S TABULA RASA

Whether Young was misguided when he ventured that the topic of his "Conjectures on Original Composition" was original—Samuel Johnson did not seem to think it was—his "Conjectures" represents an important milestone in the history of the conceptualization of originality because it is the first essay devoted exclusively and systematically to

[21] Francis Hutcheson, *An Inquiry into the Original of our Ideas of Beauty and Virtue,* 4th ed. (London, 1738), 14–15, 40. David Paxman, "Aesthetics as Epistemology, or Knowledge without Certainty," *Eighteenth-Century Studies* 26 (1992–1993): 285–306.
[22] Pope, "Preface to the Works of Shakespear," 460, 468.

that question.[23] More important, whatever else one may think of Young's "Conjectures," he did manage to turn originality into an unavoidable aesthetic category, a situation griped about ever since.[24] Moreover, the text encapsulates several important issues related to the debate on originality: it is part of the ongoing debate over the respective values of modernity and antiquity; it ties the conceptualization of originality to those of genius and imitation; and it proposes that originality also has legal implications and that authorship must be framed in terms of ownership and property.

Somewhat disappointingly—though perhaps wisely—Young states early on that he has chosen not to "enter into the curious enquiry of what is, or is not, strictly speaking, *Original,* content with what all must allow, that some compositions are more so than others" (409). Less equivocally, however, he immediately adds: "And the more they are so, I say, the better" (409), thereby emphasizing a criterion that had not always received top billing in literary criticism. Young goes on to tell us that originals are a product of genius, its "fairest flowers" (409). By comparison, "*Imitations* are of quicker growth, but fainter bloom" (409), he writes, referring to the imitation *of other authors*. Indeed, imitation is not *stricto sensu* incompatible with originality in Young's essay: "*Imitations* are of two kinds; one of nature, one of authors: The first we call *Originals,* and confine the term *Imitation,* to the second" (409). And the term is not used in a flattering way. Even the best imitator of authors "but nobly builds on another's foundation; his debt is, at least, equal to his glory; which therefore, on the balance, cannot be very great" (410).

In view of Young's strong stance on imitation, which he calls "inferiority confessed" (426), it is hardly surprising that, despite its late date of publication (1759), the "Conjectures" still echoes the rhetoric of the Quarrel between the Ancients and the Moderns. Although Young

[23] Edward Young, "Conjectures on Original Composition," in *The Great Critics: An Anthology of Literary Criticism,* ed. James Harry Smith and Edd Winfield Parks, 3rd ed. (New York: W. W. Norton, 1951), 408. Further page references to Young's "Conjectures" will be included parenthetically in the body of the text. Johnson "was surprized to find Young receive as novelties, what he thought very common maxims." James Boswell, *The Journal of a Tour to the Hebrides with Samuel Johnson, L.L.D.,* 3rd ed. (London, 1786), in vol. 5 of *Boswell's Life of Johnson,* ed. George Birkbeck Hill, revised and enlarged by L. F. Powell (Oxford: Clarendon Press, 1950), 269.

[24] See, for example, Walter Jackson Bate, *The Burden of the Past and the English Poet* (Cambridge, Mass.: Harvard University, Belknap Press, 1970), 105, and Françoise Meltzer, *Hot Property: The Stakes and Claims of Literary Originality* (Chicago: University of Chicago Press, 1994), 158.

specifies that "quite clear of the dispute concerning *antient and modern learning,* we speak not of performance, but powers" (420), that dispute still constitutes the background and even the raison d'être for his strong insistence that his contemporaries need not be exclusively restricted to imitating the classics, which stifles moderns' growth by transplanting them "in a foreign soil" (410). One of Young's objectives is indeed to demonstrate that the inferiority of the moderns in the liberal arts—which he does not dispute—does not proceed from any historical necessity: "The mind of a man of genius . . . enjoys a perpetual spring" (409). He strongly denies that one's capacity to be original might somehow be dependent on the date of one's birth and categorically rejects the claim that the practitioners of the liberal arts are merely latecomers increasingly unable to connect with the source that had nurtured Homer. Young, and by extension, his readers, must deny that "the human mind's teeming time is past" (412).

By insisting on his age, seventy-six, in the opening paragraphs of this "Letter" to Richardson, Young immediately frames his remarks in individual terms, which explains the occasionally breathless urgency of the "Conjectures." In his "evening hours" (409), "like the sepulchral lamps of old" (407), Young offers to disclose to the reader the source of originality, which he locates both in himself and in his own belated era, that "churchyard" of "monumental marbles" (407). The date of one's birth must be understood not only in sociohistorical but in biological terms. Young's denial that "the human mind's teeming time is past" is both a reference to the history of poetry and to his own history. Similarly, at the beginning of the essay, "the frozen obstructions of age" (408) refer not only to himself but to the flotsam of civilization. Age, and by association, history, become personal enemies whose power must be denied. Hence the refusal to think that composition is determined by history: "If you write naturally, you might as well charge *Homer* with an imitation of you. Can you be said to imitate *Homer* for writing *so,* as you would have written, if *Homer* had never been?" (413).

The state of the liberal arts, which "are in retrogradation, and decay" (418), parallels the description of Young's own body. Hence the seemingly paradoxical situation of the "Conjectures," in which a man who presents himself as having one foot in the grave sings the praise of "native powers" (415) and "the natural strength of the body" (415). Rejecting imitation, which causes us to sever ourselves from the nature that "brings us into the world all *Originals*" (419), Young chooses instead to present the reader with an organic theory of originality: "An *Original* may be said to be of a *vegetable* nature; it rises spontaneously from the vital root of genius; it *grows*, it is not *made: Imitations* are often a sort of *manufacture* wrought up by those *mechanics, art,* and *labour,* out of pre-existent materials not their own" (410).

Needless to say, Young resists the notion that "you must either imitate *Homer,* or depart from nature" (413) and accordingly saves his most derogatory comments for Pope, that "zealous recommender" of imitation (426). He will not even grant the truth of Pope's "True genius is but rare," claiming instead, toward the end of an embarrassed explanation, that "many a genius, probably, there has been, which could neither write, nor read" (417), an unconvincing statement, even more so from the perspective of a highly literate era. Pope's principal shortcoming, in Young's eyes, is his self-repression: "An *Original* author is born of himself, is his own progenitor. . . . Therefore, though we stand much obliged for his giving us an *Homer,* yet had he doubled our obligation, by giving us—a *Pope*" (427).

Young believes that the source of originality is within and he accordingly urges writers to "know" and "reverence" themselves so "as to prefer the native growth of [their] own mind to the richest import from abroad; such borrowed riches make us poor" (422). Originality, then, is no longer relegated to the fanciful or strange; it takes on the coloration of authenticity, of truth to the self. The more a text will be my own, the more original it will be. Originality depends on organic growth and is incompatible with foreign elements, including history. Modern writers must therefore rely "on their own native powers" (415) and connect with the "god within," genius. In this one stroke, Young turns the self into a divinity.

As death nears, he therefore urges his contemporaries to affirm their rights. Modern writers have allowed themselves to be dispossessed by writers such as Homer and Pindar who are only *"accidental Originals;* the works they imitated, few excepted, are lost: They, on their father's decease, enter as lawful heirs, on their estates in fame: The fathers of our copyists are still in possession" (411). Young's appeal to a legalistic language is important in that it signals that originality is now also a matter of property. The original author's distinguishing feature is that he alone can claim ownership of his production: "His works will stand distinguished; his the sole property of them; which property alone can confer the noble title of an *author*" (422). This authority will then affirm itself not only over its own production but also over its consumers and heirs, since a truly original author dispossesses the reader: "We have no home, no thought, of our own" (410).[25]

Significantly, it is in the land where Young's theories had the greatest impact, the land of the *Originalgenies*, that the words "original" and "*eigen*tümlich" are sometimes used interchangeably. Indeed, Young's theory understandably landed on fertile ground in a culture faced with the need to chart a tradition of its own. But even in England, the logic of a concurrent defense of originality and modern culture could lead in a nationalistic direction, and the latter half of the *"Conjectures"* does consist for the most part in waving the British banner: "Something new may be expected from *Britons* particularly; who seem not to be more sever'd from the rest of mankind by the surrounding sea, than by the current in their veins" (429). Moreover, the issue took on religious connotations when Young equated the spirit of imitation with papist idolatry and declared that Pope's "taste partook the error of his religion" (426). One must, however, note that in his praise of Shakespeare as an original author, Young conveniently ignored that he was making an argument Pope had already made, and in very much the same way.

No matter how influential Young's contribution may have been, one should be wary of ascribing too much revolutionary zeal to him. As we have seen, his defense of originality does not exclude all forms of imitation but merely restricts its field of application. Even his praise of originality is not unmixed ("as nothing is more easy than to write originally wrong; Originals are not here recommended"; 424), while his appreciation of genius is tempered with a word of caution against throwing learning to the winds. In addition, after a strong attack on the "many ill effects" (418) of the spirit of imitation, he goes on to say that "notwithstanding these disadvantages of *Imitation*, imitation must be the lot (and often an honourable lot it is) of most writers" (419).

The composition of the entire essay seems indeed to oscillate between provocative statements and shy retractions. This conservative restraint does not, however, detract too much from the power of Young's essay,

[25] For a discussion of the interplay between originality and copyright at the aesthetic, philosophical, and social levels, see Martha Woodmansee, "Genius and the Copyright: Economic and Legal Conditions of the Emergence of the 'Author,'" *Eighteenth-Century Studies* 17 (1984): 425–48. See also Raymond Birn, "The Profits of Ideas: *Privilèges en librairie* in Eighteenth-Century France," *Eighteenth-Century Studies* 4 (1970–1971): 131–68.

the title of which warns, in any case, that his thoughts are of a tentative nature. A case in point is that, though genius is "knowledge innate" (417), it "must be nursed, and educated, or it will come to nought" (416). The question is: Nursed by what, if not by that which would provide the answer to Young's anguished question: "Born *Originals*, how comes it to pass that we die *Copies?*" (419)

AUTOGENESIS

Young's denial of history could not last forever. Strangely enough, however, it was reinstated by one of the fiercest proponents of what might be called an "autogenetic" theory of composition, someone who took Young's theory much farther than Young had been willing to do. Indeed, William Duff's *Essay on Original Genius* (1767) points even more emphatically than Young's "Conjectures" to the rise of romanticism, despite Duff's derogatory use of the term "romantic."[26]

By the time Duff wrote his *Essay*, the importance of originality in a work of art no longer needed to be defended and he therefore felt free to rhapsodize without restraint. In his definition of the word *original*, for instance, at the beginning of book 2, he already makes extraordinary claims, implying that the field of application of original geniuses is unlimited. Totally gone now is the sense of human balance we associate with neoclassicism: "by the word ORIGINAL, when applied to Genius, we mean that NATIVE and RADICAL power which the mind possesses, of discovering something NEW and UNCOMMON in every subject on which it employs its faculties" (86). Novelty has turned into a religion. Original genius

> is distinguished by an inventive and plastic Imagination, by which it sketches out a creation of its own, discloses truths that were formerly unknown, and exhibits a succession of scenes and events which were never before contemplated or conceived. In a word, it is the peculiar character of original Genius to strike out a path for itself whatever

---

[26] If he does not combine judgment and taste with the imagination, the most inventive author will be nothing more than some "romantic visionary." [William Duff], *An Essay on Original Genius; And Its Various Modes of Exertion in Philosophy and the Fine Arts, Particularly in Poetry* (London, 1767), 19. Further page references to Duff's *Essay* will be included parenthetically in the body of the text.

sphere it attempts to occupy. . . . It is distinguished by the most uncommon, as well as the most surprising combinations of ideas; by the novelty, and not unfrequently by the sublimity and boldness of its imagery in composition. (89–90)

Though "ORIGINAL GENIUS . . . may be exerted in any profession" (87), poetry occupies a privileged position in Duff's theory. Indeed, "it is Poetry that affords the amplest scope . . . for the most advantageous display of ORIGINAL GENIUS" (188) because the poet, as opposed to, for example, the philosopher, "has nothing to do but to give scope to the excursions of this faculty [the imagination], which . . . will supply an inexhaustible variety of striking incidents" (129). Going further than Young, Duff not only rejects the imitation of other poets because "an original Genius in Poetry will strike out NEW SENTIMENTS, as well as NEW IMAGES, on every subject on which he employs his talents" (149), he would also like to do away with any reference to nature and goes so far as to say that "truly ORIGINAL GENIUS" (143) manifests itself in "the invention of . . . supernatural characters" (143). Any form of imitation is "a bar to ORIGINALITY" (256). As a consequence, all descriptive genres, whether in painting or poetry, cannot have "any pretensions to ORIGINALITY, strictly considered. . . . They can only be regarded at best as the first and most complete COPIES of the true ORIGINALS" (190–91).

Duff is therefore a fierce proponent of what might be called autogenetic aesthetics. An original genius expresses new sentiments that "are the natural dictates of the heart, not fictitious or copied, but original" (156). Noteworthy here, of course, is that "original" is paired with "natural" and distinguished from "fictitious." This is significant on at least two counts. On the one hand, it demonstrates that Duff is more inspired than careful in the elaboration of his theory, for what is the reader to make of his previous high regard for the invention of supernatural characters? On the other hand, this pairing does offer one possible explanation for Duff's cumulative inclusion of two apparently mutually exclusive theories: autogeneticism and primitivism.

If originality is inborn, an author's place in time should be irrelevant. That, at least, had been Young's contention. Duff, conversely, believed that the "earliest and least cultivated" (261) periods are most conducive to the production of originals, particularly in poetry: "The efforts of Imagination, in Poetry at least, are impetuous, and attain their utmost perfection at once, even in the rudest form of social life"

(262). His rationale is that "in this primitive state of nature, when mankind begin to unite in society, the manners, sentiments, and passions are (if we may use the expression) perfectly ORIGINAL. They are the dictates of nature, unmixed and undisguised: they are therefore more easily comprehended and described" (269–70). Duff's derogatory use of the word "fictitious" need not be understood, therefore, as a rejection of the theories set forth in earlier parts of the *Essay*. He is not urging the imitation of nature but is mourning society's indiscriminate loss of unity with nature.

By equating "natural" and "original" and opposing these to "fictitious," then, Duff is not retracting his earlier dismissal of the imitation of nature, though his rhetoric is somewhat misleading. The poet of original genius need not imitate nature, but can access his or her own, even though each passing century makes it more difficult to be spontaneous. Somewhat amusingly for so vehement a writer, Duff can then be viewed as simply entertaining us with his own version of Pope's equation between Homer and nature, in spite of his more primitivist invocations. Moreover, his belief that belatedness necessarily undermines poetic genius made his theory ultimately less inspiring than Young's, in spite of the more radical rhetoric put to the service of Duff's exaltation of originality.

"UN TOUT EXQUIS"

Originality did not gain acceptance steadily as the sine qua non criterion of aesthetic value, as a number of pockets of resistance will attest. Alexander Gerard, another Scottish thinker, did not, for instance, share Duff's enthusiasm for originality. In *An Essay on Genius* (1774), Gerard, Like Young and Duff before him, refers contemptuously to the "trite and unoriginal" productions of "instead of a poet, a servile imitator, or a painful translator."[27] However, his associationist propensity does not lend itself to an indiscriminate embrace of an autogenetic theory of artistic production. More scientifically inclined than most literary critics, even in an age that tended to discuss scientific and artistic genius side by side, Gerard applied to criticism the simple observation that "as we can create no new substance, so neither can we, except perhaps

[27] Alexander Gerard, *An Essay on Genius*, 1774, ed. Bernhard Fabian (Munich: Wilhelm Fink, 1966), 42 and 43. Further page references to Gerard's *Essay* will be included parenthetically in the body of the text.

in a few very peculiar instances, imagine the idea of a simple quality which we have never had access to observe" (101). As a consequence, Gerard did more than pay lip service to imagination, judgment, and observation as necessary composites of invention: "All the fine arts are, in some sense, imitative of Nature; invention in these arts is only observing and copying Nature in a certain manner: natural objects and appearances are observed by the artist, they are conceived with distinctness and with force, their characteristical circumstances are selected, and so expressed as to imprint the whole form on the mind of others, with the clearness and vivacity with which he himself apprehended it" (395). Only nature can be totally original.

Characteristically, Gerard did not put originality on a pedestal. Although he granted that "invention is the infallible criterion of Genius" (27), he also qualified that proposition by noting that inventing means rearranging and not creating elements. Genius depends on both judgment and the imagination, so that perfecting a first draft or sketch may be more an act of genius than the first attempt itself. Not at all in sympathy with the primitivists, Gerard even cites Homer as a perfect example of genius *by improvement*.

On the topic of originality, the most interesting feature of Gerard's *Essay* is that he ascribes to it a much more limited role in the production of genius. "Genius," he writes, "is properly the faculty of *invention*; by means of which a man is qualified for making new discoveries in science, or for producing original works of art" (8). This apparent endorsement of originality is, however, quickly narrowed to "unenthusiastic" proportions: Scientific invention may consist simply of improvements over preceding discoveries while, in the arts, new and different works may be created that will not necessarily surpass previous ones. Finally, originality is not a reliable criterion of aesthetic judgment because it is often impossible to distinguish between originality and imitation. This is particularly true in the case of the ancients, where "every thing is reckoned original, because we know not, who had occupied it before" (26), a state of affairs detrimental to the moderns.

Gerard's praise of regularity as a sign of genius is even more reactionary. The imagination "is far from being capricious or irregular, but for the most observes general and established rules" (39–40). However subjective a process, it still functions along potentially predictable lines. The key to this predictability is the notion that "association being an operation of fancy, common to all men, some of its effects are universal" (41), a concept that highlights the viability of Locke's thought throughout the eighteenth century despite the fact that critical methodology had moved away from a number of Lockean tenets in the early part of that century. Of course, Locke's notions would sometimes be put to new and different uses. Gerard, for instance, relied on the association of ideas to counter the notion that there might be anything unaccounted for. He also added a new twist, in that he was able to think of creation as a historical process from within a systematic position. The two were not mutually exclusive for him. Originality is grounded in earlier developments. Its site can be occupied more than once.

Gerard's is not the only discordant note in the elaboration of a critical definition of originality. The bulk of eighteenth-century French literary criticism stands in sharp contrast to that of Gerard's English predecessors. Indeed, French thinkers tended to be far less radical in their aesthetic than in their political theories, and the French climate of those decades was therefore less favorable to the development of theories on originality.[28] As conceded by Baldine Saint-Girons, "One must admit that at the beginning of the century the impetus comes from England, where empiricist and experimental philosophy forces one to ask the question of the relationship that exists between the beautiful on the one hand and the impression from the senses [*l'impression sensible*] and sentiment on the other. By the end of the century, however, Germany seems to be taking over, by seeking to reduce the wealth of speculations on art to a logic of taste."[29]

---

[28] It is symptomatic, for instance, that whereas Young was to take pains to point out that original composition "seems an original subject to me, who have seen nothing hitherto written on it" (408), Batteux did not shy away from stating that his *Beaux Arts réduits à un même principe*, first published in 1746, was based on a doctrine which "n'est point nouvelle." *Les Beaux Arts réduits à un même principle*, in *Principes de la littérature*, 5th ed. (1775; Geneva: Slatkine Reprints, 1967), 1:39. See Julie Hayes, "Plagiarism and Legitimation in Eighteenth-Century France," *Eighteenth Century: Theory and Interpretation* 34 (1993): 115–31, for a discussion of the French reluctance to praise originality, from traditionalists such as Charles Rollin, M. de Vaubrières, and Jean-François Cailhava de l'Estendoux to more progressive Encyclopedists. For a different perspective, see Bernard Magne's reflections on the sublime in *Crise de la littérature française sous Louis XIV: Humanisme et nationalisme*, thesis presented to the Université de Toulouse le Mirail, May 28, 1974 (Lille: Reproduction des Thèses, Université Lille III, and Paris: Honoré Champion, 1976), esp. 2:788–90. According to Magne, eighteenth-century aesthetics lacks "originality" in part because it had already exhausted itself in the seventeenth century, the age of the sublime, the new, the modern, and the neoclassical, the age that had claimed, as it were, that *l'origine, c'est moi.*

[29] Baldine Saint-Girons, *Esthétiques du XVIIIe siècle: Le modèle français* (Paris: Philippe Sers, 1990), 9.

This being the case, nothing could be more fitting than to begin this section with a discussion of Charles Batteux's treatise *Les Beaux Arts réduits à un même principe*. This work, influential both in France and abroad, can indeed be said to have set the tone for much of eighteenth-century French criticism. In Charles Batteux's all-subsuming principle of imitation, the issue is Cartesian-clear but unaffected by anything like Cartesian doubt: originality is strictly an attribute of nature and cannot be produced artificially. Since nothing can be created ex nihilo, all art is necessarily imitative and the logical implications of this fundamental principle are clearly stated: "To imitate is to copy a model. This notion involves two separate concepts: 1) the original, or prototype, which has the features one wishes to imitate and 2) the copy that represents them."[30] As a consequence, the category of originality is inapplicable to the fine arts. As Gerard would put it, only nature is "the great original."[31]

Batteux is not a naturalist *avant la lettre*, however. He considers imitation a highly selective process and his prototype is not nature in general but what he calls "la belle Nature," that is, "an exquisite whole [*un tout exquis*] more perfect than Nature itself, without ceasing to be natural" (*Beaux Arts* 1:29). In other words, "la belle Nature" is not God's but man's creation, which must be "checked" against the referential mirror that nature still holds out to us. This leads to a built-in contradiction that Batteux recognizes but chooses to dismiss. In his desire to be systematic and reduce aesthetics to a single principle, Batteux refuses to address the notion that if "la belle Nature" is not identical to nature itself, then its appreciation must also be dependent on criteria that cannot be found in nature. Batteux has to see this, but he will not take into consideration any theory that would ascribe the possibility of genesis to the human mind. The application of his fundamental principle is extremely strict.[32] His views on invention, for instance, have

---

[30] Batteux, *Beaux Arts*, 1:33. Further page references to Batteux's treatise will be included parenthetically in the body of the text.

[31] Gerard, *Essay on Genius*, 128. See Arthur O. Lovejoy, " 'Nature' as Aesthetic Norm," in *Essays in the History of Ideas* (Baltimore: Johns Hopkins University Press, 1948), 69–77, for an annotated list of the various meanings of the word *nature* in eighteenth-century aesthetics.

[32] Becq's claim that Batteux's association of pleasure with imitation proceeds solely from the mind and not from the object under consideration refines but does not invalidate this basic fact. Annie Becq, *Genèse de l'esthétique française: De la raison classique à l'imagination créatrice, 1680–1814*, 2 vols. (Pisa: Pacini Editore, 1984), 1:343.

very little in common with Duff's: "To invent in the Arts is not to give birth to an object, but to recognize where it is, and how it is" (*Beaux Arts* 1:32). Batteux refuses to admit that "la Belle Nature" is a construct. It is the object of imitation, not its result. There may indeed be "privileged souls" that "are strongly impressed by the things they conceive, and never fail to reproduce them along with the new agreeable and striking character they impart to them [*un nouveau caractère d'agrément & de force qu'elles leur communiquent*]" (*Beaux Arts* 1:53), but this should not undermine the foundation of his theory. As his choice of words clearly indicates, to create is to be impressed and to reproduce. Geniuses may not function exactly like photocopy machines, but they react like photographic paper.

Clear heir to a neoclassical tradition that was to flourish for several more decades, Batteux privileges craftsmanship over inspiration, and conformity over originality. "[A skillful poet] appears to be giving new things; however, this is only one of the tricks of art."[33] Even Homer, Milton, and Corneille are creators only in that they are among the few who can imitate Nature: "The Arts, which are bound to a model, almost always bear the marks of their servitude" (*Beaux Arts* 1:116). Lesser figures should limit themselves to imitating the ancients.

The obsession with nature as the source of art is symptomatic of the longing to master the universe and leave nothing out. History and its attendant beginnings presuppose a rupture from an initial "wholeness." Hence Batteux's desire to compensate and deny by creating *un tout exquis*.

The search for epistemological principles, unity, and comprehensiveness remained a central feature of eighteenth-century thought. Buffon's "Discours sur le style," delivered on his acceptance to the Académie française on August 25, 1753, illustrates this trend perfectly. The core of Buffon's argument is that we must imitate nature because she alone is an example of wholeness and, therefore, perfection.[34] Referring to

---

[33] Charles Batteux, *Traité de la poésie épique*, in *Principes de la littérature*, 5th ed. (1775; Geneva: Slatkine Reprints, 1967), 2:326.

[34] "Why are the works of nature so perfect? Because each work is a whole and because nature works according to an eternal plan from which she never deviates . . . ; she drafts in one unique act the primitive form of every living being. . . . The human mind cannot create anything; . . . however, if it imitates nature in her functioning and in her work, if it elevates itself through contemplation to the most sublime truths, if it brings and links them together, if it shapes a whole or a system out of them through thinking, it will build immortal monuments on unshakable foundations." Georges Louis Leclerc, comte de Buffon, *Discours sur le style* (Paris: Hachette, 1867), 16–17.

Fénelon's *Lettre à l'Académie*, Buffon reaffirms that "every subject is one and can, no matter how vast it is, be dealt with within the boundaries of a single discourse."[35] This insistence on comprehensiveness accounts for the continued success of Batteux's theories. D'Alembert, for instance, embraced without much argument the foundations of Batteux's *Beaux-Arts réduits à un même principe*. In the *Preliminary Discourse to the Encyclopedia* (1751), the *philosophe* defines art as "any system of knowledge which can be reduced to positive and invariable rules" and states that the fine arts are those "liberal arts that have been reduced to principles, those that undertake the imitation of Nature," which in the *Preliminary Discourse* is also to be understood as "la belle Nature."[36]

There is one significant area, however, in which d'Alembert moves away from Batteux's principles, namely, when he stresses that aesthetic perfection is reached at early stages of cultural achievement, and that eighteenth-century works tend to be "inferior to those of the preceding century."[37] Batteux had found it easy to dismiss inquiries into the origins of poetry: "To look for poetry in its first origin is to look for it before its existence" (*Beaux-Arts* 1:319). By virtue of his central principle, poetry has always already been imitation. It does not originate. In spite of Batteux's success, this prescription did not hold. Some did try to combine comprehensiveness and systematic models of knowledge with a historical method and a search for origins. Buffon's own inquiries into natural history and Condillac's answer to Locke in the *Essay on the Origin of Human Knowledge* both attest to this.

[35] Buffon, *Discours*, 15. See Ernst Cassirer, *The Philosophy of the Enlightenment*, trans. F. C. A. Koelln and James P. Pettegrove (Princeton, N.J.: Princeton University Press, 1951), esp. 275–83, on the ties between eighteenth-century aesthetics and Cartesian thought.

[36] Jean Le Rond d'Alembert, *Preliminary Discourse to the Encyclopedia of Diderot*, trans. Richard N. Schwab, with the collaboration of Walter E. Rex (Indianapolis: Bobbs-Merrill/Library of Liberal Arts, 1963), 40, 43.

[37] Ibid., 97.

CHAPTER FOUR

The Primitive Imagination

CONDILLAC: "DANS L'ORIGINE"

In 1746 Condillac argued that "the only means of acquiring knowledge is to return to the origin of our ideas, follow their generation, and compare them in terms of all their possible relations. That is what I call to 'analyze.'"[1] Condillac's genetic turn was, of course, not unheard of. Some eighty-five years earlier, Joseph Glanvill had equated true knowledge, or more accurately, the knowledge of nature, with a knowledge of *"true initial causes"* and a view of nature's *"simple Originals."*[2] There was a difference, however. Glanvill had also seen fit to remind his readers of the unreliability of appearances and of the hypothetical nature of even the "miraculous Des-Cartes['s] . . . account of the *Universal Fabrick.*" He had accordingly deplored the impossibility of true knowledge of nature's causes even though they were "the Alphabet of Science": "We know nothing but *effects,* and those but by our Senses."[3]

---

[1] Etienne Bonnot de Condillac, *Essay on the Origin of Human Knowledge,* trans. and ed. Hans Aarsleff (Cambridge: Cambridge University Press, 2001), 49. Further page references to Condillac's *Essay* will be included parenthetically in the body of the text.

[2] Joseph Glanvill, *The Variety of Dogmatizing: Or Confidence in Opinions. Manifested in a Discourse of the Shortness and Uncertainty of Our Knowledge, and Its Causes; with Some Reflexions on Peripateticism; and An Apology for Philosophy* (London, 1661), 210. Douglas Lane Patey discusses this passage in *Probability and Literary Form: Philosophic Theory and Literary Practice in the Augustan Age* (New York: Cambridge University Press, 1984), 49–50.

[3] Glanvill, *Variety of Dogmatizing,* 211, 210.

Condillac held far more sanguine views on the possibilities of human knowledge. By the time he put pen to paper, what had been thought to yield nothing but probable knowledge at best had come to be seen as belonging, quite plausibly, to the realm of the certain. Condillac's philosophy clearly reflected and participated in this revolutionary— the word *paradigmatic* would not be too strong here—epistemic shift. The new "alphabet of science" was thought to be in the mind rather than in nature. Hence Condillac's decision to devote himself to the study of a genealogy of human understanding.

Condillac took pains to distinguish his genealogy of the human mind from Descartes's philosophy: "Descartes knew neither the origin nor the generation of our ideas. To that failure we must attribute the inadequacy of [his] method"(4).[4] Going beyond his predecessor, Condillac not only believed that the most vital task of philosophy was to study the human mind rather than the nature of things but also grounded his episteme in a metaphysics that "adjusts its inquiries to the weakness of the human mind" (3), a position reminiscent of Vico's belief that human knowledge is grounded in ignorance.

In the *Essay on the Origin of Human Knowledge*, studying the mind implies, as it had for Locke, relying on a genetic method: "We must ascend to the origin of our ideas, reveal how they are generated, trace them to the limits that nature has set for them, and thereby determine the extent and limits of our knowledge and invest human understanding with new life" (5). Compared to Locke's *Essay*, which had demonstrated that the adoption of such a principle need not automatically lead to a historical method exclusively embedded in diachrony, Condillac's *Essay* makes clear that, by the mid-eighteenth century, Locke's confident synchrony was no longer a viable option. Although Condillac insists that discovery hinges on direct observation, he also contends that presence is a form of mediation that makes it possible for us to acknowledge the past. Although his discourse may not be historical (if historical knowledge is indirect vis-à-vis experience), its (auto)archeological (or, direct) dimension, at least, can hardly be ignored. Indeed Condillac is, far more than Locke, aware of the problems inherent in the development of a synchronic historical method. He tries to prevent

---

[4] I have slightly modified Aarsleff's translation, which reads "inadequacy of this method." The French reads: "l'insuffisance de sa méthode." Condillac, *Essai sur l'origine des connaissances humaines,* preceded by "L'Archéologie du frivole," by Jacques Derrida (Auvers-sur-Oise: Galilée, 1973), 100.

them in part by developing the Lockean notion of the association of ideas into a valid explanation for the presence of the past, by introducing something like a principle of autoarcheology, and by problematizing the relationship between memory and the imagination.

The association of ideas, according to Condillac, depends on attention. Once perceptions are brought to our attention, there is a spiraling codetermination of fundamental perceptions—or ideas—and signs, which add up to a signifying chain: "The attention that we give to a present perception recalls its sign, which in turn recalls others to which it bears some relation; these latter revive the ideas to which they are connected; these ideas revive other signs and other ideas, and so on" (33). Memory depends on this codetermination: "As soon as someone begins to attach ideas to signs he has himself chosen, memory is formed in him" (40).[5] This in turn *activates* the imagination, defined in part as our ability to combine ideas through signs (41).[6] The use of the imagination in turn presents certain risks, which are the necessary consequence of the ignorance and limitations caused by original sin. In postlapsarian situations, reason and its contrary are born of the same principle, which is the *liaison des idées*. As a result, Condillac believes that "imagination and madness can differ only by degrees" (57).[7]

Condillac gives more emphasis than Locke to the role language plays in the association of ideas. "Ideas connect with signs, and it is . . . only by this means that they connect among themselves" (5).[8] This accounts for his desire to bring together perception (first "operation of

---

[5] Note here that ideas come in the wake of signs—*après coup*—which is different from Locke's position (see, in particular, book 2, chapter 1 of the *Essay concerning Human Understanding*).

[6] The word *activates* is crucial here. The imagination comes into play "when a perception, by the mere force of the connection that attention has established between it and an object, is recalled at the sight of the object" ("quand une perception, par la seule force de la liaison que l'attention a mise entre elle et un objet, se retrace à la vue de cet objet"; Condillac, *Essay*, 27; *Essai*, 121). It is an operation of the mind that both logically and historically precedes the development of memory. It is an initially involuntary operation that depends on visual awareness only, but which memory, which is the faculty to recall names or abstractions of perceptions, can activate, in which case it assumes a more deliberate form (Condillac, *Essay*, 27–28).

[7] John Locke had drawn a similar parallel between madness and the imagination in his *Essay concerning Human Understanding*, ed. Peter H. Nidditch (Oxford: Clarendon Press, 1985), 160–61 and 394–95.

[8] Roger Lefèvre has underscored the importance Condillac gives to signs in the actual formation of thought in "Condillac, maître du langage," *Revue Internationale de Philosophie* 21 (1967): 393–406.

the soul") and the language of action (first stage in linguistic development) (6). The two poles fulfill different epistemological functions. Perception is open to direct observation, while the language of action represents a first step in a "history of language" that "will not, I believe, leave any doubt about the origin of our ideas" (6) and points to the possibility of a genuine historical discourse.

Although Condillac does not fully develop the second term in his discussion (his section on language is undoubtedly the weaker of the two segments that make up the *Essay*), it is clear that he recognizes the importance of something like the retrosignification of language and ideas. Hence his criticism that "it is only in the Third Book that [Locke] treated a matter that should have been treated in the Second" (7), namely, words. "But since he did not do it, he passed lightly over the origin of our knowledge" (7). This criticism notwithstanding, Condillac also sought to limit the field of application of historical knowledge. By stressing the bond between language and ideas and combining it with the notion of association of ideas, Condillac made origins knowable by annulling the distance of the past. By emphasizing that origins leave both linguistic and sensory memory traces in the here and now, he underplayed the need for a social historicization of the codetermination process.

At the same time, Condillac's most important contribution, especially vis-à-vis Locke, is that he ventures into the realm of a social history of our ideas, most noticeably in his discussion of the origin and evolution of languages. He describes, for instance, how writing evolved from the simple clarity of the early fables to the politically motivated enigmas of a certain class to a surfeit of metaphors or ornaments that have lost their original clarity, which surfeit reverses the distinction between what is necessary and what is accessory (182–84).[9]

Condillac's linguistic theories are indeed generally accompanied by considerations pertaining to history, and also to geography. Yet, in spite of his own awareness of the historicity of languages, Condillac still believes it will eventually be possible to give popular languages the

[9] Like Jean-Jacques Rousseau, Condillac describes the evolution of writing as one of decadence: "We can slow down, but we cannot prevent, the decline of a language" ("on peut retarder, mais on ne sauroit empêcher la chûte d'une langue"; *Essay*, 184; *Essai*, 259), but that does not represent his general view of historical evolution. If the history of writing is one of decadence, it is because writing itself came late. The development of languages is initially marked by progress. The decline, *la chûte*, comes after an apex.

kind of exactness proper to the language of mathematics by "reform-ing" them "without regard to usage" (200). In the meantime, he expresses the wish that, in the presence of children, people would use only words "whose sense is precisely determined" ("dont le sens seroit exactement déterminé") (*Essay*, 83; *Essai*, 166), even though he acknowledges the ultimate impossibility of perfectly carrying out such a project. It would appear, then, that Condillac undermines his burgeoning historicism by clinging to the belief that his program of study will yield scientific cer-tainty: "Now [in all the sciences as in arithmetic], the truth can be dis-covered only by composition and decomposition. If we do not for the most part reason with the same correctness in the other sciences, it is because we have not yet found dependable rules always to compose and decompose our ideas correctly, which has its source in the fact that we have not even been able to define them. But perhaps our reflections on the origin of knowledge will provide the remedy" (199).[10]

However, such an interpretation would fail to recognize that for Condillac history and science are not epistemologically antithetical. This explains why post-nineteenth-century readers are left with what they have come to think of as an impossibility: an ideal ahistorical lan-guage dependent on a genetic epistemology. Only if we accept that this does not represent an epistemological paradox for Condillac can we take seriously his statement that, to perfectly understand complex notions, "mistakes can be avoided by retracing [the] generation" of their complex notions (210).

The method to this "madness" consists in part in appeals to the imme-diacy of experience, the ultimate judge of Condillac's own *Essay:* "It seems to me that everyone can consult his own experience to be sure of the truth that is the foundation of his entire work. Perhaps people will even become convinced that the connection of ideas is, without rival, the simplest, the most lucid and most fertile principle" (216). By linking experience to the fundamental principle of the association of ideas, Condillac manages to deny the possibility of anything like a gap in our knowledge. This explains why the origin is not, for Condillac, a rupture or a unique moment in time, but something that is endlessly played out. Hence the repeated use of that strange expression, "dans

[10] I have slightly modified Aarsleff's translation, which reads, "Now, in arithmetic as in all the sciences," to have the translation conform better to the original: "Or, dans toutes les sciences comme en arithmétique" (*Essai*, 271).

l'origine," which betrays Condillac's unwillingness to speak about the origin as a fixed moment in time. History is forever recapitulated in the individual. We are still "dans l'origine."[11]

At the same time, the notion of association of ideas also becomes the condition for the development of the sequential implications of a genetic epistemology. Because there is no gap in our knowledge, we can retrace the path to our origins. The principle of "connection of ideas" (*liaison des idées*) is a scientific insurance policy against unaccountability that gives Condillac's archeological method the authority of a scientific discourse of certainty. In addition, our need to rely on the immediacy of experience must be understood as bearing the mark of our historical nature since it proceeds from our fallenness. Since the advent of original sin, the soul (*âme*) has been unable to operate without depending on the senses. The body has become primary and ignorance is a necessary condition of human knowledge. This sin was indeed *original;* it originated human knowledge and history, which are grounded in the body and in ignorance.

Condillac's description of the origin of languages illustrates this proposition. Language is originally not verbal but physical, what Condillac calls "the language of action, a language which in its early stages, conforming to the level of this couple's limited intelligence, consisted of mere contortions and agitated bodily movements" (115).[12] This first couple is of course the distorted image of the Edenic couple, masters of a perfect discourse that had not been contingent on experience. Conversely, postlapsarian experience (a redundant expression) and language are marked by need, suffering, and extreme limitations. The first communication "recorded" by Condillac consequently involves a mute request for help.

Even the imagination is affected by this unfortunate historicity since it is dependent on experience. Defined as the operation of the mind that

---

[11] In his lecture "On Historicall Composition," Adam Smith also insists on the importance of connecting all facts either chronologically, logically, or "poetically," on the grounds that "we should never leave any chasm or Gap in the thread of the narration even tho there are no remarkable events to fill up that space. The very notion of gap makes us uneasy for what should have happened in that time." *Lectures on Rhetoric and Belles Lettres* (1762–1763), ed. J. C. Bryce, general ed. A. S. Skinner, in *The Glasgow Edition of the Works and Correspondence of Adam Smith* (Oxford: Oxford University Press, 1983; Indianapolis: Liberty Fund, 1985), 4:100.

[12] The couple in question here is the first couple who engaged in "mutual discourse" ("commerce réciproque"; *Essay*, 114; *Essai*, 194).

enables us to retrace a perception visually (27), the imagination does not seem likely to be affected by history. Yet Condillac unequivocally states that it is more developed in the early stages of civilization: "Greek more than any other language felt the influence of the language of action. . . . This language was therefore especially suitable for the exercise of the imagination. French, by contrast, is so simple both in construction and prosody that it hardly requires more than the exercise of memory. In speaking of things, all we do is to recall their signs but rarely the ideas" (141). Because the imagination operates visually rather than verbally, it functions better when it is closer to the mute *langage d'action*. Anything that depends on a primarily visual faculty will accordingly be more developed in its early stages. This explains why Condillac framed his discussion of the evolution of writing—initially "a mere picture" ("qu'une simple peinture") (*Essay*, 178; *Essai* 252)—in the context of a history of decadence. This, however, is not the movement of society as a whole. Indeed, from the point of view of abstract knowledge— dependent on the operation of memory—anything had to be an improvement over the immense paucity of the earliest form of communication.

This is where Condillac's insistence that memory and the imagination are not coeval becomes particularly fruitful. There is, he writes, "between imagination, memory, and reminiscence *a progression by which they are alone distinguished*. The first revives the perceptions themselves, the second recalls only the signs or the circumstances, and the last reports those we have already had" (30, emphasis added). By separating memory and the imagination (logically and temporally antecedent or, rather, logically antecedent because temporally so), Condillac introduces historicity as such. The progress he speaks of is indeed a social/civil phenomenon. Moreover, inasmuch as there can be no *mastery* without memory—he refers to "the activity of the imagination that is produced by a capacious memory" (41)—, he is able to grant that though the imagination may well be more predominant in early stages of societal development, this does not mean that we must resign ourselves to accepting the superiority of the ancients in the arts. Talent and originality in the arts as well as in philosophy and science depend on the interplay of memory and the imagination, that is, on an "active imagination," which is itself the product of large-scale cultural developments that can be appreciated only through the medium of a historical reading: "Newton's success was prepared by the choice of signs that had been made before his time" (187). Condillac accordingly rejects the belief "that a person with Corneille's gifts would have given the same evidence of his talents regardless of the age in which he might have lived or the vernacular in which he wrote" (193).

As a result, Condillac's "historicism" is remarkably complex. Depending on a number of factors, each language will develop characteristics that make it suited for different accomplishments. Because of its dependence on the development of a highly abstract language, that is, on significant advances in memory, modern philosophy is generally superior to ancient philosophy. In works of aesthetics, where the interplay of the imagination and memory is both stronger and more volatile, no such generalization can be made: "If the Greek and Roman poets in certain genres are superior to ours, we have poets who in other genres are superior to their poets. Does antiquity have any poet who can be compared to our Corneille or Molière?" (192).

To evaluate respective productions, "the simplest way of deciding which language excels in the largest number of genres would be to take a count of the original authors in each" (192). Condillac does not elaborate on the criteria that might be used in this determination, but it is clear that these vary for historical reasons. In formative stages, originality consists in developing the generative possibilities of analogy. In late, or decadent, stages, it is a strictly individual act in opposition to socially determined products: "But since all the styles analogous to the character of the language and to his own have already been used by his predecessors, he [the talented writer] has no choice but to keep his distance from the analogy. Thus in order to be original he is obliged to contribute to the ruin of a language whose progress a century sooner he would have hastened along" (193). If analogical, originality will be positive. If not, it will be merely disassociated and negative. In either case, however, the makeup of originality is historically determined, leaving little room for individual options. There is an interdependent historical determination between the language a writer inherits, his future production, and the language that production will generate in turn (194), but the nature of a writer's contribution (analogical or negative) is not up to him.

Immediately on the heels of this strongly "historicist" position, Condillac concludes his *Essay* by expressing the hope that language will some day acquire mathematical exactness. The "French Locke" was caught between two epistemological requirements: his own awareness that knowledge must be historicized and a desire to modulate his episteme after the certainty traditionally associated with nonhistorical scientific methods. Significantly, he switched to the conditional mood in his conclusion: "In fact, a person who began making a language for himself and who decided not to communicate with others until he had fixed the meaning of his expressions by the circumstances in which he had placed himself would not have fallen into any of those mistakes we have so often landed in" (200–201). This new mood underlines that Condillac knew very well the impossibility of reoriginating. It negates the notion that we might still be "dans l'origine." The epistemological tension is real, however, and it accounts for the fact that Condillac's appeals to the immediacy of individual experience are appeals to a common sociohistorical ground.

The contrast Rousseau presents is all the more striking. Only a few years separate the *Essay on the Origin of Human Knowledge* and the Second Discourse, yet Rousseau did not see the need to ground his certainties in science or to appeal to "commonsense" experience. Social alienation and historical rupture—not individual recapitulation or analogical association—are the epistemological conditions of his portrayal of the origin, admittedly lost and incommunicable.

ROUSSEAU'S PRIMACY

The sixth-to-the-last paragraph of Jean-Jacques Rousseau's *Discourse on the Origin of Inequality* (*Discours sur l'origine et les fondemens de l'inégalité*) is dominated by the repetition of a key phrase: "one would see" ("on verrait").[13] This anaphora signals that Rousseau has abandoned the tone of historical exposition and statement of principles that had prevailed throughout the second part of the Second Discourse and has decided to return in his concluding statements to the visionary prose of the opening of the first section: "I see an animal less strong than some,

[13] This and the following five paragraphs, which I will now focus on, can be found in Jean-Jacques Rousseau, *Discourse on the Origins of Inequality (Second Discourse); Polemics; and Political Economy*, ed. Roger D. Masters and Christopher Kelly, trans. Judith R. Bush, Roger D. Masters, Christopher Kelly, and Terence Marshall, in *The Collected Writings of Rousseau*, ed. Roger D. Masters and Christopher Kelly (Hanover, N.H.: Published for Dartmouth College by University Press of New England, 1992), 3:63–67, and 189–93 of the Pléiade edition of the *Discours sur l'origine et les fondemens de l'inégalité parmi les hommes*, ed. Jean Starobinski, in *Oeuvres complètes*, ed. Bernard Gagnebin and Marcel Raymond, vol. 3 (Paris: Gallimard, 1964). Further page references to these two editions will be included parenthetically in the body of the text.

less agile than others. . . . I see him satisfying his hunger under an oak, quenching his thirst at the first Stream" ("Je vois un animal moins fort que les uns, moins agile que les autres. . . . Je le vois se rassasiant sous un chesne, se désalterant au premier Ruisseau"; 20; 134–35). This return to a visionary and conjectural style by means both semantic ("to see"/"voir") and grammatical ("would see"/"verrait") reinforces one of the key premises of the Second Discourse, namely, that Rousseau never intended to describe historically verifiable truths, but "a state which no longer exists, which perhaps never existed, which probably never will exist, and about which it is nevertheless necessary to have precise Notions in order to judge our present state correctly" ("un Etat qui n'existe plus, qui n'a peut-être point existé, qui probablement n'existera jamais, et dont il est pourtant nécessaire d'avoir des Notions justes pour bien juger de nôtre état présent"; 13; 123).

Rousseau's focus is accordingly more on the nature of things than on their origin. Or rather, in spite of Rousseau's distinction between nature and origin, which implies, as Starobinski notes, "that logical precedence necessarily leads to *historical* precedence," we must also understand origin as nature, a choice that signals a horror of the rupture implicit in any beginning and in time.[14] Hence Rousseau's memorable methodological statement:

> Let us therefore begin by setting all the facts aside, for they do not affect the question. The Researches which can be undertaken concerning this Subject must not be taken for historical truths, but only for hypothetical and conditional reasonings better suited to clarify the Nature of things than to show their genuine origin, like those our Physicists make every day concerning the formation of the World. (19)

> Commençons donc par écarter tous les faits, car ils ne touchent point à la question. Il ne faut pas prendre les Recherches, dans lesquelles on peut entrer sur ce Sujet, pour des verités historiques, mais seulement pour des raisonnemens hypothétiques et conditionnels; plus propres à éclaircir la Nature des choses qu'à montrer la véritable origine, et semblables à ceux que font tous les jours nos Physiciens sur la formation du Monde. (132–33)

[14] "L'antécédence logique entraîne obligatoirement l'antécédence *historique*." Note to Rousseau's *Discours sur l'origine et les fondemens de l'inégalité* (1285n2).

Origins introduce a rupture in static time and consequently open the possibility of conceptual oppositions, a Manichaeanism that inevitably leads to entropy in Rousseau's work. The following paragraph, in which the phrase "one would see" is repeated one more time, accordingly rests on a play of contrasts or symmetrically articulated conceptual oppositions. The adjectives "useless," "pernicious," and "frivolous" ("inutiles," "pernicieux," and "frivoles") are opposed to the notions of "reason, happiness, and virtue" ("à la raison, au bonheur, et à la vertu"); the concept of "Chiefs" ("Chefs") to that of "weaken[ing]" ("affoiblir"); "assembled men" ("des hommes rassemblés") to what "disunit[es]" ("désuni[t]") them; "an air of apparent concord" ("concorde apparente") to "a seed of real division" ("un germe de division réelle") (64; 190). These correspondences accentuate the dualistic nature of the discourse, but the terminology itself fosters disorder and undermines the careful symmetry.

This creates tensions that are further enhanced by Rousseau's switches in temporal perspective, from past to future to present. In the next three paragraphs, for instance, Rousseau becomes even more daring in his conjectures and abandons the conditional mood and the careful, "If this were the place to go into details, I would easily explain how," "I would show," "I would prove," "one would see" ("Si c'étoit ici le lieu d'entrer en des détails, j'expliquerois facilement"; "je ferois voir"; "je montrerois"; "je prouverais"; "on verrait"; 63–64; 188–90).[15] The new paragraph opens instead with an affirmation: "It is" ("C'est"). This shift paves the way for a new, more prophetic tone. Origins have been left behind and Rousseau is now focusing on what he calls a "last change" ("dernier changement"), which he describes in apocalyptic terms. In doing so, he moves away from hypothetical explanations of the origins and foundations of inequality to a futuristic vision and relies on aphorisms rather than historical descriptions. He thereby also succeeds in rhetorically bringing together beginning and ending, past and future. In the context of Rousseau's thought, *penser l'origine* leads quite naturally to thinking the apocalypse.

The next paragraph also begins with "C'est" (translated as "Here is" in this instance), but the text is no longer prophetic or aphoristic. The present tense no longer supports a general truth, but signals a new temporal perspective. The future is suddenly among us, introduced by an innocent-looking adverb: "ici" ("here"). Referring both to spatial

[15] Both "je ferois voir" and "je montrerois" are translated as "I would show."

and temporal presence, the polysemic *ici* allows Rousseau to slip into a political mode and offer a radical criticism of despotism.

In this same paragraph, Rousseau's argument proceeds along the lines of a reverse dialectic. His rhetoric rests on antinomies and a polemical dissolution of oppositions: "Here is the last stage of inequality, and the extreme point which closes the Circle and touches the point from which we started" ("C'est ici le dernier terme de l'inégalité, et le point extrême qui ferme le Cercle et touche au point d'où nous sommes partis"; 65; 191). At this "last stage" ("dernier terme"), equality suddenly hinges on nothingness: "Here all individuals become equals again because they are nothing" ("C'est ici que tous les particuliers redeviennent égaux parce qu'ils ne sont rien"; 65; 191]). It becomes impossible to distinguish the notions of law and order from those of will and passion. Even "l'Etat de Nature" is no longer a reliable concept; it takes on a new connotation: corruption. In the end, the so-called "dernier terme de l'inégalité," is marked by a dialectical dissolution (since contradictions are not overcome or resolved but negated or dissolved), in which concepts such as law and force are hopelessly contaminated. Linearity implies a circular collapse. Time, once instituted by origins, recollapses onto itself.

Rousseau's rhetorical mode then shifts one more time. In the penultimate paragraph of the Second Discourse, what was to be speculation according to the stated methodological foundation of the *Discourse,* has become discovery: "In discovering and following thus the forgotten and lost routes that must have led man from the Natural state to the Civil state . . ." ("En découvrant et suivant ainsi les routes oubliées et perdues qui de l'état Naturel ont dû mener l'homme à l'état Civil . . ."; 65; 191). Rousseau is not only the careful rationalist who knows the limits of a hypothetical discourse but also a guide who has led the reader down a quasi-initiatory road. The roads have been "forgotten and lost" to all except Jean-Jacques.[16]

---

[16] The faculty he has relied on in this process of remembrance is, as he mentions a few lines later, the imagination. This conflation of memory and imagination does not constitute a contradiction. Indeed, the eighteenth-century understanding of the term generally does not refer to the usual contemporary definition: "The ability to form images of objects one has not perceived" (*Le Petit Robert 1,* 1983), but rather to the ability to do so for objects one has perceived. Voltaire's definition, quoted in *Littré,* makes this clear: "There are two kinds of imagination: the first consists in retaining a simple impression made by objects, the second consists in arranging these received images and combining them in a thousand different ways." The *Encyclopédie* is in agreement: "This faculty depends on memory." *Encyclopédie ou dictionnaire raisonné des sciences, des arts et des métiers* [1751–1772], s.v. "Imagination, Imaginer," http://www.lib.uchicago.edu/efts/ARTFL/projects/encyc/. For Vico's definition, see *NS* §699.

In this same penultimate paragraph, Rousseau goes on to recapitulate the movements of the Second Discourse, both thematically and methodologically. At the thematic level, we witness once more:

1) Rousseau's doubts concerning philosophy's ability to be a master discourse; philosophers cannot solve a host of moral and political problems that the reader will *feel*.

2) The pervasive theme of the destructive or layering (veiling) nature of time that had been exemplified in the metaphor of the Glaucus statue and the attendant notions of fall and degradation: "The greatest of men only astonished the world, which he would have governed five hundred years earlier" ("Le plus grand des hommes ne fit qu'étonner le monde qu'il eût gouverné cinq cens ans plûtôt"; 65; 192).

3) The unresolved paradox of an irrevocably disfigured nature that nevertheless remains *the* referential source.

4) The subsequent opposition between "Savage man and Civilized man" ("L'homme Sauvage et l'homme policé") and a scathing attack on Jean-Jacques Rousseau's own era.

5) The negative connotations of the notion of labor, perceived as introducing a shift in value, primary cause of a fundamental inequality or disruption of an earlier status quo.

At the methodological level, we note

1) The quasi-simultaneous reliance on the resources of both speculation and history, the two poles between which Rousseau's argument wavers throughout the Second Discourse.[17]

2) The glorification of interiority coupled with appeals to great predecessors.

These few paragraphs offer a microcosm of Rousseau's writings on origins. Interpreting them alongside some of his other works can help us to determine with reasonable economy the complex epistemological status of the origin in Rousseau's thought.

In the *Essay on the Origin of Languages,* Rousseau notes: "Let us try to follow the very order of nature in our investigations. I am entering upon a long digression on a subject so hackneyed that it is trivial, but to which

---

[17] History itself can become hypothetical as, for instance, when Rousseau states in a seemingly descriptive/historical passage that "the soul and human passions, altering imperceptibly, change their Nature so to speak" ("l'ame et les passions humaines s'altérant insensiblement, changent pour ainsi dire de Nature"; 192). If the alteration is "imperceptible" ("insensible"), it cannot, by definition, have been observed.

one still has to return in order to discover the origin of human institutions."[18] This makes clear that for Rousseau the socio-genetic order, which lies within the purview of history, and the natural order, understood as the pure duration of stasis or prehistory, are indissoluble.

At the same time, however, the two orders stand in a clearly antagonistic relation. This results from Rousseau's idealization of a static model, an ideal realized at Clarens, where a self-sufficient economy based on recycling makes surplus unnecessary and where "each one finding in his own station everything needed to be content with it and not desire to leave it, each becomes attached to it as a lifelong commitment."[19] At Clarens, labor, otherwise unnatural and genetically disruptive, contributes to the restoration of the status quo.

This ideal does not, of course, correspond to our empirical knowledge of social history. The introduction of the origin as an epistemologically significant moment serves two purposes. Genealogically, it enables Rousseau to acknowledge the undeniable historicity of the past. Logically, it allows him to postulate something before the origin, which the origin has disrupted.[20] That postulate then allows Rousseau to negate that past, which cannot be denied. There is a logical possibility that one might return to the idealized static model, as M. and Mme. de Wolmar have demonstrated in their re-creation of a neo-Edenic orchard (see part 4, letter 11).

To bring about that return, Rousseau needs to find ways of countering what he perceives to be the rectilinear degenerescence of civil history. This desire accounts for the frequent play of antinomies and the conceptual corruption and contamination so prevalent in Rousseau's writings. For Jean-Jacques Rousseau, history is the source of negative alterations. Born

[18] Jean-Jacques Rousseau, *Essay on the Origin of Languages* and *Writings Related to Music,* trans. and ed. John T. Scott, in *The Collected Writings of Rousseau,* ed. Roger D. Masters and Christopher Kelly (Hanover, N.H.: Published for Dartmouth College by University Press of New England, 1998), 7:305. Further page references to the *Essay* will be included parenthetically in the body of the text.

[19] Jean-Jacques Rousseau, *Julie, or the New Heloise: Letters of Two Lovers Who Live in a Small Town at the Foot of the Alps,* trans. Philip Stewart and Jean Vaché in *The Collected Writings of Rousseau,* ed. Roger D. Masters and Christopher Kelly, vol. 6 (Hanover, N.H.: Published for Dartmouth College by University Press of New England, 1997), part 5, letter 2, 448. Further references to letters in *Julie* will be included parenthetically in the body of the text.

[20] The use of the singular form origin is here deliberate when speaking of Rousseau. If origins are clearly plural for Vico, such is not the case for Rousseau, who stresses instead the uniqueness of the primal scene.

of man's perfectibility, it ratifies its degenerescence: "Everything is good as it leaves the hands of the Author of things; everything degenerates in the hands of man."[21] The movement of history is essentially that of a fall and betrays an irreversible loss of a state of grace. We should therefore not be surprised if Rousseau generally invests the early stage of civilization with values such as isolation, primitive liberty, and idleness, and claims that these have been vitiated over time. By contrast to these happier times, in modern governments liberty has given way to public constraints and isolation has become a tool of political power.

This negative linear perception of history is also reflected in Rousseau's considerations on language. For the "citoyen de Genève," the language of gestures is generally preferable to that of speech. Although both are "natural," the former is less dependent on conventions and can express love more felicitously than speech, since "the most energetic language is the one in which the sign has said everything before one speaks" (*Essay* 290). In the modern era, however, even gestures have been vitiated and now betray not love but anxiety.

This entropy also manifests itself in the evolution of writing, which is itself the ultimate form of language. In general, writing is posterior to speech because it was not born of passions but of needs. It represents both an improvement and a setback.[22] More specifically, hieroglyphic writing "corresponds to passionate language, and already presupposes some degree of society and some needs to which the passions have given rise" (*Essay* 297).[23] Ideograms betray an even more elaborate level of convention but still proceed from a desire for restitution, for a "painting" of speech. Finally, the alphabet is strictly analytical and represents an attempt "to break down the speaking voice" (*Essay* 297) for the good of commerce.

---

[21] Jean-Jacques Rousseau, *Emile or On Education*, trans. Allan Bloom (New York: Basic Books, 1979), 37.

[22] As noted by Jacques Derrida, "writing is somehow fissured in its value. On the one hand, . . . it is the effort of symbolically reappropriating presence. On the other, it consecrates the dispossession that had already dislocated the spoken word." *Of Grammatology*, trans. Gayatri Chakravorty Spivak (Baltimore: Johns Hopkins University Press, 1976), 166.

[23] Let us note here that passion, like perfectibility, does not have exclusively positive connotations: "From where, then, could this origin [of languages] derive? From the moral needs, the passions. . . . Neither hunger nor thirst, but love, hatred, pity, anger, wrested the first voices from them" (*Essay*, 294). In the passage quoted in the body of the text we further see that the distinction that had seemed well established between needs and passions is now annulled.

By contrast, when Vico proclaimed the anteriority of writing vis-à-vis speech, he had a different conception of history. The Italian philosopher did not read a dangerous linearity into every historical process. Since his world of nations, deprived of any direct communication with God, is posterior to the Fall, its progression can be positive. The Vichian state of nature has therefore nothing in common with Rousseau's *âge pastoral* but corresponds instead to the barbarism of the first civil societies. Profane history describes a movement that goes from barbarism to equality, from the absolute power of the fathers to a tenderness on their part.

The historiographies of both Rousseau and Vico become even more distinct when one compares their respective descriptions of the salient moments in the formation of languages and societies.

In Rousseau's scheme, popular languages were born at the stage of pastoral life, near the watering holes of southern lands.[24] They were the children of pleasure and desire. (In northern areas, on the other hand, the climate forced inhabitants to be industrious, "and the first word among them was not 'love me,' but 'help me'" [*Essay* 316]). New needs progressively modified these—southern—languages and "forced each to consider only himself and to withdraw his heart within himself" (*Essay* 315). In the modern era, "societies have assumed their final form" and languages are no longer popular, made to be heard and "favorable to liberty" (*Essay* 332).

Unlike Rousseau, Vico did not introduce any geographical distinction; every nation experiences the same development, going through *corsi* that comprise three different ages to which three kinds of nature, government, and language correspond. In the age of gods, language was in the hands of those giants who, frightened by thunder, had mistakenly but

---

[24] In the *Essay* Rousseau does not reject the premises concerning the *état de nature* he had developed in the Second Discourse. If he no longer returns to this topic in the *Essay*, it is because language presupposes the existence of a society. The "first times" he describes in the *Essay* (305) are those in which families have already been constituted but in which men live in isolation once again (following natural disasters such as the Flood). They are neither savage nor truly civilized (*policés*). In this era of dispersion and isolation—Rousseau's golden age—people are ignorant of the fact that they belong to a species. Between this era and the age of patriarchs (separated by ten generations) a combination of natural factors and the necessity of feeding themselves gradually brought human beings together. They generally devoted themselves to pastoral life, which best suited their natural penchant for laziness. The social state proper constitutes a third era, whose beginnings can only be described through an appeal to supernatural elements: "He who willed that man be sociable touched his finger to the axis of the globe and inclined it at an angle to the axis of the universe" (*Essay*, 310).

providentially turned it into a god and had founded the first societies, which were regulated by auspices and oracles. It was a "mute language of signs and physical objects having natural relations to the ideas they wished to express."[25] Corresponding to the heroic age, the age of aristocratic republics, is an unconsciously symbolic language that makes communication possible "by means of heroic emblems, or similitudes, comparisons, images, metaphors, and natural descriptions" (*NS* §32). Finally, in the age of men, "in which all men recognized themselves as equal in human nature" (*NS* §31), language is totally articulated, made up of words "agreed upon by the people, a language of which they are absolute lords . . . ; a language whereby the people may fix the meaning of the laws by which the nobles as well as the plebs are bound" (*NS* §32).

For Vico, there is not one origin of languages but multiple and independent origins organized along the same principles and corresponding to the same institutions. The first grapheme, for instance, always proceeds from an error that comes to have institutional as well as religious consequences. It also proceeds from fear rather than pleasure. Hence its mute nature.

Indeed, Vico maintains that hieroglyphic writing must have preceded speech. In the *Essay*, conversely, though Rousseau admits that "the art of writing does not at all depend upon that of speaking" (*Essay* 298), he also evokes "those who first took it into their heads to resolve speech into elementary signs" (*Essay* 297). Writing is therefore considered de facto posterior to speech. Writing alters speech and deprives it of vivacity and energy through a process of "dissolution."

The play of antinomies and the conceptual corruption and contamination that dominate Rousseau's work are the rhetorical means by which he seeks to negate the components of dynamic time and thereby regenerate stasis. There is a price to pay for this process, however: this new stasis also turns out to be negative; it no longer refers to an "état de grâce/état de nature" but to nothingness. Indeed, the preface to the *Letter to M. D'Alembert* contains a dire warning: "In returning to my natural state, I have gone back to nothingness."[26]

---

[25] *The New Science of Giambattista Vico: Unabridged Translation of the Third Edition (1744) with the Addition of "Practic of the New Science,"* trans. Thomas Goddard Bergin and Max Harold Fisch (Ithaca, N.Y.: Cornell University Press, 1984), §32.

[26] Jean-Jacques Rousseau, *Politics and the Arts: Letter to M. d'Alembert on the Theatre,* trans. Allan Bloom (Glencoe, Ill.: Free Press, 1960), 7. By contrast, Vico's philosophy of history offers a possibility of recovery through the *ricorsi* of history, which not only involve return or repetition, but theoretically present an opportunity for *recourse* or redress.

We still need to address the question of the epistemological foundation of this rhetoric. To do so we must look at the status of both logic and history in Rousseau's epistemic system. Memory and the imagination combined allow Rousseau to give a genetic meaning to the origin, which is always understood to be historically antecedent, as Starobinski has rightly pointed out. They allow him to write in the descriptive mode of the historian and in the visionary mode of the master. This "empirical" foundation then merges with the logical necessity of the origin, which is an internalized necessity that proceeds in part from self-observation. Indeed, the notions of stasis and the subsequent equation of origin with rupture are strictly Rousseau's postulates. His reliance on memory and the imagination must then be understood as crucial since they allow him to convince the reader of his ability to recapture the origin by buttressing his admittedly hypothetico-deductive and psychological method with the possibilities of a descriptive discourse. The two factors constantly reinforce each other, which accounts for the obsessive use of the verb *voir* in Rousseau's writings. Sight is both an empirical and a visionary faculty.

The *Essay on the Origin of Languages* is a case in point. It begins with a warning that limits the possibilities of strictly descriptive/historical discursive practices and indirectly authorizes the reliance on subjectivity: "One has to go back to some reason that pertains to locality, and precedes even morals" (289). The *Essay* accordingly marshals an abundance of erudite references and presents arguments along primarily chronological lines in order to give the text a quasi-scientific appeal. However, these scientific trappings are not valued as such but merely provide a foundation of credibility that eventually allows Rousseau to blithely move from description to vision, from history to *imaginaire*, and from facts to hypotheses:

> Assume a perpetual spring on earth; assume water, livestock, pasturage everywhere; assume men leaving the hands of nature, once dispersed throughout all this: I cannot imagine how they would ever have renounced their primitive freedom and forsaken the isolated and pastoral life so suited to their natural indolence, in order needlessly to impose on themselves the slavery, the labors, the miseries inseparable from the social state.
>
> He who willed that man be sociable touched his finger to the axis of the globe and inclined it at an angle to the axis of the universe. With this slight movement I see the face of the earth change and the

vocation of mankind decided: I hear from afar the joyous cries of a senseless multitude; I see Palaces and Towns raised; I see the arts, laws, commerce born; I see . . . (*Essay* 310)

The scientific coloring of Rousseau's argumentation is a rhetorical device that gives him the support he needs to make his own claims, which are based on the belief that "he is able to evoke the language of the beginning because this initial language has not grown silent in him. . . . He recapitulates internally and dramatically the whole history of language."[27] This is in keeping with the bulk of Rousseau's writings, which indicate that for him "the self is its own origin; better yet, it retains the memory of its origin and coincides with it in and through remembering."[28]

The *New Science*, by proclaiming the authority of the *coscienza*, had also implicitly glorified interiority. As we saw in chapter 2, the *New Science* describes "a metaphysics of the human race" that tries to recapture the principles of its genesis and is based on a philological hermeneutic, that is, a hermeneutic grounded as much in memory (imagination, invention) as on reason.[29] Since institutions (*cose*) and consciousness are interdependent in the *New Science*, Vico's history of institutions was able to proceed in part from an autoarcheology. According to the logic of the *New Science*, an external or purely rational approach cannot hope

[27] "Il peut évoquer le langage du commencement parce qu'en lui ce langage initial ne s'est pas tu. . . . Il récapitule en lui, dramatiquement, toute l'histoire du langage." Jean Starobinski, "Rousseau et l'origine des langues," in *Jean-Jacques Rousseau: La transparence et l'obstacle, suivi de sept essais sur Rousseau* (Paris: Gallimard, 1971), 379. See also Jean-François Perrin, *Le chant de l'origine: La mémoire et le temps dans les "Confessions" de Jean-Jacques Rousseau*, Studies on Voltaire and the Eighteenth-Century 339 (Oxford: Voltaire Foundation, 1996).

[28] "Le moi est à lui-même son origine, ou pour mieux dire, il garde la mémoire de son origine, et, dans ce souvenir, il coïncide avec elle." Jean Starobinski, "Rousseau et la recherche des origines," in *Jean-Jacques Rousseau*, 329. It is this very conception of the self that allows for the creation and continued existence, or re-creation, of the quasi-tautology that is human society. As Steven Affeldt notes, "the individual's movement beyond natural independence is itself to be made continuously and may only be made through his and her continuous turn toward participation in the continuous constitution of a general will." Steven G. Affeldt, "The Voice of Freedom: Rousseau on Forcing to Be Free," *Political Theory* 27 (1999): 312.

[29] Giambattista Vico, *The Autobiography*, trans. Max Harold Fisch and Thomas Goddard Bergin (Ithaca, N.Y.: Cornell University Press, 1975), 167. Let us note that for Vico memory is a retrosignifying faculty only inasmuch as it is coupled with imagination. Indeed, memory is a threefold faculty. As Donald Phillip Verene notes, "memory (*memoria*) is memory (*memoria*), imagination (*fantasia*), and invention (*ingegno*)." *Vico's Science of Imagination* (Ithaca, N.Y.: Cornell University Press, 1991), 96.

to account for the history of the human mind. Any hermeneutic that pertains to secular history must be internalized.

This common reliance on interiority notwithstanding, the status of historical knowledge through self-observation is not the same for Vico and for Rousseau. For the Italian thinker, interiority is not external to culture. There is a principle of mutual determination that gives a rational foundation to his autoarcheology. Moreover, the *New Science* clearly sets aside temporal considerations that would pertain to anything other than the "world of nations," whereas Rousseau's *état de nature* lies outside the realm of civil history and cannot be determined by it.

Both men wished to overcome the disciplinary schism inherited from the seventeenth century, which pitted history against reason and the study of language and institutions against that of mathematics and science. Their antisystems rest on a critique of Cartesianism. They proceeded in different ways, however. Vico rehabilitated history by systematizing both history and consciousness, while Rousseau proclaimed the almost incommunicable uniqueness of his psyche. As a result, Vico's origins are plural whereas Rousseau's origin refers to a singular moment. In the end, by referring to historically necessary repetitions, Vico's genetic principle allows for the possibility of appropriating the past. Rousseau's origin negates it.

Finally, by grounding his thought in subjectivity, Rousseau contributed in spite of himself to the systematization of originality, an aesthetic quality he never wrote about. Indeed, if we add Rousseau's dismissal of facticity to his claims to uniqueness, we arrive at the perfect formula for autogenesis: the self as origin, that is, as necessarily original, whose potential he proclaimed at the beginning of the *Confessions:* "I am forming an undertaking which has no precedent, and the execution of which will have no imitator."[30] As Roland Mortier notes, in spite of his apparent lack of interest in originality as a criterion of aesthetic judgment, "Rousseau will contribute more than anyone to the invasion of the *I* [*moi*] in literature and to the emergence of originality."[31]

[30] Jean-Jacques Rousseau, *"The Confessions" and "Correspondence,"* including the Letters to Malesherbes, ed. Christopher Kelly, Roger D. Masters, and Peter G. Stillman, trans. Christopher Kelly, in *The Collected Writings of Rousseau,* ed. Roger D. Masters and Christopher Kelly (Hanover, N.H.: Published for Dartmouth College by University Press of New England, 1995), 5:5.
[31] Roland Mortier, *L'originalité: Une nouvelle catégorie esthétique au siècle des Lumières,* Histoire des Idées et Critique Littéraire 207 (Geneva: Droz, 1982), 151.

At least two late-eighteenth-century strands lead back to Rousseau on this issue: the elaboration of the concept of *Originalgenie* and Adam Smith's views on labor and propriety.

FROM ORIGINALITY TO *EIGENTÜMLICHKEIT*

Unburdened by a compelling critical tradition and in search of literary references of their own, the German critics were understandably more receptive than the French to the notion of originality as a criterion of literary value.[32] The success of Young's "Conjectures," translated twice within months of publication, should not, however, mislead us into thinking that the Germans embraced originality unquestioningly, even in the late 1760s and the 1770s, the high point for the theorization of original genius.[33] What follows is therefore a brief overview of the positions adopted by some of the more prominent protagonists.

In his "Thoughts on the Imitation of the Painting and Sculpture of the Greeks" (1755), Winckelmann, whose writings were a frequent source of inspiration for late-eighteenth-century critics, had dismissed the imitation of nature as inappropriate, suggesting instead that artists must first let themselves be guided by Greek art, the original source of art. Only at a later stage can an artist "embark on the imitation of nature, as in those instances where his art allows him to deviate from his marble models."[34] Even those artists favored by nature have to *become* original. Originality is secondary, a belated occurrence that depends on one's having first learned the rules of Greek beauty.

[32] It is not until Mme. de Staël's *De la littérature* (1800) that we find the concept of originality used in an unabashedly positive fashion in French criticism. Originality is not even an entry in Jean François Marmontel's *Eléments de littérature*, a two-volume critical dictionary published in 1787. Even at the turn of the nineteenth century, praise on the basis of originality was not yet part of mainstream French literary criticism. In his influential eighteen-volume *Cours de la littérature ancienne et moderne*, first published between 1799 and 1805, Jean-François de La Harpe clearly chose to ignore the concept. Deeply reactionary, he rejected the new cult of genius without rules and dismissed neologisms by appealing to old criteria of taste. The virulence of his criticism does suggest, however, that the new cult had gained ground, even in France.

[33] See M. H. Abrams, *The Mirror and the Lamp: Romantic Theory and the Critical Tradition* (Oxford: Oxford University Press, 1971), 201–3, on the reception of Young's "Conjectures" in Germany.

[34] Johann Joachim Winckelmann, "Thoughts on the Imitation of the Painting and Sculpture of the Greeks," trans. H. B. Nisbet, in *German Aesthetic and Literary Criticism: Winckelmann, Lessing, Hamann, Herder, Schiller, Goethe*, ed. H. B. Nisbet (Cambridge: Cambridge University Press, 1985), 38–39.

Winckelmann's theories were vigorously debated in literary circles. Even Johann Georg Hamann felt compelled to address the issue of the excellence of the ancients versus that of the moderns: "If our theology is not worth as much as mythology, then it is simply impossible for us to match the poetry of the Heathens, let alone excel it." For Hamann, the true sources of poetry are nature and the scriptures; they "are the materials of the beautiful spirit which creates and imitates." There is no need to either "stop at the fountain of the Greeks, all riddled with holes as it is" or embrace the cult of original genius: "The birth of a genius will be celebrated, as usual, to the accompanying martyrdom of innocents—I take the liberty of comparing rhyme and metre to innocent children, for our most recent poetry seems to put them in mortal danger." Although Hamann rejected Winckelmann and contemporary poetry, his positions remain within the purview of much of eighteenth-century aesthetics. I am thinking in particular of his desire to salvage poetic traditions and, above all, of his insistence that "to speak is to translate," an aphorism that acknowledges poetic creativity (in the sense that something can be "made") but limits the role of originality.[35]

By contrast, Gotthold Ephraim Lessing would grant that originality is a determinant factor in aesthetic appreciation, but only in the case of poetry. Because of the consecutive and arbitrary nature of linguistic expression, nature cannot be depicted verbally with any degree of success: "I hear the poet at work, but I am a long way from seeing the object itself."[36] As a result, whereas painters and sculptors ought to be judged on the basis of the *execution* of their representation, poetry should instead be evaluated in terms of originality and invention. In general, the distinction between the original and the copy or between imitating a model and imitating an imitation, still crucial at this late date (1766), is therefore applicable only to poetry.

Heinrich Wilhelm von Gerstenberg made no such distinction and presented his reader with the kind of unabashed glorification of originality that has become one of our cultural staples. In his *Briefe über Merkwürdigkeiten der Litteratur*, published the same year as Lessing's *Laocoön* (1766), Gerstenberg celebrated the link between originality and genius, the former described as a necessary element of the latter: "Where

[35] Johann Georg Hamann, "Aesthetica in Nuce: A Rhapsody in Cabbalistic Prose," trans. Joyce P. Crick, in Nisbet, *German Aesthetic and Literary Criticism*, 144, 147, 149, 142.
[36] Gotthold Ephraim Lessing, *Laocoön: An Essay on the Limits of Painting and Poetry*, trans. Edward Allen McCormick (Baltimore: Johns Hopkins University Press, 1984), 88.

there is genius, there is invention, there is novelty, there is the original."[37] As is often the case with extreme positions, Gerstenberg did not elaborate a great deal. We are told, for instance, that Shakespeare is an original genius but are not given the benefit of the slightest explanation, even though Gerstenberg's use of terminology is quite different from that of earlier critics such as Pope.

Johann Georg Sulzer's entries on "Originalgeist" and "Originalwerk" in his *Allgemeine Theorie der schönen Künste* (1771–1774) are somewhat less cryptic than Gerstenberg's letters. First, Sulzer disagrees with Gerstenberg's theory that poetic geniuses express themselves better in new genres. Taking Young's cue, Sulzer believes instead that such poets are merely "accidental Originals." Originality according to Sulzer is far more akin to authenticity or truth-to-the-self, *das Eigene*, than to novelty. Indeed, Sulzer pounds away at the notion that the more important criterion of aesthetic appreciation is no longer external: "We have remarked in various parts of this work that the true origin of all the fine arts is to be found in the nature of the human soul [*des menschlichen Gemüthes*]." Because of this global principle, Sulzer tends to describe originality from the point of view of the author rather than in terms of the work of art. The truly original is equated with the truly expressive, even though this makes it even more difficult to determine whether individual works are indeed originals, a difficulty Sulzer recognizes but tends to minimize. In a language reminiscent of Rousseau, he prefers to emphasize instead that original geniuses are "stimulated by their own inclination and not by an alien example." According to Sulzer, "they are *Originalgeister* inasmuch as they have made works of art not in the spirit of imitation but out of the impulse of their own genius." Within such a framework, self-knowledge understandably becomes an extremely valuable commodity and Sulzer, disciple of both Young and Rousseau, accordingly saves his highest praise for Laurence Sterne. *The Life and Opinions of Tristram Shandy* will have imitators, he writes, "because Sterne's way of viewing the most common incidents of daily life is definitely important and will lead many to know themselves more precisely than with any other method one could devise toward that end."[38]

[37] [Heinrich Wilhelm von Gerstenberg], *Briefe über Merkwürdigkeiten der Litteratur*, ed. Alexander von Weilen, in *Deutsche Litteraturdenkmale des 18. und 19. Jahrhunderts*, no. 29/30, ed. Bernhard Seuffert (Stuttgart: G. J. Göschen, 1890), 228.
[38] Johann Georg Sulzer, *Allgemeine Theorie der schönen Künste in einzeln, nach alphabetischer Ordnung der Kunstwörter . . .* , 2nd ed. (Leipzig: Weidmann, 1793), 3: 625, 628.

In the second essay of *Vom Erkennen und Empfinden der menschlichen Seele* (1778), "Einfluß beider Kräfte in einander und auf Charakter und Genie des Menschen," Johann Gottfried Herder appears to be following Sulzer's lead when he stresses that every book should ideally be the "offprint [*Abdruck*] of a living human soul." In retrospect, he even seems to be calling for the perfect interior monologue: "Were a man able to depict the deepest, most individual foundation of his particular tastes and feelings, of his dreams and thought processes, what a novel!" For Herder, beginnings and first impressions are consequently to be treasured: "The first candid work of an author is hence most often his best: his bloom is just beginning, his soul is like a sunrise."[39]

Like Young, Herder tends to use organic metaphors. "Bacon," he writes, "put classifications and scholastic speculations aside and went back to first concepts, things, nature. He searched . . . for a treasure and the rich crop grew of itself in the field he had ransacked." This clearly links the discussion of originality to the epistemology of origins prevalent in other fields. Moreover, this choice of words emphasizes Herder's resolve to limit the excesses of rationalism. Undeniably, the key word in the essay is not *reason* but *Wahrheit* (it appears five times in one short paragraph), which is perceived as standing in an antagonistic relationship to culture. For instance, like Rousseau, Herder believes that a young man should not be taught worldliness too early: "Better to grow up rocked by biting winds and experience necessity, danger, and poverty so that your knowledge become action and your shy, pure, and sealed feelings truth, truth for the rest of your life." This recommendation is accompanied by a call for authenticity, primitivism, and rustic simplicity: "The common man and the peasant know and feel more healthily than the aristocrat and the scholar; the moral wildman more sanely than the polite but immoral European; the man of deliberation and action better than the idle, half-mad genius."[40]

[39] Johann Gottfried Herder, *Vom Erkennen und Empfinden der menschlichen Seele,* in *Sämmtliche Werke,* ed. Bernhard Suphan (Berlin: Weidmannsche Buchhandlung, 1892), 8:208, 207, 209. In his "Correspondence on Ossian and the Songs of Ancient Peoples" (1773), he had similarly sided with Rousseau against Voltaire, feeling regret only "for the philosopher of mankind and culture who thinks that his scene is the only one, and misjudges the primal scene to be the worst and the most primitive!" Johann Gottfried Herder, "Extract from a Correspondence on Ossian and the Songs of Ancient Peoples," trans. Joyce P. Crick, in Nisbet, *German Aesthetic and Literary Criticism,* 157. Hamann, too, in his anti-Enlightenment stance, had already made the claim that philosophy and dicta had crippled nature.

[40] Herder, *Erkennen,* 8:211, 216–17.

Interestingly enough, however, Herder is not as radically antirationalist as Hamann. Truth is a matter of both sensibility and reason and his essay accordingly calls for a balance between understanding and feeling. Already by 1778 Herder's intent was to avoid not only the excesses of a strict rationalism but also of the *Geniekult*. This is particularly striking, especially in view of his lineage. Not only does he not glorify genius, dismissed, as we have seen, as "idle" and "half-mad" (and even, elsewhere, as nonexistent), his essay also illustrates a shift away from originality as novelty to originality as authenticity, from *Originalität* to *Eigentümlichkeit*. The "old" concept of originality is no longer welcome. On the contrary, it is now time, according to Herder, to expose the category of genius as "hostile" ("feindselig") and to dismiss it along with its attendant "attributes of enthusiasm, creativity, originality, self-generating, heaven-climbing *Ur*power and the like."[41]

This rejection is even more striking when one realizes that it comes from a man who, only eleven years earlier, had published a short essay entitled "Über die Mittel zur Erweckung der Genies in Deutschland" (1767). In this introduction to the second collection of fragments, *Über die neuere Deutsche Litteratur*, Herder had recommended observation over speculation: "We limit ourselves with the latter, but spread ourselves out through observation." Observation, moreover, has the added advantage of allowing us to distinguish between true originality and mere *Originalsucht* by bringing us into immediate contact with instances of original genius, of which Young's "Conjectures" is a prime example. This work captivates and inspires "because Young's spirit presides over it and, as it were, speaks directly from his heart to ours, from his genius to ours."[42]

By 1778, however, in a remarkable about-face, Herder believed that "every man of noble and active dispositions is a genius in his own right, achievement and sphere and, truly, the best geniuses are not to be found in the library." What now mattered were "the healthy human understanding and character which are the only true geniuses."[43] With Herder, we witness in one thinker the unfolding of a more widespread trend,

---

[41] Ibid., 8:225. The German reads: "Attributen von Begeisterung, Schöpferkraft, Originalität, himmelauftrebender, sich aus sich selbst entwickelnder Urmacht u.dgl."
[42] Johann Gottfried Herder, "Einleitung in die Fragmente: Über die Mittel zur Erweckung der Genies in Deutschland," in *Über die neuere Deutsche Litteratur: Zwote Sammlung von Fragmenten. Eine Beilage zu den Briefen, die neueste Litteratur betreffend* [Riga, 1767], 204.
[43] Herder, *Erkennen*, 8:223, 231.

which favored a balance between early- and late-eighteenth-century values or emphases, dramatically illustrated by his inclusion of a passage from Pope's *Essay on Criticism* that describes the play between memory, understanding, and the imagination.

SMITH'S LABOR THEORY OF VALUE

The notion of *Eigentümlichkeit* focused the debate on expression rather than execution. Propriety no longer referred only to an adequation between subject matter and result but also, and primarily, between producer and output. Adam Smith's *Lectures on Rhetoric and Belles Lettres*, transcribed by a student in 1762–1763, demonstrates that the second meaning did not displace the first in one stroke. In the eighth lecture, for instance, we hear echoes of Buffon in Smith's contention that "one who has such a complete knowledge of what he treats will naturally arrange it in the most proper order." In lecture 11, conversely, the focus is quite different, though still framed by neoclassical considerations. Here "the perfection of stile consists in Express[ing] in the most concise, proper and precise manner the thought of the author, and that in the manner which best conveys the sentiment, passion or affection with which it affects or he pretends it does affect him and which he designs to communicate to his reader."[44]

Smith then goes on to develop a somatic theory that leads him to give a lopsided explanation for the impropriety of style in Shaftesbury, whose "puny and weakly constitution" supposedly accounts for his adoption of a "stile abstracted from his own character." The problem with this theory is that, as Smith himself recognizes, this constitution is "natural" and proper to Shaftesbury: "His weakly state of body as it prevented the violence of his passions, did not incline him greatly to be of any particular temper to any great height. His Stile therefore would not be naturally more of one Sort than another. As therefore he was not lead to have any particular Stile, by the prevalence of any particular inclination, it was natural for him to form some Model or Idea of perfection which he should always have in view." Despite Smith's "progressive" statements about propriety of expression, what really galls him about Shaftesbury is not that he had no style of his own, should

[44] Smith, *Lectures*, 4:43, 55.

we even want to grant that such was the case, but that he chose to imitate the ancients and used the same "pompous, grand and ornate Stile" no matter what he wrote about. Clearly, character alone is far from a sufficient criterion of stylistic propriety. Smith even falls back on the traditional rhetorical notion of the topos precisely at the point when he is apparently trying to move away from that tradition.[45]

It is indeed not in Smith's contribution to rhetoric that we find the most telling echoes of the debate over *Eigentümlichkeit*, but rather in his analysis of labor as the foundation of economic wealth. His seminal theory of labor is more closely tied to the issues of origins and originality discussed so far than either his *Lectures on Rhetoric and Belles-Lettres* or his "Considerations concerning the First Formation of Languages," even though these works have more immediate thematic points of contact.[46]

For the sake of the present argument, three points should be made regarding Smith's selection of labor as "original foundation":

1) Smith's economic analysis is inherently Vichian inasmuch as he is trying to systematize the history of nations by focusing on the interplay of human actions rather than on climates or soil fertility, the then standard explanations.

2) More specifically, economics (also read: poetry) must be interpreted from the point of view of the producer (poet) rather than, though not to the exclusion of, nature or society, not to mention the consumer (reader).

3) Not only does Smith's emphasis on labor find obvious resonances in the emphasis on *Eigentümlichkeit* noticeable in certain critical circles of the time, it must also be understood within the context of primitivism, especially as exemplified by Rousseau.

Although labor is obviously secondary to raw materials and to the land, as Smith never tires of repeating, the foundation of the wealth of nations is labor rather than nature. In this he echoed Locke's insistence that property rights were grounded in every man's ownership of his own

---

[45] Ibid., 4:56, 58, 59.

[46] In recent years economic and intellectual historians have significantly broadened the contextualization of Smith's economic thought. I have provided a more detailed account of some of these recent developments and of the link between eighteenth-century aesthetics and Adam Smith's labor theory of value in "The Aesthetics of Adam Smith's Labor Theory," *Eighteenth Century: Theory and Interpretation* 38 (1997): 134–49.

body and, therefore, of its labor and its fruits: "Whatsoever then he removes out of the State that Nature hath provided, and left it in, he hath mixed his *Labour* with, and joyned to it something that is his own, and thereby makes it his *Property*."[47] Only toward the end of volume 1, book 2, does Smith even mention the role of nature and its share in the products of agriculture, a significant delay and a reminder, at the level of organization, of Smith's priorities.[48]

By choosing the unit of labor as the absolute standard of value, Smith fulfills a threefold requirement: this standard is at once natural/analogical and dependent on human will but not on the vagaries of history. Not only did Smith want to have an absolute standard of value, he also wanted this standard to have a natural referent. The category of labor was meant to meet both goals. In the pre-Marxist labor theory of value that Smith originated, "the *rate* of exchange between goods is always equal to the ratio of the labour *embodied* in them."[49] For Smith, this principle is both historically and logically justified. In the stage of social development that antedates ownership of stock and land, "the proportion between the quantities of labour necessary for acquiring different objects seems to be the only circumstance which can afford any rule for exchanging them for one another. If among a nation of hunters, for example, it usually costs twice the labour to kill a beaver which it does to kill a deer, one beaver should naturally exchange for or be worth two deer. It is natural that what is usually the produce of two days or two hours labour, should be worth double of what is usually the produce of one day's or one hour's labour" (WN 65).

According to Smith, the centrality of labor as a determinant of value still holds in later stages of societal development: "The real value of all the different component parts of price, it must be observed, is measured by the quantity of labour which they can, each of them, purchase or command. Labour measures the value not only of that part of

[47] John Locke, *The Second Treatise of Government* in *Two Treatises of Government*, ed. Peter Laslett (Cambridge: Cambridge University Press, 1988), §27, p. 288.

[48] Adam Smith, *An Inquiry into the Nature and Causes of the Wealth of Nations*, in *The Glasgow Edition of the Works and Correspondence of Adam Smith*, vol. 2, bks. 1 and 2, textual ed. W. B. Todd, general eds. R. H. Campbell and A. S. Skinner (Oxford: Oxford University Press, 1976; Indianapolis: Liberty Fund, 1981), 363–67. Further references to this work will be included parenthetically in the body of the text, preceded by the abbreviation *WN*.

[49] *The New Palgrave: A Dictionary of Economics*, ed. John Eatwell et al. (New York: Stockton Press, 1987), s.v. "Smith, Adam," (by Andrew S. Skinner).

price which resolves itself into labour, but of that which resolves itself into rent, and of that which resolves itself into profit" (*WN* 67–68).

As a result, wages and prices have an immediate referent. Wages are "the produce of labour" and that produce "constitutes the natural recompense or wages of labour" (*WN* 82). This in turn accounts for the very notion of such a thing as the "natural price" of commodities: "When the price of any commodity is neither more nor less than what is sufficient to pay the rent of the land, the wages of the labour, and the profits of the stock employed in raising, preparing, and bringing it to market, according to their natural rates, the commodity is then sold for what may be called its natural price" (*WN* 72). The natural price is then further defined as "the price of free competition" (*WN* 78), as opposed to the inflated pricing found under monopolies.[50] Smith is opposed to economic excess in the same way one might disparage the kind of inflation so necessary to an appreciation of the sublime or for the same reasons Rousseau had longed for stasis.[51] The natural price is even described as a "centre of repose and continuance" toward which the prices of commodities constantly tend (*WN* 75).

Needless to say, whatever unit of labor one could devise as a standard measure would necessarily be somewhat arbitrary, but such a standard is less abstract in the case of labor than in that of money or stocks. Whereas it had been painfully obvious since at least the seventeenth century that the referential nature of money and stocks could be quite insignificant, labor, defined as "the first price, the original purchase-money that was paid for all things" (*WN* 48), "is the only universal, as well as the only accurate measure of value, or the only standard by which we can compare the values of different commodities at all times, and at all places" (*WN* 54). The labor price of goods is real; the money price merely nominal. "Labour, it must always be remembered, and not any

---

[50] The distrust of monopoly was a hallmark of mercantilism. For a discussion of Locke's distrust of monopoly and the concept of natural price, see chapter 3 of Karen Iversen Vaughn, *John Locke: Economist and Social Scientist* (Chicago: University of Chicago Press, 1980). Note also that the natural price is not identical to the market price but "is, as it were, the central price, to which the prices of all commodities are continually gravitating" (*WN* 75). See G. Vaggi's entry on "natural price" in the *New Palgrave: A Dictionary of Economics* for a brief introduction to the concept.

[51] The first term of this analogy is authorized as much by my reading of Smith as by the forceful parallel Peter de Bolla has drawn between the "discourse of the sublime" and the "discourse of debt." See *Discourse of the Sublime: Readings in History, Aesthetics, and the Subject* (Oxford: Basil Blackwell, 1989), esp. 12–15 and 103–12.

particular commodity or sett of commodities, is the real measure of the value both of silver and of all other commodities" (*WN* 206).

This emphasis on what could be called the referentiality of human production is then explained in historico-deductive terms. Labor is idealized for "historical" reasons as well. The ideal form of labor is agriculture, in part because it is the earliest form of labor: "And as to cultivate the ground was the original destination of man, so in every stage of his existence he seems to retain a predilection for this primitive employment" (*WN* 378).[52] Not only had this held true, it could still be recommended as economically sound in 1776: "Of all the ways in which a capital can be employed, it is by far the most advantageous to the society" (*WN* 364).

Smith further underlines the positive connotations of labor as the only original source of value by presenting it as the element that only *adds* value. Labor *supplies*. By contrast, rent and the profit made from the lending of stock are presented strictly in terms of *deductions* "from the produce of the labour which is employed upon land" (*WN* 83). Hence the opening statement of Smith's magnum opus: "The annual labour of every nation is the fund which originally supplies it with all the necessaries and conveniences of life which it annually consumes" (*WN* 10).

Labor is primary both logically and historically. Moreover, labor's primacy is precisely what allows Smith to cling to the wish that history might be eradicated. By turning the unit of labor into the standard of value, Smith also makes a case for earlier over later modes of production, that is, for agriculture over manufacture. Not only is agriculture more labor-intensive, it is a mode of production so dependent on and limited by nature that its introduction cannot disrupt too irreparably what is undeniably an idealized primitive status quo. In the case of agriculture, where "nature labours along with man" (*WN* 363), supply can never run wild. Consumption and production, being therefore equal, cancel each other out as it were, which helps to maintain an ideal original balance.

Let us make no mistake about it; Smith does not eradicate history. In *The Wealth of Nations* the circumstances that determine the so-called natural rate of wages and rate of profit are undeniably affected by the

---

[52] Here Smith echoes Rousseau's remark that "country labor . . . is man's first vocation, it recalls to the mind a pleasant notion, and to the heart all the charms of the golden age" (*Julie*, part 5, letter 7, 493).

stage of societal development in which they take place ("advancing, stationary, or declining"; *WN* 80).[53] A dedicated heir to Rousseau, however, Smith also postulates an "original state of things, which precedes both the appropriation of land and the accumulation of stock, [and in which] the whole produce of labour belongs to the labourer. He has neither landlord nor master to share with him" (*WN* 82).[54]

This unmistakable nostalgia proceeds from an evaluation of modern society similar to Rousseau's, whose *Discourse on the Origins of Inequality* the Scottish philosopher had reviewed and excerpts of which he had translated in a letter published in the *Edinburgh Review* of 1755–1756.[55] The similarity is particularly striking in Smith's discussion of a "natural order of things," which echoes the conclusion of the Second Discourse: "But though this natural order of things must have taken place in some degree in every such society, it has, in all the modern states of Europe, been, in many respects, entirely inverted" (*WN* 380).

Anything that is late accordingly tends to be interpreted negatively by Smith. For instance, the value of labor offers a better standard than prices in part because it is less abstract, a historically laden term. (As the third lecture of the *Rhetoric* and the bulk of the "Considerations concerning the Formation of Languages" make clear, the clearest sign of the evolution of languages is an increased penchant and need for abstraction.) Not only does Smith recognize and include in his *Wealth of Nations* a historicity that takes into account time-invested concepts such as history, abstraction, and manufacture, he also tries to neutralize these by investing the polar concepts of nature, referentiality, and agriculture with positive, that is, primitive, connotations. While he has

[53] Note, however, that Smith does not develop any systematic theory of development. The succession of these stages varies from country to country (*WN* 99–100).

[54] Although Rousseau is not mentioned here, it is clear that Smith implicitly accepts Rousseau's hypothetical primal scene of division, in which "the first person who, having fenced off a plot of ground, took it into his head to say *this is mine* . . ." (*Discourse*, 43). Hence the surprise of finding in what one tends to think of as a founding text of capitalist economics a proto-Marxist defense of laborers against masters and merchants, who are generally described as oppressive conspirators (see, for example, *WN* 83–91, 114–15, 146).

[55] Smith's "Letter to the *Edinburgh Review*," ed. J. C. Bryce, can be found in *Essays on Philosophical Subjects, The Glasgow Edition of the Works and Correspondence of Adam Smith*, vol. 3, ed. W. P. D. Wightman and J. C. Bryce, general eds. D. D. Raphael and A. S. Skinner (Oxford: Oxford University Press, 1980; Indianapolis: Liberty Fund, 1982), 242–54.

to and does write economic history—in more ways than one—in his more hypothetical and prescriptive moments he also erects obstacles to minimize its development, thereby reflecting an unease, common to both sides of the Atlantic, with the economic modernity he did so much to conceptualize.

"MEER PRIORITY"

The 1770s saw the acceptance and elaboration of standards of value such as *Eigentümlicheit* and labor in part because these terms were being defined independent of the ebb and flow of history; the poet as source is unburdened by his predecessors while the unit of labor transcends time. Yet, in a reversal of the earlier "paradox" of the "synchronic historical method," these "timeless" standards also became historicized. The key to this turnabout was primitivism. Indeed, in the later part of the eighteenth century, origins were often valued less for their ability to give the appearance of logical causality than for the way they evoked the past and gave atemporal values the stamp of historical corroboration. This was particularly evident in the 1770s. Smith, who was no exception to this trend, repeatedly went back, if only summarily, to the hypothetical beginnings of society.

As can be seen from Robert Wood's *Essay on the Original Genius and Writings of Homer,* first published in London in 1775, the terms of the equations remained problematic and their definitions varied. In Wood's essay the various aspects of the problem are still, from a postnineteenth-century perspective at least, highly unsettled or, rather, unsettling. By reemphasizing Homer's old status as the absolute fount of Western literature and using him as an example of original genius, Wood attempted to give a relatively recent major criterion of aesthetic judgment a foundation in history. In his *Essay*, primitivism is intimately linked to originality. This should not be interpreted as the triumph of a historical perspective, however, since Homer's primacy, both temporal and qualitative, is said to depend primarily on his ability to depict faithfully a natural environment still visible over two thousand years later. Homer was original because of his ability to paint. What allows us to appreciate the Greek poet's originality is our ability to stand where he stood and see what he saw. "We should place ourselves on the spot, or in the point of view, where the Painter [the reference is

specifically to Homer] made his drawing." Homer's "primitive simplicity" is directly observable. Wood's goal is therefore "to carry the
Reader to the Poet's Age, and Country."[56]

As can be observed from Wood's evaluation of Homer's original
genius, he did not find that the categories of time and nature, history
and painting, were antithetical. The past is not necessarily distant. One
can travel to primitivism. Originality is a sign both of individual presence and of historical primacy. The original is opposed to the copy, which
it precedes in an absolute linear sense. At the same time, Homer's temporal primacy can be ascertained on the basis of the adequacy between
Homer's descriptions and a geography that cannot, by definition, have
changed. This in turn lends credence to Homer the historian, since "a
review of Homer's scene of action leads naturally to the consideration
of the times, when he lived; and the nearer we approach his country and
age, the more we find him accurate in his pictures of nature, and that
every species of his extensive Imitation furnishes the greatest treasure
of original truth to be found in any Poet, ancient or modern" (vi). Scenery
"verifies" history and the travelogue becomes a historical genre. Homer
is a trustworthy historian because he can be shown to have been a faithful painter. In such a context, we can hardly be surprised if it is Wood's
own "*map* of Troy" (223) that turns out to offer the best support for his
contention that the *Iliad* can be read "as a *journal* of the siege of Troy"
(223, emphasis added). Using, in a new context, the old distinction
between imitation of nature and imitation of other writers, Wood can
therefore assert "that however questionable Homer's superiority may
be, in some respects, as a perfect model for composition, in the great
province of Imitation he is the most original of all Poets, and the most
constant and faithful copier after Nature" (4–5).

If painting is what confers on Homer the qualities of the historian,
it is in part because Wood had to counter the then popular notion
that our primal scene of culture is really Egypt, not Greece. Because
Wood, unlike Vico,[57] could not very well deny that Egyptian culture

---

[56] Robert Wood, *An Essay on the Original Genius and Writings of Homer: With a Comparative View of the Ancient and Present State of the Troade* (London, 1775), 19, 144, 300.
Further page references will be included parenthetically in the body of the text.

[57] Vico had denied the extreme antiquity of Egypt's culture on the grounds that
those who supported this theory were gullible and naively ignorant of the "conceit
of nations," a tendency shared by all civilizations which consists in exaggerating
one's antiquity.

had antedated Homer, he tried to preserve the epic poet's primacy by claiming that there had been no cultural contamination between Egypt and Greece. This could be demonstrated, he believed, by pointing out what he took to be the ridiculous nature of Egypt's monuments—"Egypt has, no doubt, produced the most stupendous and amazing, but I must add, the most absurd and unmeaning public works, to be seen in any country: I mean pyramids, obelisks, labyrinths, artificial lakes, which are without art, elegance, or public utility" (120)—and by contrasting their artificiality to the mimetic accuracy of Homer's epics. This stylistic difference allowed Wood to devote some pages to dismissing the notion that Homer had inserted allegorical meanings learned in Egypt into his poetry: "But though we are apt to trace every thing back to Egypt, I believe, in those the Greeks are entirely original, and took their ideas from nature alone" (119).

Wood's argument is, at the very least, somewhat circular. Homer may well have had Egyptian predecessors, but this is dismissed through ridicule and on the grounds that Homer's proven talent as a painter—Wood, after all, had taken the trouble of going and standing where Homer had stood—establishes a de jure (and consequently de facto) primacy and originality. And, since primitivism bears the inescapable mark of originality, Homer is the true primitive, no matter who came first. Why Wood found it necessary to link originality and temporal primacy is not clear, but these somersaults in the face of evidence indicate this was an imperative he could not dispense with: "Homer must stand unrivalled, as the Father of History: to him we owe the earliest accounts of Arts, Science, Manners, and Government; and without him, no just ideas can be formed of the state and true character of primitive society. . . . I am therefore entirely within my subject, when I attempt to show, that Homer was a faithful Historian, because he was a correct Painter" (181).

One of the fascinating implications of this argument is that, for Wood, the historian does not profess an occupation marked by secondariness. This is further corroborated by Wood's insistence that Homer had known some of the participants in the Trojan War. He could be a historian of that war only because he was close to the events he described, just as, by definition, he painted only what was in front of him. Painting and history both are dependent on direct observation. By way of contrast, Wood insisted that Virgil had not been a historian and even devoted some twenty pages to denying that Aeneas had ever been to Rome.

At the same time, Wood makes the point that it may well have been the "Roman copy" that caused us to grant the "Greek original" its primacy (137). Indeed, though we must acknowledge that, for Wood, Homer's originality undeniably hinges on his position as the absolute primal father of literature's "legitimate sons" (139), we must not ignore the fact that Wood clearly indicates that in this case it is the son who begot the father: "Though Homer was born with a genius, that must have figured, if not taken the lead, in any age; and wrote under greater advantages, than ever fell to the lot of any Poet; there is still a peculiar circumstance of meer good fortune, that attended his productions, to which they perhaps owe more reputation, than to their intrinsic value: viz. that they were presented to the golden age of letters, by the most acute and distinguishing genius of that or any other period; who was in a great measure allowed to judge for the rest of the world, both in matters of Taste and Philosophy, for above two thousand years" (232). Temporal originality, a recent notion, is then taken down from its pedestal by one of its very proponents and becomes "meer priority": "For had Virgil written first, I doubt not but Homer would have copied him. Indeed, the importance of meer priority, if properly considered, will appear much greater, than we are apt to imagine" (231–32). Wood goes on to compare the *Aeneid* favorably to Homer's epics on the grounds "that the Greek Poet found great part of his moral in his fable; and did not, like Virgil, invent a fable for his moral" (234–35).

Another remarkable element of Wood's argumentation is that it is precisely within the context of a discussion of Homer as original genius (a criterion obviously meant to be interpreted positively) that those features most associated with originality collapse before our very eyes. Homer's originality is linked to his primacy, which is then dismissed as mere priority. To be original is to be lucky. But then, why the emphasis on the category of original genius, which is so obviously dependent on primitivism? Similarly, though the foundation of Homer's originality is his ability to paint, and his visual accuracy is a proof of his antiquity, one should not suppose that painting is a primitive art form. On the contrary, painting—identified as the master art—is also last in order of appearance, after poetry and sculpture. Homer himself did not know it (271). This development further undermines the importance of temporal priority. It also raises the question of what Wood meant by painting. If Homer did not know painting, how did he become a painter?

To answer that question, we must obviously think of painting as a mental faculty as much as a specific art form. Indeed, for Wood painting is associated with the communication of clear and distinct ideas: "I have already observed the advantage, which Painting has over Poetical imitation, in conveying clear and distinct ideas, by the help of minute circumstances" (226). By contrast, poetry shared this advantage only in its early stages. Primitive life was simple, and it was easy to see it more clearly and distinctly because there was less to see. The "uniformity of manners" (246) characteristic of primitive society therefore turned Homer into a painter and gave early poetry its perfection (248). Hence Wood's goal: to focus on scenery, that is, give a *visual* defense of Homer's poetry and prove that "every sketch of this great Master is an exact transcript of what he had either seen, heard, or felt" (294). Painting is the activity most likely to capture origins; it enables us to bridge the historical distance imposed by the temporal dimension of the primacy of origins. By doing so, it both acknowledges and negates that dimension.

Eighteenth-century discourses of origins and originality crystallized an epistemic mode that has since been dominant in Western thought: aesthetic knowledge, or an episteme that recognizes the human both as mind and as senses, as the sole source of understanding, that is to say, as supplier of the only valid objects and as the only valid means of inquiry. The eighteenth-century fascination with origins played a crucial role in this regard because the inherently conjectural character of origins made thinkers crave the conceptualization of a mode of understanding that revolved around the imagination. Thanks to this faculty, traditionally linked to the sense of sight and to memory, the human mind came to be depicted as an entity that recapitulated both space and time, that is, as the source of both spatial and temporal knowledge. Hence the never fully resolved tension in eighteenth-century thought between genetic epistemology as a synchronic and as a diachronic model of knowledge. Armed with the "law of the imagination," Baumgarten initially defined aesthetics as a branch of knowledge. This original definition has often been forgotten, since aesthetics has come to be defined more narrowly as the branch of philosophy dedicated to the fine arts. This narrowing of the field was never final, however. Aesthetic thinking quickly exceeded these short-lived bounds and seeped into a variety of discourses, as we saw in the case of Smith's otherwise illogical preference for agriculture over later modes of production. A once marginal discourse was now at the center of a wide variety of discursive practices. We should therefore not be surprised that Kant reinstated the epistemological dimension of aesthetics when he defined judgment as mediating between the concept of nature and the concept of freedom, or between the understanding (*Verstand*) on the one hand and reason (*Vernunft*) on the other.

CHAPTER FIVE

Kant's Abyss:
Serialization and Originality

*Tombs and mausoleums are signs of our remembering the dead. So too
are pyramids, which are also imperishable mementoes of the great
power a king once had.—Strata of seashells in regions far from the
sea, holes of Pholades in the high Alps, or volcanic residue where no
fire now erupts from the earth signify to us the ancient state of the
world and establish an* archeology *of nature. But they are not such
clear signs as the scars of a soldier.—The ruins of Palmyra, Baalbek
and Persepolis are eloquent reminders of the artistic level of* ancient
states, *and melancholy indications of the way* all things change.
Anthropology from a Pragmatic Point of View §39.

Infinite and eternal, right and ordered, spherical and centrifugal, the universe is an edifice that evolves according to absolutely necessary and
unchanging laws. Such is, at least, the position adopted by Immanuel
Kant in his *Allgemeine Naturgeschichte,* or, to give the full English title,
*Universal Natural History and Theory of the Heavens, or An Essay on the Con-
stitution and Mechanical Origin of the Entire World-Edifice Treated according
to Newtonian Principles,* first published in Königsberg and Leipzig in 1755.

The very attributes of the universe assigned by Kant make it clear that
his goal, the description of a "mechanical origin of the entire world-edifice," did not entail reliance on a genetic mode of explanation in the
Vichian sense. On the contrary, in the context of Enlightenment genetic

epistemology, one of the distinctive features of Kantian philosophy is that it put severe constraints on the permissibility of genetic explanations. This chapter is therefore devoted to an investigation of Kant's views on the proper epistemological place of origins. This will help us put in perspective the various ways that place was reassigned over the one-hundred-year period that separated the publications of Locke's *Essay concerning Human Understanding* (1690) and Kant's *Critique of Judgment* (1790), a task I shall undertake in the postscript, in part by sketching a comparison between the Vichian and Kantian models. What do they have to offer regarding the limits and possibilities of genetic epistemology in general and of Enlightenment genetic epistemology in particular?

The range of Kant's own thought is such that it can be said to represent the "crowning phase" of the Enlightenment, to borrow a phrase from the title of R. A. C. Macmillan's important work on the *Critique of Judgment*. Indeed, Kant did bridge many gaps, including those that separate figures as distinct as Newton and Rousseau. It is therefore particularly unfortunate that most studies sharply isolate Kant's aesthetic, scientific, and ethical concerns from one another. The reception of the Third Critique is a case in point. In their interpretations of this particular work, critics tend to focus on either the Critique of Aesthetic Judgment or the Critique of Teleological Judgment and usually go about their business as though the other half, usually the Critique of Teleological Judgment, did not exist or was something of an embarrassment.[1] Needless to say, I wish to avoid breaking up Kant's thought along strict disciplinary lines. Instead, my objective is to bring together the various areas of concern that have been dealt with in the preceding chapters and turn to a topic that has so far been left out, at least with respect to the eighteenth century: the question of the origin(s) of nature itself, rather than of our ideas, our languages, our societies, or our art.

"THE SEQUENCE OF ETERNITY"

As the full title of the *Universal Natural History* makes clear, in 1755 Kant believed that the genesis of nature could be accounted for by relying on a mechanical explanation. This raises a number of questions, in particular: How, in his early work on cosmology, did Kant reconcile the

---

[1] Howard Caygill's *Art of Judgement* (Cambridge, Mass.: Basil Blackwell, 1989) represents a notable exception to this generalization; see esp. 284–395.

need for a mechanistic genetic explanation with the claim that the world is eternal?[2] Theological considerations are primary here inasmuch as eternity, as well as infinity, are presented as the necessary attributes of God, who is eternally creating, which makes the "world-edifice" eternally in process and infinitely expandable (*ANG* 151).[3] As a result, Kant repeatedly stresses the notion of creation as process: "Creation is never completed. Though it has once started, but will never cease. It is always busy in bringing forth more scenes of nature, new things and new worlds" (*ANG* 155).[4]

This claim highlights one of the contextualizations in the *Universal Natural History*, in which the origin functions as both a diachronic and

---

[2] Although I begin this chapter with a discussion of the Cosmology, this should not be interpreted as signaling a desire to minimize the uniqueness of the Critical phase of Kant's thought, which will constitute, as one would expect, my main focus. I merely wish to suggest that revolutionary though it was, it did not exist in a vacuum, either with respect to Kant's non-Critical writings or in terms of the preoccupations of other eighteenth-century figures.

[3] Unless otherwise noted, all quotations are from published translations of Kant's works: *Universal Natural History and Theory of the Heavens*, trans. Stanley L. Jaki (Edinburgh: Scottish Academy Press, 1981); *Critique of Pure Reason*, trans. Norman Kemp Smith (New York: St. Martin's Press, 1965); *Critique of Judgment*, trans. Werner S. Pluhar (Indianapolis: Hackett, 1987); and *Anthropology from a Pragmatic Point of View*, trans. Mary J. Gregor (The Hague: Martinus Nijhoff, 1974). Further page or section references will be included parenthetically in the body of the text, preceded, wherever appropriate, by the relevant abbreviation: *ANG* (for *Allgemeine Naturgeschichte*), *KrV* (for *Kritik der reinen Vernunft*), *KU* (for *Kritik der Urtheilskraft*), or *Anthropology*. As is customary, page numbers for the First Critique are preceded by the letters A or B, which refer to the first and second editions of the *Kritik der reinen Vernunft* as they appear in the *Gesammelte Schriften* (known as the *Akademie* edition); they are also given in the margins of Pluhar's translation. Unless otherwise noted, references to the Third Critique and the *Anthropology* will be to section (§) numbers. Page numbers for the Cosmology refer exclusively to Jaki's translation.

[4] This claim is what allowed him, of course, to make the daring suggestion that "perhaps a series of millions of years and centuries will have flown past before the sphere of developed nature in which we find ourselves, arrived at the [stage of] perfection, which now attends it" (*ANG* 154), even though he shied away from explicitly discussing the age of the earth itself: "Perhaps our earth had been around a thousand or even more years before it found itself in the condition to support men, animals, and plants" (*ANG* 184). For discussions of Kant's predecessors, including Robert Hooke, Nicholas Steno, Thomas Burnet, Descartes, Newton, and Buffon, and the movement away from a reliance on the Mosaic account in matters of cosmogony and geogony, see Stephen Jay Gould, *Time's Arrow, Time's Cycle: Myth and Metaphor in the Discovery of Genealogical Time* (Cambridge, Mass.: Harvard University Press, 1987); John C. Greene, *The Death of Adam: Evolution and Its Impact on Western Thought* (Ames: Iowa State University Press, 1959); Paolo Rossi, *The Dark Abyss of Time: The History of the Earth and the History of Nations from Hooke to Vico*, trans. Lydia G. Cochrane (Chicago: University of Chicago Press, 1984); and Stephen Toulmin and June Goodfield, *The Discovery of Time* (Chicago: University of Chicago Press, 1982).

a synchronic concept. In the latter case, genetic inquiries are framed in theological rather than "historical" or "archeological" terms. Instances of this thinking abound—one can choose examples almost at random: "But even in the essential properties of the elements, which constitute the chaos, one can notice the hallmark of that perfection which they have from their origin on, insofar as their essence is a consequence of the eternal idea of the divine mind. The simplest, the most universal properties which seem to have been planned without intent, the [very] matter, which seems to be purely passive and in need of forms and arrangements, has in its simplest state a tendency to develop through natural development into a perfect constitution" (*ANG* 114).

This theo/teleological origin, different from the mechanical origin promised in the title, is never forgotten. The two genetic models are actually interdependent. The former legitimizes the latter, in part by relying on a visionary mode with familiar characteristics: "I assume the matter of the entire world to be universally scattered and I make a perfect chaos out of it. I see, in accordance with the established laws of attraction, the stuff forming itself and through repulsion modify its motion. I enjoy the satisfaction of seeing, without the aid of arbitrary notions, a well-ordered whole arise under the direction of established laws, a whole so similar to that world system which we have before our very eyes that I cannot prevent myself from holding it to be the same" (*ANG* 84–85). This, of course, brings to mind the rhetoric that dominates the beginning and end of the Second Discourse, published the same year as the *Universal Natural History*. Moving beyond the limits of civil society, however, Kant, unlike both Rousseau and Vico, does not hesitate to affirm in the Cosmology that even the knowledge of the origins of natural phenomena is inherently visionary and dependent on a single and isolated consciousness. It is indeed his awareness of what he perceives to be harmony and order and his assumption that they have a purpose that allow him to claim access to origins.

In addition, Kant does not hesitate to rely on hypothetical reasoning: "One could, if one were to go into details, finally arrive, through a series of conclusions drawn from one another according to the manner of a mathematical method with all the pomp which it entails and with a greater probability than what its application in physical topics commonly appears to be, at the very plan which I will lay out about the origin of the world-edifice, but I prefer to present my views in the form of a hypothesis" (*ANG* 113). This is particularly significant, not only because it reinforces the kinship with Rousseau, but also because it forces us to address the issue of the admissibility of hypotheses and their function regarding claims of certainty, claims Kant is undoubtedly also making here, the hypothetical presentation notwithstanding. Must we, with Stanley L. Jaki, the irascible translator of the *Universal Natural History*, dismiss this conjunction as a mere contradiction (see, for example, 257n8)? Or does it not suggest instead that even in the Cosmology hypotheses are not uniform or univocal but can function at different levels of certainty? More specifically, can we not reconcile the reliance on a hypothetical rhetoric with a) Newton's well-known "I frame no hypotheses" (especially in view of Kant's grounding of the *Universal Natural History* in "Newtonian principles")[5] and b) the statement made in the *Critique of Pure Reason* that "hypotheses are . . . , in the domain of pure reason, permissible only as weapons of war, and only for the purpose of defending a right, not in order to establish it" (A777/B805).

The first objection can be easily dealt with. As Kant himself points out, Newton's stricture apparently did not apply when the English scientist appealed to "the direct hand of God" (*ANG* 113), that is, precisely what Kant was eventually to dismiss as the worst kind of hypothesis, the "hyperphysical hypothesis, such as the appeal to a divine Author, assumed simply in order that we may have an explanation" (A773/B801). In any case, even if this element were not present, as Gordon G. Brittan Jr. remarked, "the significance of the words 'deduced,' 'derived,' and 'inferred,' even 'phenomena,' is far from clear," so that even Newton's apparently straightforward rejection of hypotheses needs qualification.[6]

---

[5] I am referring here, of course, to the famous claim made by Newton in the General Scholium appended to the *Principia*: "I frame no hypotheses; for whatever is not deduced from the phenomena is to be called an hypothesis; and hypotheses, whether metaphysical or physical, whether of occult qualities or mechanical, have no place in experimental philosophy. In this philosophy particular propositions are inferred from the phenomena and afterwards rendered general by induction." Isaac Newton, *Mathematical Principles of Natural Philosophy and System of the World*, trans. Andrew Motte (1729), rev. ed. by Florian Cajori, 2 vols. (Berkeley and Los Angeles: University of California Press, 1934), 547. For discussions of the nature of the relationship between Newtonian and Kantian science, see Gordon G. Brittan Jr., *Kant's Theory of Science* (Princeton, N.J.: Princeton University Press, 1978), esp. 117–42, and Robert Hahn, *Kant's Newtonian Revolution in Philosophy* (Carbondale: Southern Illinois University Press for *The Journal of the History of Philosophy*, 1988). In particular, see Hahn, *Kant's Newtonian Revolution*, 56–60, for observations on the role of hypotheses in Kant's Critical philosophy.

[6] Brittan, *Kant's Theory*, 6.

This is already apparent in the *Critique of Pure Reason* (A769–82/B797–810). Here Kant, moving away from the apparent simplicity of Newton's dismissal, distinguishes between metaphysical and physical hypotheses and allows that, under certain conditions, physical hypotheses may be legitimate. In particular, and here I am following the argument made by Robert E. Butts, hypotheses are acceptable if they are explanatory but not if they are regulative. In other words, scientific hypotheses are legitimate if they "fulfill the requirement that propositions offered in explanation of sensory experience be connected with possible objects of experience by laws of connection that are themselves certain, even though the details of this contention are not free from dispute." This allowed Kant to avoid the trap of an "infinite regression of explanatory bases," a point of particular importance for genealogical debates. This does not rule out all genealogical explanations, but merely "hyperphysical" ones. Indeed, as Butts noted, causal hypotheses are not unwarranted under these conditions: "We are entitled on Kant's theory to make guesses about the causes of an event because of the certainty—the universality and necessity—of the causal principle. If we have a rule for connecting events of type X with events of type Y (the rule of understanding associated with the category of causality) we may, on appearance of Y_1 hypothesize X_1 as its cause. The guess may be wrong, but in Kant's theory we are entitled to make it, since *a priori* we can account for Y_1 by means of X_1. We can so account for Y_1 by means of X_1 only because the causal principle guarantees that every event has a cause."[7]

The certainty of the causality principle is not as free from dispute as Butts suggests in this particular context, an issue I expand on in the next section. For now, however, it suffices to note that though, in the Cosmology, Kant did rely on the type of hyperphysical hypothesis he would later denounce, he also distinguished between hypothesis as mere probability and hypothesis as proceeding from something certain. The statement that he chose "to present [his] views in the form of a hypothesis" (*ANG* 113) may well strike the reader as an acknowledgment that the mathematical presentation Kant set aside would not have been "pretentious" but impossible. At the same time, we must note that this remark is preceded by a) a reminder that certain elements of his arguments are empirically certain (there *are*, for instance, six planets

[7] Robert E. Butts, "Hypothesis and Explanation of Kant's Philosophy of Science," *Archiv für Geschichte der Philosophie* 43 (1961): 162, 163, 165–66.

moving in a specific direction) and b) an evaluation of the validity of two sets of considerations regarding the mechanical origins of the world in terms of a gradation in certainty, from the probable to the certain, with something in between. Finally, though he does refer to something "above the probability of a hypothesis" (*ANG* 113), which would therefore be preferable, he also insists that his choice of a hypothetical framework is merely a matter of rhetorical preference, not an indication that mathematical certainty is impossible. By preferring a hypothetical presentation to what he calls a "pretentious" mathematical demonstration, Kant implies that mathematical certainty lies behind and supports the hypotheses he is about to present.

In the Cosmology, then, hypotheses belong to the realms of both the probable and the certain, and Kant plays on both registers to reach his stated goal, namely, a mechanistic genesis of the universe, a genesis distinct yet inseparable from the theological origin: "I hope to found on incontrovertible grounds a firm conviction, [*first*] *that the world recognizes for the origin of its constitution a mechanical development unfolding from the general laws of nature; and second, that the kind of mechanical genesis which we have presented is the true one*" (*ANG* 170). Methodologically, this genesis can then be reduced to the simplest and most basic laws, which, one supposes, are intended to counter the hypothetico-probabilistic elements of his cosmogony: "I have in fact decided with the greatest caution to forego all arbitrary speculation, I have, after I have set the world in the simplest chaos, applied no other forces than the forces of attraction and repulsion for the development of the great order of nature, two forces which both are equally certain, equally simple, and also equally primary and universal. Both are borrowed from the Newtonian philosophy of nature" (*ANG* 91). These basic mechanisms are then used to buttress Kant's overall goal, which is to provide a cosmology "whereby the edifice of creation is secured from collapse and made fit for an imperishable duration" (*ANG* 104).

This still does not account for and even seems antithetical to the need for a mechanistic genesis. To support this part of the equation, Kant divides eternity into an endless sequence of finite periods during which individual worlds are subject to decay and inevitably collapse back into chaos. Nature itself, as the object of creation, even "demonstrates her richness in a kind of waste [exchange] which, while some parts pay tribute to transitoriness, maintains itself undamaged through innumerable new products in the entire extent of her perfection" (*ANG* 158).

This even holds true at the universal level. Should nature collapse back into chaos, "can one not believe that nature, which was capable of placing herself from chaos into a regular order and a skillful system, will not be in the position to restore herself from the new chaos, into which the diminution of her motions had lowered her, just as easily and to renew the first combination?" (*ANG* 159).

Cosmology, then, is marked by endless expansion and recollapse. Cosmogony, by contrast, depends on sequentiality, that is, the breaking up of eternity into finite parts. Sequentiality becomes the condition of creation, a conceptual bulwark against the threat of a world always already there. The "sequence of eternity" (*ANG* 159) counterbalances the "abyss of eternity" (*ANG* 157), just as the linearity of sequence and duration mingles with the cyclicality inherent in the concept of a return to chaos. Sequentiality is not to be equated with absolute linearity, however. First, linearity is more limited in its application. Chaos and development can coexist: "The developed world finds itself confined in between the ruins of a collapsed and the chaos of an undeveloped nature" (*ANG* 159). Second, linearity is applicable only to the development of individual worlds before the collapse, which reminds us, of course, that teleology and linearity do not necessarily go together.

There is therefore in the *Universal Natural History* a pervasive tension between duration, collapse, and the rules of succession and sequence on the one hand and the rules of the supposedly ordered abyss and chaos on the other. This tension is not a problem at a strictly theological level, where one can adhere to both "the traditional Christian doctrine of creation" and to the view that the world is eternal.[8] Such a view no longer holds, however, once one introduces a mechanistic requirement. From within a mechanistic cosmogony, it is not unproblematic to state that the world has no end but does have a beginning, that is, that eternity is only forward-looking, a position even less tenable once one links eternity to infinity and insists that the world has a center (*ANG* 152–53). In the end, Kant's own edifice holds only if one views *origin* as a misnomer in the expression *mechanical origin*. The introduction of sequentiality, necessary though it may be for the elaboration of a mechanical origin, does not carry enough weight to convince the reader that the "abyss of eternity" or the "worlds without number and without end" (*ANG* 152) can have a knowable beginning.

---

[8] Jaki, in Kant, *Universal Natural History*, 284n29.

Permanence and Causality
in the *Critique of Pure Reason*

By the time Kant wrote the *Critique of Pure Reason,* he had clearly become aware of the fact that he had painted himself into a corner in the *Universal Natural History.* In the *Critique,* first published some thirty years later, the mechanistic fallacy that had limited the successful elaboration of the Cosmology is displaced by the crucial notion that though we may, by virtue of the makeup of our reason, presuppose a primal scene of creation, we cannot claim that it corresponds to any objective reality lying outside the confines of our reason. Indeed, in a position reminiscent of Vico's hermeneutic theory, which, as discussed earlier, rests on the notion "that the world of civil society has certainly been made by men, and that its principles are therefore to be found within the modifications of our own human mind,"[9] Kant underlines in his Critical philosophy "that reason has insight only into that which it produces after a plan of its own, and that it must not allow itself to be kept, as it were, in nature's leading-strings, but must itself show the way with principles of judgment based upon fixed laws, constraining nature to give answer to questions of reason's own determining" (Bxiii).

Problematically, one such principle is permanence, which Kant defines as

> what alone makes possible the representation of the transition from one state to another, and from not-being to being. These transitions can be empirically known only as changing determinations of that which is permanent. If we assume that something absolutely begins to be, we must have a point of time in which it was not. But to what are we to attach this point, if not to that which already exists? For a preceding empty time is not an object of perception. But if we connect the coming to be with things which previously existed, and which persist in existence up to the moment of this coming to be, this latter must be simply a determination of what is permanent in that which precedes it. (A188/B231)

[9] *The New Science of Giambattista Vico: Unabridged Translation of the Third Edition (1744) with the Addition of "Practic of the New Science,"* trans. Thomas Goddard Bergin and Max Harold Fisch (Ithaca, N.Y.: Cornell University Press, 1984), §331.

The permanence principle plays a complex role in the study of origins. By definition, origins and permanence are antithetical. Kant rejects neither, however, but ascribes separate functions to them, while also claiming that permanence is the condition of genetic inquiries. Permanence, which Kant describes as a condition of perception, "cannot," he writes, "be something in me" (B275). By contrast, according to Kant's hermeneutic principle, the reverse holds true for genetic explanations. This distinction frees origins from the empirical fallacy that generally pervades genetic explanations and rests on the assumption "that there is an actual object corresponding to the idea" (A482/B510). As a result, in the *Critique* Kant no longer insists that infinity is a necessary component in the elaboration of a cosmology. The dominant principle is now that of "the greatest possible continuation and extension of experience, allowing no empirical limit to hold as absolute" (A509/B537). Accordingly, "I cannot say, therefore, that the world is *infinite* in space or as regards past time. Any such concept of magnitude, as being that of a given infinitude, is empirically impossible, and therefore, in reference to the world as an object of the senses, also absolutely impossible. Nor can I say that the regress from a given perception to all that limits it in a series, whether in space or in past time, proceeds to *infinity*; that would be to presuppose that the world has infinite magnitude. I also cannot say that the regress is *finite*; an absolute limit is likewise empirically impossible" (A520/B548).

This new perspective is another sign that Kant "extended" to concepts pertaining to natural history the principle Vico had limited to his "world of nations."[10] This principle signals a significant departure from the mechanistic perspective idealized in the Cosmology and forces a restructuring of epistemic goals. In the *Critique* nature cannot itself be understood with any great degree of accuracy because "natural appearances are objects which are given to us independently of our concepts" (A480/B508). The study of origins, by contrast, presents the possibility of absolute certainty since they are strictly conceptual entities. This severely limits the claims of what could be labeled geneticism, but does

---

[10] I would indeed argue that the primal intellectual genesis of institutions elaborated by Vico is akin to the claim made in the *Critique of Judgment* that "we have complete insight only into what we can ourselves make and accomplish according to concepts" (*KU* §68), with the important caveats that Kantian concepts are not to be understood genetically and that, except for the primal scene, Vichian ideas are not primary but are motivated by institutions in a process of codetermination.

not dismiss it: "We cannot, therefore, escape by complaints of the narrow limits of our reason, and by confessing, under the pretext of a humility based on self-knowledge, that it is beyond the power of our reason to determine whether the world exists from eternity or has a beginning. . . . All these questions refer to an object which can be found nowhere save in our thoughts" (A481/B509).

Kant's views and methodology on this issue are strikingly similar to James Hutton's, whose perspective is best encapsulated in the famous ending of his *Theory of the Earth*: "We find no vestige of a beginning,—no prospect of an end."[11] As noted by Stephen Jay Gould, Hutton constructed a system that was eminently a priori in character and rested on the twin concepts of a final cause for inanimate objects and a denial of history.[12] Kant was therefore not the only one to set aside the issue of infinity in the 1780s; his epistemic choice regarding not only infinity but also the attendant issues of temporality and causality proceeded in part from the state of scientific knowledge in the late eighteenth century. P. F. Strawson has already pointed out that this also affected the structure of Kant's argument:

> It must have seemed plausible enough at the time at which Kant wrote, though it seems less clear now, that there could never be adequate empirical grounds for opting for either the finite or the infinite alternative in the case of any of the cosmological questions, i.e., that the ideas in question are essentially *transcendent* of any possible experience. . . . By the same token, it would seem entirely reasonable to claim for the idea of the infinite alternative in each case the status of a necessary *directive* or *regulative* idea in science, thus setting ourselves a task of inquiry which we could never declare to be completed.[13]

If the foregoing reading suggests a deep kinship between Kant and Vico regarding the link between the study of origins and the quest for certainty, it also illustrates a major gap between the two thinkers.[14]

[11] James Hutton, *Theory of the Earth*, in *Transactions of the Royal Society of Edinburgh* 1 (1788): 304.

[12] See Gould, *Time's Arrow*, esp. 61–97.

[13] P. F. Strawson, *The Bounds of Sense: An Essay on Kant's "Critique of Pure Reason"* (London: Methuen, 1966), 159.

[14] Another link between the two thinkers that would be worthy of exploration but which I cannot dwell on here also manifests itself in their common reliance on the language of geometry. See, for example, *KrV* Bx–xiii, A87–92/B120–24, A162–66/B202–7, A712–38/B740–66, and A837–44/B865–72. For related discussions on Kant's use of

As we saw in the chapter devoted to the Italian philosopher, Vico's masterstroke consisted in developing a theory of reciprocal determination between institutions and ideas, which allowed him to claim access to "the modifications of our own human mind." This represented one way out of what Kant was to perceive to be the genetic fallacy par excellence. In the *New Science,* there is, therefore, to use Kant's own words in a different context, "an actual object corresponding to the idea" (A482/B510) and hence no genetic fallacy in the sense excoriated by Kant in the *Critique,* since, in the case of the *New Science,* the "object" does not belong to the "world of nature." This made it possible for the Italian philosopher to develop a genuine philosophy of history, but excluded natural history.

By contrast, not only does the *Critique of Pure Reason* focus primarily on the world of nature, it is quite blatantly marked by a desire to denounce the supposedly excessive claims of Locke's "historical method."[15] Indeed, it is hardly coincidental that the preface to the first edition opens with a statement of opposition to Locke and the "fictitious" claims of experimental genealogies, while the second edition of the *Critique* ends with a reference to the English philosopher, "who, after having derived all concepts and principles from experience, goes so far in the use of them as to assert that we can prove the existence of God and the immortality of the soul with the same conclusiveness as any mathematical proposition—though both lie entirely outside the limits of possible experience" (A854–55/B882–83). Kant's own goal in the *Critique* is to answer the question "whether there is any knowledge that is thus independent of the senses" (B2) and to find a priori conditions in which to ground our knowledge in any area. Indeed, the crux of Kant's rejection of the Lockean tradition of experimental genealogies lies in his contention that "though all our knowledge begins with experience, it does not follow that it all arises out

---

geometry from three widely different perspectives, see Brittan, *Kant's Theory,* 68–89; Claudia J. Brodsky, *The Imposition of Form: Studies in Narrative Representation and Knowledge* (Princeton, N.J.: Princeton University Press, 1987), 21–87; and Jaakko Hintikka, "Kant on the Mathematical Method," in *Kant Studies Today,* ed. Lewis White Beck (La Salle, Ill.: Open Court, 1969), esp. 125–40.

[15] Even in the Critique of Aesthetic Judgment, Kant is more concerned with the beautiful in nature than in art (even though purposiveness in nature can only be conceived by analogy to purposiveness in art). See *KrV* A86–87/B118–19 for a discussion of genealogy as "practiced" by Kant's predecessors, including Locke.

of experience" (B1). This is accompanied by a consequent setting aside of a posteriori claims, which would seem to exclude all forms of historical knowledge from the Critical realm. Yet this exclusion is never completed. As is particularly evident in Kant's treatment of causality, apriority and permanence condition temporality, historiography, and a posteriori judgments.

To fully appreciate this, we must start by looking at the relationship between temporality and causality in the Analogies of Experience. On the one hand, Kant eliminates temporal predication from his definition of causality: "Let us take the proposition, 'Everything which happens has its cause.' In the concept of 'something which happens,' I do indeed think an existence which is preceded by a time, etc., and from this concept analytic judgments may be obtained. But the concept of 'cause' lies entirely outside the other concept, and signifies something different from 'that which happens,' and is not therefore in any way contained in this latter representation" (A9/B13). On the other hand, temporality is reinstated in the Second Analogy (A189–211/B232–56), where causality is presented as the condition of our knowledge of succession. In other words, Kant's goal in the Second Analogy is to demonstrate that though the law of cause and effect must not hinge on temporality, "laws allow us to order events causally and the causal order of events allows us to order them in time empirically and objectively."[16] This reverses the Lockean order of things. In the *Essay concerning Human Understanding* our knowledge of succession is not dependent on any a priori principle such as causality, but is derived from the direct observation of our own ideas: "By observing what passes in our Minds, how our *Ideas* there in train constantly some vanish, and others begin to appear, we come by the *Idea* of Succession."[17]

By contrast, in the Second Analogy, succession is not a concept derived from experience but is determined by the necessary law of causality. This does not, however, deny the empirical reality of time (see A30–37/B46–54). Kantian time, Ingeborg Schüssler notes, "is never present or existent [*existant*] except to the extent that an empirical content is present and existent [*existant*] in it."[18] The task of the Second Analogy

---

[16] Brittan, *Kant's Theory*, 173.

[17] John Locke, *An Essay concerning Human Understanding*, ed. Peter H. Nidditch (Oxford: Clarendon Press, 1985), 195.

[18] Ingeborg Schüssler, "Causalité et temporalité dans la *Critique de la raison pure* de Kant," *Archives de Philosophie* 44 (1981): 45.

is therefore partly to distinguish causality from temporality while also making causality a condition of serialization or "eventiality."[19]

As stated in the second edition, the Second Analogy is devoted to proving that "all alterations take place in conformity with the law of the connection of cause and effect" (B232). An essential element of the proof is that "we must derive the *subjective succession* of apprehension from the *objective succession* of appearances" (A193/B238). Apprehension is always subjective and successive. In the case of an inanimate object, the order of succession is arbitrary—though not necessarily irrelevant in that it alerts us to the necessity of sequentiality. In the case of an event, however, that order cannot be reversed and "the *subjective succession* of apprehension," which is also at work in this instance, is determined by an "*objective succession* of appearances" (A193/B238).[20]

In other words, an event exists only as something that is preceded by another event. Hence the need to think serially. In addition, "there must lie in that which precedes an event the condition of a rule according to which this event invariably and necessarily follows. I cannot reverse this order, proceeding back from the event to determine through apprehension that which precedes" (A193–94/B238–39). We cannot, according to Kant, think otherwise and it is this necessity that accounts for the primacy of the law of causality:

> Thus the relation of appearances (as possible perceptions) according to which the subsequent event, that which happens, is, as to its existence, necessarily determined in time by something preceding in conformity with a rule—in other words, the relation of cause to effect—is the condition of the objective validity of our empirical judgments, in respect of the series of perceptions, and so of their empirical truth; that is to say, it is the condition of experience. The principle of the

[19] This insight also indirectly supports Nathan Rotenstreich's argument that one of the key differences between Kant and Vico lies in the understanding of causality. To summarize Rotenstreich's point: Vico's rejection of Descartes's "je pense, donc je suis" on the grounds that I can know only what I have *caused* (or *made*) rests on an essentialist definition of causality. By contrast, Kantian "causality is the principle, not of the emergence of the manifold, but of the regularity of succession and relation within the manifold." Nathan Rotenstreich, "Vico and Kant," in *Giambattista Vico's Science of Humanity*, ed. Giorgio Tagliacozzo and Donald Phillip Verene (Baltimore: Johns Hopkins University Press, 1976), 223.

[20] As Brittan notes, this represents a significant departure from Newtonian mechanics, where "temporal parameters are reversible" (*Kant's Theory*, 175).

causal relation in the sequence of appearances is therefore also valid of all objects of experience ([in so far as they are] under the conditions of succession), as being itself the ground of the possibility of such experience. (A202/B247)

The logical necessity that requires us to assume that an event can be caused only by another event is not a matter of perception but of understanding. In many cases, the *"lapse* of time" itself is irrelevant. The perception of the cause may well follow the perception of the effect. Causality is therefore primary, just as the *"order* of time" is primary vis-à-vis chronicity or the *"lapse* of time" (A203/B248). It is not our experience of things happening in time—historicity—that leads us to discover the concept of cause; it is causality as a pure concept of the understanding that is a priori: "When, therefore, I perceive that something happens, this representation first of all contains [the consciousness] that there is something preceding, because only by reference to what precedes does the appearance acquire its time-relation, namely, that of existing after a preceding time in which it itself was not. But it can acquire this determinate position in this relation of time only in so far as something is presupposed in the preceding state upon which it follows invariably, that is, in accordance with a rule" (A198/B243). In sum, to follow is always to follow according to the rule of cause and effect and experience is possible only because of this concept of the understanding. One might ask why—and reams have been written on the subject—the necessity of serialization has to be identified with causality.[21] After all, in the first edition of the *Critique,* the principle of the Second Analogy did not

[21] Critics generally tend to support the basic thread of Kant's argumentation in the Second Analogy, the most notable exceptions being Prichard, Strawson, and Suchting. For a small but representative sample of the Anglo-American reception of Kant's views on causality, see, in order of publication, H. A. Prichard, *Kant's Theory of Knowledge* (Oxford: Clarendon Press, 1909), esp. 268–307; A. C. Ewing, *Kant's Treatment of Causality* (1924; [Hamden, Conn.]: Archon, 1969), esp. 72–103; D. P. Dryer, *Kant's Solution for Verification in Metaphysics* (London: Allen and Unwin, 1966), esp. 403–46: Strawson, *Bounds of Sense*, esp. 118–52; W. A. Suchting, "Kant's Second Analogy of Experience," in *Kant Studies Today*, ed. Lewis White Beck (La Salle, Ill.: Open Court, 1969), 322–40; Wrynn Smith, "Kant and the General Law of Causality," *Philosophical Studies* 32 (1977): 113–28; Brittan, *Kant's Theory*, esp. 165–87; William A. Harper and Ralf Meerbote, eds., *Kant on Causality, Freedom, and Objectivity* (Minneapolis: University of Minnesota Press, 1984); and Paul Guyer, *Kant and the Claims of Knowledge* (Cambridge: Cambridge University Press, 1987), esp. 237–66. Also see Béatrice Longuenesse, *Kant and the Capacity to Judge: Sensibility and Discursivity in the Transcendental Analytic of the "Critique of Pure Reason"* (Princeton, N.J.: Princeton University Press, 1998), esp. 345–75.

include any reference to causality but simply read: "Everything that happens, that is, begins to be, presupposes something upon which it follows according to a rule" (A189).

Rather than step into this black hole, however, it suffices to note that, as far as Kant is concerned, the appearances of events are always already connected in a time series. This element, which echoes the intense eighteenth-century preoccupation with associationism but tries to ground it in something other than psychology, reflects a desire to serialize the abyss and would certainly seem to set genetic considerations aside. This, however, is only a preliminary gesture. Serialization merely precedes a shift to the other side, an other side henceforth defined by serialization and which it therefore cannot negate. Indeed, even when it is determined that the knowledge of events depends on serialization—not to mention permanence and causality—, Kant still feels the need to account for the ultimate abyss of spontaneous generation, an abyss he hopes to close by introducing the distinction between causality from *freedom* and causality according to *nature* (A532–33/B560–61) and by claiming that the two are not mutually exclusive. This, of course, raises the question of how causality from freedom, or "the power of beginning a state *spontaneously*" (A533/B561), can be reconciled with the earlier connection made between causality and necessity. How do serialization and freedom coexist?

Ultimately the answer hinges on whether one interprets Kant's position as suggesting that there are two radically distinct types of causality (one depending on nature and the other on teleology), or whether one accepts Kant's claim that the two "feed off" each other. Kant's own answer is to introduce a distinction between natural and human events. Indeed, not only is the "eventiality" discussed in the Second Analogy not limited to natural events, but the concept of causality from freedom can only be conceived by analogy with historical events.[22] Causality according to nature involves a certain degree of predictability, which is missing from human events. For instance, if event y takes place on, say, September 11, 2001, I have to assume that it was preceded by an earlier event x. Even more clearly than in the case of a natural event, however, I may not know the exact cause of y, just that there was causality. To stretch the point beyond its Kantian limits, in the case of human

---

[22] See Ralf Meerbote, "Kant on the Nondeterminate Character of Human Actions," in Harper and Meerbote, *Kant on Causality, Freedom, and Objectivity*, 3–19.

events, causality and randomness—hence freedom—are not mutually exclusive. Vico's theory, for instance, that there can be causality from *error*, could be said to be a form of causality from freedom.[23]

To fully appreciate Kant's argument, one would have to deal with his views on morality and the role of the *Critique of Practical Reason* in the architecture of the Critical philosophy. For the purposes of the present discussion, however, we need only recognize a number of key procedural elements. First, by establishing the conditions of knowledge according to nature (according to our understanding) and determining that it depends on serialization, Kant defines the boundaries of geneticism. Having done so, he turns to the realm in which genetic explanations are required. In this case, by distinguishing between causality according to nature and causality from freedom, setting strict epistemic limits to each and making both necessary, Kant intends to retain both types of causality and avoid Humean skepticism and the need to appeal to a "Divine mathematics or metaphysical mechanics" or to inherently self-contradictory concepts such as Leibniz's "ultimate origination."[24] Moreover, since causality from freedom is arrived at by analogy with human events, and since both forms of causality are determined by our understanding, Kant is able to suggest that we cannot think one type of causality without the other. To even try would constitute, in his own words, "a truly disjunctive proposition" (A536/B564). Finally, nature is described as keeping freedom within certain limits (a point that will be crucial to the elaboration of Kant's views on genius in the *Critique of Judgment*). At the same time, however, he introduces the notion that empirical causality may be the effect of an intelligible original causality (A543–45/B571–73). This then leads to the notion that origins do have a reality of their own, though only in the particular sense that time too can be said to be real, that is, "not indeed as object but as the mode of representation of myself as object" (A37/B54). The

---

[23] See Brodsky, *Imposition of Form,* for a discussion of what she calls "the striking marginalization of the problem of error in Kant," (39) which she persuasively interprets as suggesting that "errors in themselves are in no way centrally disruptive of his conception of knowledge" (35).

[24] Gottfried Wilhelm Leibniz, "On the Ultimate Origination of Things. 1697," in *The Monadology and Other Philosophical Writings,* trans. and ed. Robert Latta (New York: Garland, 1985), 342. Kant's views on causality are generally presented, at least in the Anglo-American tradition, in conjunction with Hume's, and only to a lesser extent with Leibniz's. See, for instance, Meerbote and Harper's introduction to *Kant on Causality, Freedom, and Objectivity,* 3–19; and Guyer, *Kant,* 237–38.

reality of origins even proceeds from the nature of time's reality. This, in turn, allows for the inclusion of genetic considerations in certain contexts, which is what will happen in the *Critique of Judgment*.

Before one can reach that point, however, one must note that the reality of time and origins and, with it, the validity of temporal and genetic determinations are grounded in what Kant calls the "original synthetic unity of apperception." This rests in part on the notion that the representation of the cogito "is an act of *spontaneity*, that is, it cannot be regarded as belonging to sensibility" (B132). This original apperception is then linked to a transcendental and a priori "necessary *unity* of apperception" (A177–B220), or, to co-opt a Vichian notion, the definite nature of the cogito. Time determinations proceed from this unity (A177–B219), as do genetic claims.[25]

Depending on the nature of the claim, origins may therefore be considered a legitimate or an illegitimate preoccupation. Although a posteriori claims are not possible in this context, a priori ones are. Translated into a non-Kantian vocabulary, claims pertaining to origins are valid if they are genetic (or theoretical) rather than genealogical (or historical) in kind. This then constitutes Kant's answer to "the veritable abyss" that is "unconditioned necessity" (A613/B641). Causality must occur from both within and without. And though series and origins are antithetical (as are historiography and geneticism), one is no less real (in the sense that time is real for Kant) than the other. Looking at this through a Vichian prism, rather than wistfully maintaining that "freedom is at least *not incompatible with* nature" (A558/B586), we could even say that the two are mutually determinative, which would then make it possible to graft historiography onto genetic epistemology.

In the end, though Kant severely limits the explanatory potential of geneticism, he does not deny it all epistemological validity. Genealogical explanations are not, for instance, precluded by the permanence principle, which functions only at the theoretical level. Moreover, contrary to what would be the case in a traditional empiricist framework, the reality of origins is reminiscent of the hermeneutic principle discussed earlier. The object of the *Critique of Pure Reason* is not antithetical to it but actually proceeds from it. It fits with the notion that Kantian apriority does not rest on a rejection of the thinking subject

---

[25] Within this framework of epistemological limits and possibilities, we can begin to see how even permanence can be viewed as the condition of origins.

since "nothing in *a priori* knowledge can be ascribed to objects save what the thinking subject derives from itself" (Bxxiii), and it is consonant with the necessity for synthetic judgments.

Mechanism and Regression versus Causality and Purpose in the *Critique of Judgment*

Set aside in the *Critique of Pure Reason*, the mechanistic approach so dear to the Enlightenment resurfaces three-quarters of the way through the *Critique of Judgment*. This time, however, it is set against a discursive pattern that is radically different from the weave of the *Universal Natural History*. Indeed, mechanism now functions in the context of a discussion of whether and under what conditions an *"archeology of nature"* is possible. All of a sudden, it is the search for a "common archetype" or a "common original mother" (*KU* §80) that makes mechanistic explanations potentially fruitful. This introduction of archeological motivations is not, however, accompanied by any in-depth consideration of the possibilities of historiography, since mechanism is presented as "necessarily subordinated" to teleology.

Indeed, what the Third Critique and the *Anthropology* make clear is that though there is room for something like an archeology of nature, this type of explanation is preempted by another. Although the "archeologist of nature" ought to look at nature as a mechanism (*KU* §70), "we must regard mechanism as originally subordinated to a cause that acts intentionally" (*KU* §81). A nonmechanistic approach is therefore also needed, one that rests on "the principle of final causes" (*KU* §70). In this context, genetic considerations are subsumed under a preoccupation with both purposiveness and finality. This fits into Kant's distinction between determinative (*bestimmend*) and reflective (*reflektierend*) judgment (see *KU* §IV). Determinative judgment proceeds from the universal to the particular and is suitable to the study of nature's mechanism. The apprehension of origins, by contrast, which depends on the subjective notion of possibility, rests on the principle of final causes, which constitutes an instance of reflective judgment, that is, of judgment from the particular to the universal.[26]

---

[26] See O. Chédin, *Sur l'esthétique de Kant et la théorie critique de la représentation* (Paris: Librairie Philosophique J. Vrin, 1982), 30–32, on the distinction between reflexive and determinative judgment.

This Kantian problematic lies at the heart of the study of origins in the Third Critique. At a mechanistic/determinative level, only regressive analyses are possible, a fact that, as already determined in the *Critique of Pure Reason,* renders any consideration of genetic issues moot. These are eventually not dismissed, however, even though the other option (to redefine causality and introduce a principle of causality according to purpose) would at first glance seem to crowd them out even further. This alternative form of causality is meant to mediate the distinction between causality according to nature and causality from freedom and brings together some of the key elements of the *Critique of Pure Reason* and the stated goals of the *Critique of Judgment.* This mediation, successfully accomplished in the Critique of Aesthetic Judgment, does not, however, dilute the distinctive attributes of causality according to nature and causality from freedom. This is particularly evident in the Critique of Teleological Judgment, where the awareness of the limits of mechanistic explanations for the reality of origins leads at one point to an apparently complete dismissal of geneticism. According to Kant, the limitations of mechanistic explanations suggest that "we must think a causality distinct from mechanism—viz., the causality of an (intelligent) world cause that acts according to purposes. Applied to reflection, this principle is a mere maxim of judgment; and the concept of that causality is a mere idea. We make no claim that this idea has reality, but only use it as a guide for reflection" (*KU* §71). This then results in the conviction that "we must judge certain things in nature (organized beings) and their possibility in terms of the concept of final cause . . . *without presuming to investigate their origin*" (*KU* §72, emphasis added). This position synthesizes the synchronicity inherent in much Enlightenment genetic epistemology and Rousseau's conflation of the origin and the apocalypse. This synthesis occurs through a determination of the need for and limits on a regressive analysis (now linked to mechanism) that builds on the *Critique* but departs from it on the notion of causality.

This recontextualization of causality would seem to leave little room for questions of a genetic nature. It did not, however, preclude the elaboration of a theory of originality, nor did it close the door on the belief that nature can be archeologized. To understand how the concept of causality as elaborated in the *Critique of Judgment* is meant to give a theoretical foundation to the Enlightenment's preoccupation with natural history, we need to look at the nature of the relationship between causality and purpose in the last of Kant's Critical works.

If we follow the Critique of Aesthetic Judgment, a purpose is the object of a concept, which concept is that object's cause. In a reversal of the argument made in the Second Analogy, Kant also specifies that "a causal relation (among objects of experience) can never be cognized otherwise than a posteriori and by means of experience itself" (KU §12). It is not always clear how this can be reconciled with the notion that causality is embedded in purposiveness or even "*forma finalis*" (KU §10). Moreover, the juxtaposition of these two requirements would seem to negate temporality, though one must keep in mind that causality, like purpose, is and is not a temporal concept. Or rather, it is precisely the investigation of the temporal aspect that demands the elaboration of something other than temporality. The a posteriori cognition of causal relationships is a condition of archeology. This observation, in turn, shows the limits of regressive analyses and the need to posit something else, which Kant chooses to call purposiveness.[27]

Historiography is therefore not completely absent from Kant's Critical philosophy; it is evoked both for its own sake and because studying it demonstrates the need to assume that the world is purposive by bringing to the fore the limitations of mechanistic explanations. The archeologist of nature may work from the assumption that the animal world has a "universal mother"; all the same, this assumption would not account for the fathering of the universe itself. Beyond the reality of a common and possibly knowable mother, there remains a final problem: "Once I have determinately stated that certain things are products of divine art, how can I still include them among products of nature, when it was precisely because nature cannot produce such things

[27] Although one must keep in mind Pluhar's warning in "How to Render 'Zweck-mäßigkeit' in Kant's Third Critique" (in *Interpreting Kant*, ed. Moltke S. Gram [Iowa City: University of Iowa Press, 1982], 85–98)) that the recourse to what Pluhar calls a "finality terminology" rather than a "purposiveness terminology" to translate the concepts of *Zweck* and *Zweckmäßigkeit* has generally been a major source of confusion in Kantian scholarship, one must not forget that purposiveness and finality are sometimes linked in the *Critique of Judgment*, as the above discussion shows. Indeed, I generally agree with Jean-François Lyotard's statement that "Kant's emphasis on judgment . . . indicates a reversal of the problematic of the origin in favor of the question of ends." *L'enthousiasme: La critique kantienne de l'histoire* (Paris: Galilée, 1986), 17–18n3. Let me specify, however, that this reversal involves the telescoping or conflating of two concepts that are not always defined in temporal terms. In addition, I would suggest that the reversal is not so much between questions of origins and questions of ends as between a priori knowledge of causality in the First Critique and a posteriori judgments of causality in the Third Critique, and between two kinds of causal connections, one "efficient" and the other "final" (see KU §65).

in terms of its [own] laws that I had to appeal to a cause distinct from it?" (*KU* §74). Without the introduction of causality and purposiveness, we are restricted to a regressive analysis that can never be completed.

This fact affects even Kant's optimistic prediction that we can discover a principle of production in the field of "comparative anatomy," a field that includes the history of the earth as well as of the species. As the following passage makes clear, Kant's views on species bear only a superficial resemblance to those now current: "He [the archeologist of nature] can make mother earth (like a large animal, as it were) emerge from her state of chaos, and make her lap promptly give birth initially to creatures of a less purposive form, with these then giving birth to others that became better adapted to their place of origin and to their relations to one another, until in the end this womb itself rigidified, ossified, and confined itself to bearing definite species that would no longer degenerate, so that the diversity remained as it had turned out when that fertile formative force ceased to operate" (*KU* §80). Indeed, Kant's "comparative anatomy" does not yield a theory of evolution in the Darwinian or even Lamarckian sense.[28] Faced with a choice between epigenesis, in which an organic being is seen as a product of another being of the same kind that gives it its form, and evolution, in which the new organic being is an educt, that is, something with an absolutely predetermined form, Kant chooses epigenesis. This presents a number of advantages. Unlike the theory of evolution described above, which rests on the notion of preformation and forces one to go back to origins ("as if it made a difference whether they had these forms of supernatural origin come about at the beginning of the world or in the course of it"; *KU* §81), epigenesis does not depend on a genetic analysis. New characters can be developed at any point in time while the original stock, which is permanent, remains unaffected. Epigenesis therefore leaves out the need to account for a number of first beginnings. By contrast, a theory of evolution would seem to require a regressive genetic epistemology, which Kant long dismissed as an impossibility and a contradiction in terms. Even at the heart of what would seem to cry out for a linearly regressive explanation, Kant chooses precisely the theoretical explanation that limits as much as possible the need for genetic

---

[28] For a review of key eighteenth-century views on the history of man and species in the context of natural history and social theory, see Greene, *Death of Adam*, esp. 175–247.

considerations. Instead, epigenesis reconciles the requirements of mechanism and purposiveness. It limits appeals to supernatural explanations to the first beginning; every other occurrence is a product of nature and is potentially accountable mechanistically. This can, in turn, be achieved only within a framework of purposiveness. Randomness (or "occasionalism") is not an acceptable alternative because it would mean that we could not hope to discover rules of organic formation and would have to give up on "comparative anatomy."

This development puts even more severe limitations on the explanatory potential of genetic epistemology than was the case in the *Critique of Pure Reason.* Necessary though mechanical explanations may be, they are never fully attuned to the need to account for nature itself. Mechanism and geneticism are therefore kept apart, a separation that much of the eighteenth century had tried to bridge or ignore. Hence Kant's reminder that "it is beyond our reason's grasp how this reconciliation of two wholly different kinds of causality is possible: the causality of nature in its universal lawfulness, with [the causality of] an idea that confines nature to a particular form for which nature itself contains no basis whatsoever" (*KU* §81). In the *Critique of Judgment*, it is then precisely the archeologist of nature who highlights for us the limitations inherent in historiography and "the character of our understanding and of our reason is such that the only way we can conceive of the origin of such [natural] beings is in terms of final causes" (*KU* §82). Hence the need, for Kant, for a "moral teleology," which "compensates for the deficiency of *physical* teleology and for the first time supplies a basis for a *theology*" (*KU* §86).

The movement from an awareness of the unbridgeable gap between historiography and geneticism to the positing of an ethical postulate is not as unidirectional as the preceding argument would seem to suggest, however. Not only does causality through purposes in nature not have any objective reality "for reason is quite unable to prove the concept of a natural purpose, i.e., that it has objective reality" (*KU* §74), but in the *Critique of Judgment* it is generally posited by analogy with causality through purpose in art (see, for example, *KU* §§V, VIII, and 68). To paraphrase Kant, what gives the rule to ethics is indeed aesthetics as much as the realization that, since mechanistic explanations cannot encompass the origin, we need to posit something outside mechanism and history. That something is purposiveness, of which the most exemplary instance is originality. Antithetical to the spirit of imitation, it provides a complementary alternative to regressive thought and a criterion of judgment that emphasizes the product rather than the educt.[29]

AESTHETICIZING THE PARAMETERS:
CAUSALITY FROM ORIGINALITY

Kant's analysis of originality is not extensive, covering only a handful of pages in the *Critique of Judgment*. In some superficial respects, his views are not particularly original themselves, but are clearly derived from the ravings of the 1770s, to which Kant was perhaps not quite as hostile as John H. Zammito has recently claimed.[30] Like his predecessors, Kant contrasts originality to imitation and sees it as the necessary attribute of genius. Yet in the Third Critique these views acquire a new resonance as Kant uses them to redefine nature's primacy.

Kant's theory of genius centers on the notion that nature is not the mind's referent, a position that proceeds from a desire to be rid of the twin tyrannies of empiricism and associationism.[31] This, however, leaves genius's productions open to the charge of nonsense. To circumvent this, Kant introduces the claim that genius is exemplary. In this case, genius's legitimacy rests on what I would call, by analogy with Kant's own causality according to nature and causality from freedom, causality from or according to originality.

Causality from/according to originality emphasizes production over reproduction. This is potentially troublesome because it would seem to condemn judgment to a perpetual forward deferral (since originality and exemplariness can be appreciated only in hindsight). To free aesthetic judgment from the backward-looking secondariness of

[29] See Pluhar's definitions: "To *produce* (which means, even literally, to 'bring forth') something includes giving it its form; to *educe* something is merely to 'bring out' something that already has a (predetermined) form" (*KU* 250n31).
[30] John H. Zammito, *The Genesis of Kant's "Critique of Judgment"* (Chicago: University of Chicago Press, 1992), 8–44.
[31] For a review of eighteenth-century aesthetic uses of the concept of association of ideas, especially in literary theory, see Walter Jackson Bate, *From Classic to Romantic: Premises of Taste in Eighteenth-Century England* (New York: Harper and Row, Harper Torchbook, 1961), esp. 93–128; Ralph Cohen, "Association of Ideas and Poetic Unity," *Philological Quarterly* 36 (1957): 465–74; Wallace Jackson, *The Probable and the Marvelous: Blake, Wordsworth, and the Eighteenth-Century Critical Tradition* (Athens: University of Georgia Press, 1978); and Martin Kallich, *The Association of Ideas and Critical Theory in Eighteenth-Century England: A History of a Psychological Method in English Criticism* (The Hague: Mouton, 1970).

the mimetic tradition is indeed not enough. There still has to be some method whereby the mind's ability to produce can be gauged in the here and now while also satisfying the criterion of universality. In an attempt to frustrate the deferral of judgment implicit in the concept of originality, Kant therefore reintroduces nature in the guise of the twin concepts of permanence and presence. This is nature redefined, however; what is at stake here is nature in the artist, not an external point of reference, which, the First Critique had already established, has no knowable reality and whose beauty can henceforth be understood only by analogy with artistic beauty.

Let us consider this process in greater detail, beginning with the notion that originality represents an opportunity for Kant to distance himself once again from the empiricist tradition represented by Locke. Genius offers one clear example of "freedom from the law of association" (*KU* §49), the principle that had dominated eighteenth-century thought from Condillac to Smith, to name but two of Locke's followers. Although the equation between association and regress had not been foreseen by Locke, it was inescapable for Kant, who needed to specify that one can have recourse to associationist types of explanations only under specific epistemic conditions, conditions that do not adequately allow us to conceptualize genius and originality. Kant's views on these two criteria of aesthetic judgment are perfect examples of the limitations of associationism and experimentalism. By defining genius as "the exemplary originality of a subject's natural endowment in the *free* use of his cognitive powers" (*KU* §49), Kant appealed to something other than regression and experience, "something that surpasses nature" (*KU* §49) yet is still natural: "The imagination ([in its role] as a productive cognitive power) . . . creates, as it were, another nature out of the material that actual nature gives it. . . . We may even restructure experience; and though in doing so we continue to follow analogical laws, yet we also follow principles which reside higher up, namely, in reason (and which are just as natural to us as those which the understanding follows in apprehending empirical nature)" (*KU* §49).

Again and again, the *Critique of Judgment* illustrates the notion that aesthetic ideas are ideal instances of our ability not to be limited by nature or our experience. The opposition to Locke is particularly evident in Kant's discussion of the sublime, which "must not be sought in things of nature, but must be sought solely in our ideas" (*KU* §25). It also manifests itself in the notion that implicit in any aesthetic judgment is the expectation that all others will assent—though they may not actually do so (*KU* §§8, 38). There is indeed, according to Kant, a "presumed necessity" of aesthetic judgments, which "lifts them out of [the reach of] empirical psychology, in which they would otherwise remain buried among the feelings of gratification and pain (accompanied only by the empty epithet of being a *more refined* feeling)" (*KU* §29).

On what grounds is this necessity justified? According to the argument put forward in the Third Critique, two related conditions of aesthetic judgment must be fulfilled. First, aesthetic judgment must be disinterested or free (*KU* §§1–8) even though "what is merely subjective in the presentation of an object, i.e., what constitutes its reference to the subject and not to the object, is its aesthetic character" (*KU* §VII). Second, it must be universally communicable. These conditions are buttressed by a link between moral and aesthetic considerations. This link affects not only the condition that aesthetic judgment be free, but also that it be universal. As Kenneth F. Rogerson notes, *muten* and *fordern* are used interchangeably in the Third Critique, in the context both of epistemological claims and of appeals to morality. This, as Rogerson persuasively argues, can be taken to indicate that "a legitimate demand for agreement *is* just what Kant means by the universality of judgments of taste, and this demand is not different from the one supported by morality."[32]

This identity between the presumption of universal agreement and moral exaction corroborates—and is corroborated by—Kant's claim that genius is primarily "productive" rather than "eductive." The same "identity" that can be seen between practical and aesthetic demands exists between the power of desire and the requirement of exemplariness that Kant associates with originality: "Since nonsense too can be original, the products of genius must also be models, i.e., they must be *exemplary*; hence, though they do not themselves arise through imitation, still they must serve others for this, i.e., as a standard or rule by which to judge" (*KU* §46). This, in turn, allows us to speak of a "causality from originality" by analogy with Kant's own "causality from freedom."

Causality from originality shifts the focus away from mimetic theories and toward the ability to project. In matters of genius we are, according to Kant, dealing with expectations rather than imitations

---

[32] Kenneth F. Rogerson, "The Meaning of Universal Validity in Kant's Aesthetics," *Journal of Aesthetics and Art Criticism* 40 (1982): 305.

or memories, *Vorstellung* rather than *Form, Vor-stellungen* rather than re-presentations, productions rather than reproductions. Originality, "the foremost property of genius" (*KU* §46), sets aside the very usefulness and sense of the past since its gauge is exemplariness, that is, genius's ability to generate future productions. Or rather, genius will generate the means by which communication can be established. Future geniuses will, once again, owe their productions only to their genius. Earlier examples do not give the rules for future production, except in the case of lesser artists, whose work is but a gloss that relies on the "vocabulary" generated by original works.

An evaluative problem remains. As the attribute of a work of art, originality is recognizable only *après coup*. At that point, however, its originality is gone or meaningless, or rather, only exemplariness remains. One therefore needs to find a way of anchoring originality in the present rather than subject it to perpetual deferral. Since the work of genius loses its originality precisely at the point when its originality is perceived and it becomes open to judgments of taste, that is, becomes part of the canon and hence the past, this quality must have another point of origin, which for Kant will be, yes, the producer, but more precisely, nature in the artist. Not only is genius precisely what is not determined by the past, it is "nature in the subject . . . that gives the rule to art" (*KU* §46). Even geniuses themselves cannot account for their production "since talent is an innate productive ability of the artist and as such belongs itself to nature" (*KU* §46). Having redefined nature in sensual—that is, aesthetic—terms, Kant is eventually free to reintroduce it as the ground and anchor of the *Originalgenie*. This enables him to avoid both referentiality and solipsism.

This development gave a new foundation to the concept of originality. In Germany, the discussion had petered out, as we saw, in part because the parameters of the debate had been limited to an either/or formulation: either originality or tradition, either nonsense or sense, either nature or genius. Kant conceptualized originality so as to free it from endlessly referring either backward or forward. First, he weaned it from the past by stressing productivity. Then, he anchored the future in the present of nature's permanence.[33] Exemplariness may well be

---

[33] Although my use of the term *regress* always occurs in the context of serialization and linearity, I basically agree with Rudolf A. Makkreel's distinction between "cosmological regress"—closer to my own usage and which Makkreel sees as applying primarily to the *Critique of Pure Reason*—and what he calls the "regress of the imagination

"unnatural" and genius may well have nothing in common with the spirit of imitation, but genius is nevertheless "innate" and a product of nature. In this instance, however, we are dealing with a "nature methodized" by genius itself. Nature must here be understood primarily as a temporal entity; it corresponds to the present value of what will be perceivable only in the future. In the process, the future becomes a function of inner sense while nature and time ("the form of inner sense" according to the *Critique of Pure Reason*; A33–B49) become indistinguishable.

Kant's definition of originality accounts for his preference for *Originalität* over *Eigentümlichkeit*. The latter term is used only once, and in the derogatory sense of originality for its own sake, that is, without exemplariness.[34] This choice does not just underline Kant's attempt to avoid solipsism and idiosyncrasy, but also emphasizes the peculiar redefinition of temporality that occurs in the theorization of originality. Although it emphasizes production and hence, it would seem, the future, originality ultimately enables Kant to eliminate temporality (in its linear acceptation) altogether. The past is of little value while the future can be recollapsed into the present. Eventually, however, temporality is reintroduced in the guise of communicability, the interplay between producer and consumer where the twin demands of exemplariness and judgment are met.

The artist of genius may well be defined as the author (*Urheber*) through whom nature—rather than tradition—speaks, but he is hardly passive. It may be that "an author owes a product to his genius" (*KU* §46), which is itself a product of nature, but nature itself—and, eventually, the rules of communicability—are redefined by the "authoring." This accounts for some of the apparent paradoxes to be found in Kant's discussion

---

in the sublime." In the latter case, linearity implodes, as it were, or, in Makkreel's words: "The regress of the imagination in the sublime does not involve a temporal synthesis; it is instantaneous." *Imagination and Interpretation in Kant: The Hermeneutical Import of the "Critique of Judgment"* (Chicago: University of Chicago Press, 1990), 80. See also Makkreel's "Imagination and Temporality in Kant's Theory of the Sublime," *Journal of Aesthetics and Art Criticism* 42 (1983/84): 303–15.

34 "*Mannerism* is a different kind of aping; it consists in aping mere *peculiarity* (originality) as such, so as to distance oneself as far as at all possible from imitators, yet without possessing the talent needed to be *exemplary* as well" ("Das *Manieriren* ist eine andere Art von Nachäffung, nämlich der bloßen *Eigenthümlichkeit* [Originalität] überhaupt, um sich ja von Nachahmern so weit als möglich zu entfernen, ohne doch das Talent zu besitzen, dabei zugleich *musterhaft* zu sein"; KU §49; *Gesammelte Schriften*, 5:318).

of the sublime.[35] On the one hand, *"Sublime is what even to be able to think proves that the mind has a power surpassing any standard of sense"* (*KU* §25); it "must not be sought in things of nature, but must be sought solely in our ideas" (*KU* §25). On the other, "the sublime *in art* is always confined to the conditions that [art] must meet to be in harmony with nature" (*KU* §23, emphasis added).[36] This primacy of nature is not, however, accompanied by any praise of painting. Indeed, it is in poetry, the least "mimetic" of all arts, "that the power [i.e., faculty] of aesthetic ideas can manifest itself to full extent" (*KU* §49). It relies on the most human of constructs, language, which enables it to surpass sense, yet it is not nonsense since nature speaks through genius (see *KU* §53).

Similarly, originality consists precisely in the "freedom from the constraint of rules" (*KU* §49) and of the past—but not from the constraint of the future (via exemplariness) or of nature. It allows one to go beyond the hope expressed in the *Critique of Pure Reason* that "freedom is at least *not incompatible with* nature" (A558–B586) and to claim that, in this one instance at least, freedom *cannot* be incommensurate with nature. Originality is a break from the past, but not from being or becoming. By demonstrating, via the conceptualization of originality, that the imagination can be productive, the Critique of Aesthetic Judgment is able to annul in at least one instance the demands of mechanism and regression. It is in this sense that aesthetic judgment is more than just an afterthought, or even a mediating point. It does not just mediate causality according to nature and causality from freedom but validates them and indicates the possibility of generation without association.

---

[35] I will not be comparing Kant's treatment of the sublime with his conceptualization of the beautiful. An excellent introduction to this issue can be found in Caygill, *Art of Judgement*, 320–47.

[36] For a discussion of the ties between theories of original genius and the sublime, see Samuel Holt Monk's classic study, *The Sublime: A Study of Critical Theories in XVIII-Century England* (Ann Arbor: University of Michigan Press, 1960), esp. 101–33. More generally, the sublime has undergone something of a revival in recent years. Key recent texts that focus on the Kantian sublime include Jean-François Courtine et al., *Du sublime* (Paris: Belin, 1988), translated as *Of the Sublime: Presence in Question* by Jeffrey S. Librett (Albany: State University of New York Press, 1993); Paul Crowther, *The Kantian Sublime: From Morality to Art* (Oxford: Clarendon Press, 1989); Thomas Huhn, "The Kantian Sublime and the Nostalgia for Violence," *Journal of Aesthetics and Art Criticism* 53 (Summer 1995): 269–75; Jean-François Lyotard, *Le différend* (Paris: Minuit, 1983), translated as *The Differend: Phrases in Dispute* by Georges Van Den Abbeele (Minneapolis: University of Minnesota Press, 1988), and *Leçons sur l'Analytique du sublime (Kant, "Critique de la faculté de juger," §§23–29)* (n.p.: Galilée, 1991), translated as *Lessons on the Analytic of the Sublime: Kant's "Critique of Judgment," §§23–29* (Stanford, Ca.: Stanford University Press, 1994).

The imagination plays a crucial role here. To put things as concisely as possible, let me follow in this particular case the argument made by Kant in the *Anthropology*.[37] In this work, Kant specifies that the imagination "cannot bring forth a sense representation that was *never* given to the power of sense" (*Anthropology*, §28). Yet, "as a power of [producing] intuitions even when the object is not present, imagination (*facultas imaginandi*) is either *productive* or *reproductive*—that is, either a power of exhibiting an object originally and so prior to experience (*exhibitio originaria*), or a power of exhibiting it in a derivative way, by bringing back to mind an empirical intuition we have previously had (*exhibitio derivata*)" (*Anthropology*, §28). The imagination, though dependent on the senses, is nevertheless able to function in at least one capacity independent of experience, that is, it is able to generate concepts, a capacity without which experience would be impossible. In other words, concepts are not motivated by experience but are legitimized by the role of the imagination as defined in the Third Critique (and the *Anthropology*).

Nowhere is this more obvious than in Kant's notion that "if originality of imagination (as distinguished from imitative production) harmonizes with concepts, it is called *genius*" (*Anthropology*, §30). Originality also reinforces the primacy of poetry, defined as nonmimetic or conceptual painting: "Only the painter of *Ideas* is the master of fine art" (*Anthropology*, §71). Sight may be "the noblest of the senses" (*Anthropology*, §19) as it "comes closest to a *pure intuition*" (*Anthropology*, §19), but it cannot compete with the imagination in its productive capacity.

In the Third Critique the rationale behind the possibility of originality becomes the model for causality according to nature and from freedom. This sheds new light on the remarks made early in this chapter regarding the role of the imagination in the framing of hypotheses. We see more clearly now why, as Butts correctly underlined, Kant insisted in the First Critique that it is "necessary to deal with hypotheses as functions of the *imagination*."[38] This realization allows us to deal swiftly

---

[37] For fuller discussions of Kant's treatment of the imagination, in both the First and Third Critiques, see O. Chédin, *Sur l'esthétique de Kant;* Rudolf Makkreel, *Imagination and Interpretation in Kant;* and Eva Schaper, *Studies in Kant's Aesthetics* (Edinburgh: Edinburgh University Press, 1979). For a discussion of the nature and extent of interpolations between the *Anthropology* and the Kantian corpus, including the critical works, see Frederick P. van de Pitte, *Kant as Philosophical Anthropologist* (The Hague: Nijhoff, 1971), esp. 1–6, 14–16, and 108–16.

[38] Butts, "Hypothesis," 159.

with the frequent misconception that Kant's aesthetics and the structure of the Critical philosophy reinforce the primacy of nature over that of the poet. This case is often made on the basis of Kant's injunction that, should a conflict arise between genius and either sense or lawfulness, genius must be sacrificed to taste (*KU* §50), which is interpreted as "depreciating" originality and reinstating the primacy of nature over judgment, and by extension, of the First over the Third Critique.

Two preliminary points need to be made on this issue. First of all, it is not clear why such a sacrifice should ever have to be made. After all, since genius is exemplary by definition (*KU* §46; *Anthropology*, §57), there can never be any need to sacrifice it on the grounds it is nonsensical. Second, one should not assume that what holds for originality is also true for judgment. Although genius and its attendant characteristics of originality and exemplariness involve a denial of the past, it does not follow that Kant is a "naturalist" or a "primitivist." Like the imagination, aesthetic judgment can be both productive and reflexive or secondary. Although the artist's "natural endowment must give the rule to (fine) art, . . . the rule must be abstracted from what the artist has done, i.e., from the product, which others may use to test their own talent, letting it serve them as their model, not to be *copied* [*Nachmachung*] but to be *imitated* [*Nachahmung*]" (*KU* §47).[39] In any case, judgment's ability to recognize exemplariness underlines that, though Kant's aesthetics does proceed in part from a desire to bracket the past, it does not annul the past, but recognizes its ineradicability and its role in the process of communicability. When Kant cautions that "if there is a conflict between these two properties [taste and genius] in a product, and something has to be sacrificed, then it should rather be on the side of genius" (*KU* §50), he does not renege on his validation of originality. On the contrary, causality from/according to originality forces one to reemphasize tradition. After all, the study of models becomes even more crucial once one cannot hope to know the rules of their production.

In the end, Kant's statement that "fine art would seem to require *imagination, understanding, spirit,* and *taste*" (*KU* §50) does more than demonstrate the philosopher's affinity with the dominant eighteenth-century views on aesthetics. It illustrates his success in synthesizing

---

[39] See Martin Gammon, " 'Exemplary Originality': Kant on Genius and Imitation," *Journal of the History of Philosophy* 35 (1997): 563–92, on the concepts used by Kant in conjunction with the notion of imitation and on their genealogy.

Enlightenment aesthetics and overcoming the dilemma it had faced when conceptualizing originality. Being nature's elect no longer cuts the *Originalgenie* off from society because his conceptualizations become rules. By making exemplariness a criterion of originality, Kant reintroduces communicability and tradition. Communicability, Pope's criterion,[40] is not jettisoned but rather linked to originality. The past, never dismissed but merely suspended for the sake of argument, is hereby reinstated. This is not utterly surprising, though it is at times disconcerting. The causality of originality is, after all, a by-product of causality from freedom, which was in turn conceived only by analogy with historical events.[41]

Having celebrated genius and originality, Kant can then turn around and pay tribute to the classics: "Only those models can become classical which are written in the ancient, dead languages, now preserved only as scholarly languages" (*KU* §47). This is not accompanied by any despondent or primitivist looking back. The classics must be studied, not for their own sake, but because they can help latecomers "adopt their own and often better course" (*KU* §32). These statements are commonplaces of Enlightenment aesthetics. In the context of the Third Critique, however, they emphasize the fact that Kant glorified neither "the state of nature" nor nature itself, but nature in me, thereby redefining the parameters of the debate on originality and nature. In the process he was able to subsume a haphazard tradition under the requirement of universality.

We can therefore dispense with the usual caveat that the *Critique of Judgment* focuses primarily on nature rather than art, the beautiful rather than the sublime. Art and nature are not antithetical; the latter can be understood only in reference to the former, just as "the sublime is the counterpoise but not the contrary of the beautiful. It is the counterpoise because our effort and attempt to rise to a grasp (*apprehensio*) of the object awakens in us a feeling of our own greatness and strength; but [it is not the contrary of the beautiful because] when the sublime is *described* or exhibited, its representation in thought can and must always be beautiful" (*Anthropology*, §68). Similarly, though our interest in nature is "morally" superior to an interest in art (*KU* §42), the purposiveness

---

[40] Although there are no references to Pope in the *Critique of Judgment*, the *Epistle of Man* is frequently quoted in the *Allgemeine Naturgeschichte*.

[41] In the *Anthropology* Kant even draws a rare parallel between natural and civil history (§39). See epigraph to the present chapter.

of nature is conceived only by analogy with art. One would be wrong to interpret Kant's statement that "a natural beauty is a *beautiful thing*; artistic beauty is a *beautiful presentation* of a thing" (*KU* §48) to mean that natural beauty is superior to artistic beauty. Indeed, the paragraph that immediately follows this proposition makes the conceptual primacy of aesthetic judgment abundantly clear: "In order to judge a natural beauty to be that, I need not have a prior concept of what kind of thing the object is [meant] to be; i.e., I do not have to know its material purposiveness (its purpose). Rather, I like the mere form of the object when I judge it, on its own account and without knowing the purpose. But if the object is given as a product of art, and as such is to be declared beautiful, then we must first base it on a concept of what the thing is [meant] to be, since art always presupposes a purpose in the cause (and its causality)" (*KU* §48). As a result, Kant's frequent use of the word "presentation" in connection with natural things is no contradiction, but emphasizes that judgments pertaining to the beautiful in nature are legitimized by our ability to make judgments on the beautiful in art. I know a beautiful thing only because I can conceptualize a beautiful presentation of a thing. In addition, not only is beauty "the symbol of morality" (*KU* §59), but the modalities of this analogy depend on a conceptualization of aesthetic judgment, that is, a conceptualization, not of a beautiful thing, but of a beautiful presentation of a thing.[42] This explains in part why the concept of genius dominates the Critique of Aesthetic Judgment, as the heading of section 46, "Fine Art Is the Art of Genius," makes clear, and why the *Critique of Judgment* opens with the Critique of Aesthetic Judgment and not with the Critique of Teleological Judgment. The former analogically provides the latter with the grid that makes it possible to investigate nature by providing purposive causal explanations when regressive genetic explanations prove inadequate (see *KU* §§61 and 65). This development confirms the hermeneutic principle Kant had affirmed in the *Critique of Pure Reason* and which he reiterated in the *Critique of Judgment*: "We have complete insight only into what we can ourselves make and accom-

---

[42] Kant is particularly blunt on this point in part 2 of the *Anthropology*: "Man is destined by his reason to live in a society with men and in it to *cultivate* himself, to *civilize* himself, and to make himself *moral* by the arts and sciences" (*Anthropology*, 186). See Ted Cohen, "Why Beauty Is a Symbol of Morality," in *Essays in Kant's Aesthetics*, ed. Ted Cohen and Paul Guyer (Chicago: University of Chicago Press, 1982), 221–36; and Terry Eagleton, *The Ideology of the Aesthetic* (Cambridge, Mass.: Basil Blackwell, 1990), 78–84.

plish according to concepts" (*KU* §68). This also delineates the respective roles of mechanism and geneticism, which, in the end, are not mutually exclusive:

> The character of our understanding and of our reason is such that the only way we can conceive of the origin of such beings [organic natural beings] is in terms of final causes. And hence we are certainly permitted to strive as hard and even as boldly as possible to explain such beings mechanically. Indeed, reason calls on us to make this attempt, even though we know that there are subjective grounds why we can never make do with a mechanical explanation, grounds that have to do with the particular kind and limitation of our understanding (and not with any intrinsic contradiction between a mechanical production and an origin in terms of purposes). (*KU* §82)

The proposition that judgments pertaining to the beautiful in nature can be arrived at only by analogy with the beautiful in art is not unproblematic. It accounts for the presence of such apparent paradoxes as "subjective universal" (*KU* §22), "free lawfulness of the imagination" (*KU* §22), and "purposive play of the imagination" (*KU* §22). The frequently quoted "lawfulness without law" and "purposiveness without purpose" obviously also belong to this category. An interpretation limited to the Third Critique could emphasize that no conflation is involved here and that this oxymoronic tension only exemplifies the particular role of judgment in Kant's Critical philosophy, as "a mediating link between understanding and reason" (*KU*, preface to the first edition, 1790), that is, between freedom and necessity, including purpose and mechanism. The ability to originate in art demonstrates the limits of mechanical regressive explanations for works of nature. One might add that it merely reflects a duality between taste and genius that was intricately woven into the fabric of eighteenth-century aesthetics. Any reading, no matter how justified, that limited itself to the Third Critique would be too narrow, however. There is in the Critical philosophy as a whole a refusal to jettison one element of an antinomy in favor of the other, a tendency to let them be concurrent and even interdependent. Nature and freedom, for instance, are concurrent, just as mechanism and theo/teleology were already interdependent in the *Universal Natural History*. Paradoxes are indeed not limited to the *Critique of Judgment*. The concept of a priori synthetic unity, for example, is, as we discussed earlier, an intrinsic part of the epistemic pattern of the *Critique of Pure Reason,* which also brings together permanence and origins. Could it be that the seemingly heterogeneous nature of these and other Kantian concepts are somehow essential to the successful elaboration of the Critical works?

Lyotard has correctly recognized that the Third Critique merely "dramatizes" heterogeneity: "In the Introduction to the Third Critique, the dispersion of families of sentences is not only recognized, but dramatized to the point where the problem posed is that of finding 'passages' (*Übergänge*) between these kinds of heterogeneous sentences."[43] These passages reveal the incommensurability of the different groups into which concepts are organized—yet these *Übergänge* are also necessary. The particular brilliance of Kant's aesthetics is that it emphasizes the need to let heterogeneity and synthesis coexist.[44] At the same time, as Derrida contends, the recognition of heterogeneity opens an abyss that no analogy can bridge.[45] However, in the *Critique of Judgment,* Kant is no longer trying to "economize on the abyss" ("faire l'économie de l'abîme").[46] Such a contention should be limited only to cosmological inquiries as delineated in the *Critique of Pure Reason.* In the aesthetic mode, analogical passages—such as the concepts of genius and the sublime—attempt not to bridge the abyss but to emphasize heterogeneity and thereby "*maintain* the abyss."[47] As we have just seen, heterogeneity allows for the coexistence of questions pertaining to both mechanism and originality. It is deliberately supported by Kant's recourse to analogical reasoning, which underscores the failure of associationism. Not only are analogies inherently heterogeneous, the analogical law is antecedent to experience, just as judgment precedes the concept.[48]

[43] Lyotard, *Enthousiasme,* 32.

[44] Ibid., 42–43.

[45] Jacques Derrida, *The Truth in Painting,* trans. Geoff Bennington and Ian McLeod (Chicago: University of Chicago Press, 1987), 35–36; *La vérité en peinture* (Paris: Flammarion, 1978), 42–44.

[46] Derrida, *Truth in Painting,* 37; *Vérité en peinture,* 44.

[47] Referring to Kant's comparison between different forms of government and his discussion of the shifts in representation that obtain when one moves from a monarchical to a republican system, Lyotard points to another analogy: "One can see that one must not be mistaken about this *Repräsentativität,* which is not at all a *Vorstellung,* but the name of a 'passage' between two families of heterogeneous sentences, which is used as a marker of their heterogeneity and therefore as a means of maintaining the abyss that exists between them" (*Enthousiasme,* 106–7).

[48] "L'antériorité du jugement sur le concept" is the touchstone of Chédin's *Sur l'esthétique de Kant* (129).

Risking collapse, but buttressed on every side by claims of universality and commonality, Kant's edifice is precariously poised over the abyss. Its fleeting equilibrium is laid bare by the origin, a concept that forces a recognition of heterogeneity and an aestheticization of knowledge. And if the Kantian pose seems both too restrictive and too permissive, at least it resists the temptation to synthesize the antinomies away and erase the abyss without falling into the exclusionary trap of an either/or proposition. In the end, Kant's achievement rests in part on his redefinition of authorship and authority and his allocation of a foundational role to aesthetics in his Critical philosophy. Originality negatively demonstrates the primacy of judgment while the imagination in its productive capacity functions independent of experience.

Postscript

Part of the difficulty we encounter when dealing with the Enlightenment stems from our tendency to impose current definitions of words
such as *nature, cause,* or *origin* on a deceptively familiar episteme and
filter through what I have come to view as our own epistemic paucity
an almost inconceivable flowering of approaches to knowledge we have
since elected to see—and in some cases dismiss—as heterogeneous.
Methodological approaches coexisted in the eighteenth century that
were later segregated or considered to be mutually exclusive, two forms
of epistemological retrenchment we now scramble to undo, in part
by being self-consciously interdisciplinary.

When one looks at pre-eighteenth-century preoccupations with origins, it becomes clear that, far from consolidating an episteme that was
to become ours by a process of exclusion or a narrowing down earlier discursive possibilities, the eighteenth century was characterized by a volatile
explosion of the sayable. It is as though, giddy from the possibilities offered
by the major epistemic restructuring of the seventeenth century, Western
thought experienced a century or so of epistemological luxuriance before
streamlining itself down to fighting capacity. A brief comparative review
of some of the key features of Vico's and Kant's stands on the limits and
possibilities of human epistemology and of their implications for the
nature of genetic claims highlights this discursive pluralism as well as
some core configurations of Enlightenment genetic epistemology.

Without undue violence, Vico's and Kant's hermeneutics can be narrowed down to a triad of connected propositions: a) human knowledge

is grounded in ignorance; b) we must nevertheless delineate the conditions under which certain knowledge is conceivable; and c) we can know only our own constructs. In the *New Science* the initial movement of consciousness was generated by a first instance of the "Vichian slip," which in Vico's system accounts for the human beginnings of the world of nations.[1] In the Third Critique, as Macmillan already recognized, "the whole teleological procedure is due to a defect in our intelligence"; causality and purposiveness in nature are mere postulates, conceived by analogy with practical purposiveness and the "technical" use of reason.[2] This instance, however, is but an extreme consequence of Kant's basic hermeneutic principle, namely, that "reason has insight only into that which it produces after a plan of its own."[3]

This shared premise rests in part on unmistakably religious underpinnings of which one finds traces in other works by Vico and Kant. In *De antiquissima* Vico stated that "human science was born of the vice of our mind, specifically from its extremely narrow compass, in that it is outside of everything and does not contain what it affects to know, and because it does not contain them, it does not actualize the truths it aims at. The most certain sciences are those that wash away the blemish of their origin and that become similar to divine science through their creative activity inasmuch as in these sciences that which is true and that which is made are convertible."[4] Of course, the *New Science* no longer defined origins as blemishes that must be washed away for scientific certainty to obtain, but its findings did rest in part on the old equation between human knowledge, ignorance, and vice, an equation Kant was to echo once more in the "Conjectural Beginning of Human History." Here, in an account that is deliberately modeled

[1] Note that this human engendering represents a significant departure from the position adopted by Vico in *De antiquissima*, where "the human mind makes truths ex hypothesis, while the divine mind makes true [things] absolutely." Giambattista Vico, *On the Most Ancient Wisdom of the Italians: Unearthed from the Origins of the Latin Language*, trans. L. M. Palmer (Ithaca, N.Y.: Cornell University Press, 1988), 110. In the *New Science*, the human mind makes its truths absolutely as well.

[2] R. A. C. Macmillan, *The Crowning Phase of the Critical Philosophy: A Study in Kant's Critique of Judgment* (London: Macmillan, 1912; reprint, New York: Garland, 1976), 256. See Immanuel Kant, *Critique of Judgment*, trans. Werner S. Pluhar (Indianapolis: Hackett, 1987), §68.

[3] Immanuel Kant, *Critique of Pure Reason*, trans. Norman Kemp Smith (New York: St. Martin's Press, 1965), Bxiii. Further references will be included parenthetically in the body of the text, preceded, wherever necessary, by the abbreviation *KrV*.

[4] Vico, *Most Ancient Wisdom*, 52.

on Genesis, Kant assumes that as we emerged "from the tutelage of nature to the state of freedom"—which was caused by our first awareness of choice, that is, by the first use of our reason—our "animality" rebelled.[5] The ensuing conflict was the source of all evils. Human reason was therefore born along with vice. Unlike divine reason, it is conditioned primarily by ignorance.

The nature of human epistemology therefore condemns us not only to evil but also to uncertainty and a partial idealization of mathematics and, more precisely, geometry, activities that most closely simulate God's "purest intelligence."[6] This idealization can be seen in an unusual sketch of the Vichian primal scene: "At length the sky broke forth in thunder, and Jove thus gave a beginning to the world of men by arousing in them the conatus which is proper to the liberty of the mind, just as from motion, which is proper to bodies as necessary agents, he began the world of nature" (NS §689).[7] This isolated description should not, however, distract us from the realization that the New Science is above all an acknowledgment that the world of human institutions has been made by men through ideas—no matter how erroneous, as in the Lacanian mirror stage—not given to us by God.

One finds another mirror stage in the Critical philosophy. As Terry Eagleton has pointed out, in aesthetic judgment "an imaginary misrecognition takes place, although with a certain reversal of subject and object from the mirror of Lacan to the mirror of Kant."[8] Basically, Vico and Kant equate knowing and creating and agree that the object of this creation is concepts that are in some respects flawed. They disagree on the nature of the flaw. Having set the world of nature aside, Vico was free to see ignorance not as a negative quality but as the positive

---

[5] Immanuel Kant, "Conjectural Beginning of Human History," trans. Emil Fackenheim, in Kant on History, ed. Lewis White Beck (New York: Macmillan, 1963), 60.

[6] The New Science of Giambattista Vico: Unabridged Translation of the Third Edition (1744) with the Addition of "Practic of the New Science," trans. Thomas Goddard Bergin and Max Harold Fisch (Ithaca, N.Y.: Cornell University Press, 1984), §376. Further references will be included parenthetically in the body of the text, preceded, wherever necessary, by the abbreviation NS.

[7] For an eighteenth-century definition of conatus as "the law of the geometrical composition of forces," see Gottfried Wilhelm Leibniz, "On the Ultimate Origination of Things. 1697," in The Monadology and Other Philosophical Writings, trans. and ed. Robert Latta (New York: Garland, 1985), 344. For an excellent discussion of conatus, or momentum, in Vico's work, see Mark Lilla, G. B. Vico: The Making of an Anti-Modern (Cambridge, Mass.: Harvard University Press, 1993), 40–45.

[8] Terry Eagleton, The Ideology of the Aesthetic (Cambridge, Mass.: Basil Blackwell, 1990), 87.

condition of any human knowledge. His "slips" are providential and can be corrected by the same mind that has committed the error, even from a distance of many generations. The certainty of the *New Science* is therefore not dependent on external corroboration. By contrast, Kant's recognition of ignorance is akin to an admission of guilt and his epistemology is consequently modeled on a grim and demanding resignation that causes him to restrict severely the range of epistemological certainty. For Kant, our concepts are flawed because they cannot receive the external validation Vico had dismissed but that Kant still craved.

The most important restriction of the Critical philosophy is that we can provide certain answers only to theoretical questions, which, contrary to Rudolf A. Makkreel's claim, should not be confused with "theoretical reason and its access to nature." Makkreel's argument is that "Kant does not think that we can know cultural history, which is man-made, better than nature. Because our own inner experience and the historical consequences of our actions are not readily subjected to experimentation and mathematical measurement, they are considered to be less accessible to theoretical reason than are natural processes." However, and this is made abundantly clear in both the Critique of Teleological Judgment and the *Critique of Pure Reason,* Kant never claimed that we can know nature absolutely. Makkreel is quoting out of context when he contends that the "questions of reason's own determining" (Bxiii) are those "that admit of *'confirmation or refutation by experiment'* " (Bxix,n).[9] As Kant goes on to explain in this note, "the propositions of pure reason . . . cannot be brought to the test through any experiment with their *objects,* as in natural science" (*KrV* Bxix,n). The test of our own concepts is only "modelled" (*KrV* Bxix,n) on the natural sciences and applies only to theoretical reason—not nature. At best, one can claim only that the nature of our understanding is such that the presupposition of an external world is a necessary epistemological condition of self-awareness.[10] Like the mathematician, the Critical philosopher knows only his own constructs.

Vico subscribed to and problematized this idealization of mathematical discourse. For our present purposes its importance lies primarily in the belief shared by both thinkers that epistemological certainty is a

[9] Rudolf A. Makkreel, *Imagination and Interpretation in Kant: The Hermeneutical Import of the "Critique of Judgment"* (Chicago: University of Chicago Press, 1990), 168.

[10] Robert Hahn, *Kant's Newtonian Revolution in Philosophy* (Carbondale: Southern Illinois University Press for *Journal of the History of Philosophy,* 1988), 117–18.

function of the particular constraint that limits our knowledge to the only thing we can make, namely, concepts. This common hermeneutic principle yielded radically different applications, however, highlighted by the two thinkers' respective treatments of geneticism. As we discussed in chapter 2, this principle is at the heart of Vico's genetic historiography in that history is, according to the *New Science*, a certain science (see, for example, §349). For Vico, the primal scene is merely the first instance of a process that will be repeated and which individual members of a society have internalized. Origins can therefore be unveiled; their truth is an *aletheia*, an a-forgetfulness. For Kant, by contrast, the origin is a singular moment I am compelled to posit. Its truth is theoretical. I cannot be certain that it corresponds to any actual occurrence; I know only that the makeup of my understanding is such that I am forced to think genetically. Created in accordance with the notions of possibility, projection, and final cause, the origin is, in this context, necessarily unique. Moreover, as Kant's description of the apparition of choice and thought—and by extension, freedom—in "Conjectural Beginning" indicates, to think in terms of origins is to confront an epistemological abyss.[11]

The abyssal nature of the origin compelled Kant to subordinate geneticism to teleology. Only in this context can the abyss eventually be closed and the negative origin erased. Like Rousseau, Kant believed that the apparition of culture was a lapse and that culture must solve the conflict by turning itself into a second nature. This second nature is not Rousseau's nothingness, however, but a state of perfection. Its creation will even show that "culture . . . has perhaps not even begun properly," which constitutes as drastic an elimination of the origin as one can possibly imagine.[12]

Kantian genetic epistemology depends on the conciliation of two organizing concepts: the abyss and the series. The need for serialization and regressive mechanisms actually proceeds from the abyssal rupture that he believes originating entails. Unlike Vico, Kant could neither historicize conceptualization itself nor see history as certain. Tales of historical beginnings can only be conjectural. In the end, Kant's statement that "absolute necessity is a necessity that is to be found in

[11] Kant, "Conjectural Beginning," 56.
[12] Ibid., 62. Note that, for Kant, vertigo is not disabling. The German philosopher is not like Schiller's initiate, who, in "Das verschleierte Bild zu Sais," dares lift the veil of the deity but is later found dead at her feet. (Kant refers to the Isis myth in *KU* §49n.)

thought alone" (*KrV* A617/B646) holds true but must be historicized. A comparison with Locke makes this particularly clear. Indeed, as amply demonstrated by the *Essay concerning Human Understanding*, regress is not an absolutely necessary modality of thought in the quest for origins. Kant's need to rely on regress and serialization is clearly the product of a different epistemological framework.

As the contrast with Locke reveals, Kant's epistemic position is still very much our own. Kant's dilemma, illustrated in part by his anguished references to an abyss and his final recourse to the least empirical of all forms of causality, a primordial being, isolated him from the thinkers who had preceded Rousseau. In this separation lies the origin of our own association between origin and regress. Since at least the 1780s, history has been recognizably anxiety-producing. We cannot think like Locke any more than Kant could.

It remains to be determined whether Kant's approach to geneticism did not generate, as the comparison with Vico might suggest, a fallacy of its own, a conceptual fallacy. Because the origin is not grounded in anything extrinsic to itself, its object is potentially solipsistic, which is hardly acceptable in the context of the Critical philosophy. Indeed, as Strawson notes, "There is no evidence whatever in the *Critique* that Kant seriously considered embracing solipsism. The style in which he presents transcendental idealism is consistently the collective style."[13] Vico's memory traces had sheltered the *New Science* from this particular objection. As for Kant, once he had successfully laid the objective fallacy to rest and set limits to geneticism in the *Critique of Pure Reason*, he still needed to answer the question of how we can think genetically.

Contrary to what a first reading of the end of the *Critique of Pure Reason* might suggest, in the *Critique* Kant did not revert to the type of extramundane explanations he had resorted to in the *Universal Natural History*. In his first Critical work the origin is understood in semitheological terms, but this is meant in part to reinforce our awareness of the perimeters of human knowledge: "The object of the ideal of reason, an object which is present to us only in and through reason, is therefore entitled the *primordial being* (*ens originarium*). As it has nothing above it, it is also entitled the *highest being* (*ens summum*); and as everything that is conditioned is subject to it, the *being of all beings* (*ens entium*). These terms

---

[13] P. F. Strawson, *The Bounds of Sense: An Essay on Kant's "Critique of Pure Reason"* (London: Methuen, 1966), 197.

are not, however, to be taken as signifying the objective relation of an actual object to other things, but of an *idea to concepts*. We are left entirely without knowledge as to the existence of a being of such outstanding pre-eminence" (*KrV* A578–79/B606–7). In this case, the recourse to spatial concepts where one would expect temporal ones ("above" rather than "before," for instance) signals a desire to nullify temporality, and emphasizes what has come to be seen as its inescapability as well as the limits of our knowledge, since the categories of time and space—necessary to our understanding—are no longer reliable.

Kant came to terms with the epistemological consequences of genetic thinking in the Third Critique. His answer to Vico's memory traces lies in his theory of the subjective universality of aesthetic judgments. In aesthetic judgment, knowledge becomes a collective entity, a development that deflects the possible charge of solipsism. The apriority with which Kant's philosophy is so closely associated did not, then, shut the door on the study of origins. Immanuel Kant painted the primal scene of nature and the mind, an inherently impossible task according to his own system (though not Vico's), were it not for the assumption that it can be communicated to and appreciated by all.

As this brief comparison between Vico and Kant suggests, the value of studying the Enlightenment lies in part in the coexistence of related yet very different epistemic models. The century that produced Locke, Vico, Rousseau, and Kant was also the century for which, most notably, origins could be conceived synchronically as well as diachronically. And indeed, the claims of each thinker varied tremendously: Locke proposed a synchronic genetic history of the mind; Vico developed a synchronic-diachronic genetic principle and connected it to the history of nations; Rousseau, giving up on certainty, emphasized the hypothetical nature of his thoughts on society and limited his truth claims to individual history; finally, Kant did not archeologize the mind, yet his hermeneutics, close to both Vico's and Rousseau's, allowed him to archeologize nature.

More work remains to be done if these issues are to be fully understood and appreciated. In particular, the Enlightenment's contributions should be contrasted to the genetic epistemology embedded in romanticism, starting with Wordsworth's *Prelude* and the preface to the *Lyrical Ballads*. In the meantime, we can now safely say that "the blurring of the notion of origins" Victor Brombert described as a key feature of contemporary literary theory is hardly unique to postmodernism.[14] Brombert's offhand remark actually makes one wonder what has happened between the Enlightenment and the late twentieth century that could make us suppose that, as a concept, origins ought to be, or have ever been, clear.

[14] Victor Brombert, "Mediating the Work: Or, The Legitimate Aims of Criticism," *PMLA* 105 (1990): 393.

WORKS CITED

PRIMARY WORKS

Addison, [Joseph]. ["On the Pleasures of the Imagination"]. Nos. 411–421. In vol. 3 of *The Spectator,* edited by Donald F. Bond. Oxford: Clarendon Press, 1965.

Aristotle. *The Nicomachean Ethics.* Translated by W. D. Ross. Translation revised by J. O. Urmson. In *The Complete Works of Aristotle. The Revised Oxford Translation,* edited by Jonathan Barnes, 2:1729–1867. Bollingen Series 71. Princeton: Princeton University Press, 1984.

Bacon, Francis. *The Wisedome of the Ancients.* Translated by Arthur Gorges Knight. London, 1619.

Batteux, Charles. *Les Beaux-Arts réduits à un même principe.* Vol. 1 of *Principes de la littérature.* 5th ed. (1775). Geneva: Slatkine Reprints, 1967.

——. *Traité de la poésie épique.* In *Principes de la littérature,* 2:195–443. 5th ed. (1775). Geneva: Slatkine Reprints, 1967.

Baumgarten, Alexander Gottlieb. *Meditationes philosophicae de nonnullis ad poema pertinentibus/Philosophische Betrachtungen über einige Bedingungen des Gedichtes.* Latin and German. Translated and edited by Heinz Paetzold. Hamburg: Feliz Meiner Verlag, 1983.

——. *Metaphysica.* Part 3: "Psychologia," §§501–623. In *Texte zur Grundlegung der Aesthetik,* translated and edited by Hans Rudolf Schweizer, 1–65. Latin and German. Hamburg: Felix Meiner Verlag, 1983.

——. *Theoretische Ästhetik: Die grundlegenden Abschnitte aus der "Aesthetica" (1750/58).* Latin and German. Translated and edited by Hans Rudolf Schweizer. Hamburg: Felix Meiner Verlag, 1983.

Boileau-Despréaux, Nicolas. "L'Art poétique." In *Oeuvres,* edited by Sylvain Menant, 2:85–115. Paris: Garnier-Flammarion, 1969.

Boswell, James. *The Journal of a Tour to the Hebrides with Samuel Johnson, L.L.D.* 3rd ed. London, 1786. In vol. 5 of *Boswell's Life of Johnson,* edited by George Birkbeck Hill, revised and enlarged by L. F. Powell, v–425. Oxford: Clarendon Press, 1950.

Buffon, Georges Louis Leclerc, comte de. *Discours sur le style.* Paris: Hachette, 1867.
———. *Les époques de la nature.* Critical edition of the manuscript by Jacques Roger. Paris: Editions du Muséum, 1962.
———. *Histoire naturelle, générale et particuliere.* 4 vols. in 54 books. N.p.: Aux Deux-Ponts, 1785–1790.
Castelvetro, Lodovico. *[Selections from] The Poetics of Aristotle Translated and Annotated.* Translated by Allan H. Gilbert. In *Literary Criticism: Plato to Dryden,* edited by A. H. Gilbert, 304–57. 1940; Detroit: Wayne State University Press, 1962.
Condillac, Etienne Bonnot de. *Essai sur l'origine des connaissances humaines.* Preceded by Jacques Derrida, "L'Archéologie du frivole." Auvers-sur-Oise: Galilée, 1973.
———. *Essay on the Origin of Human Knowledge.* Translated and edited by Hans Aarsleff. Cambridge: Cambridge University Press, 2001.
———. *Lettres inédites à Gabriel Cramer.* Edited by Georges Le Roy. Paris: Presses Universitaires de France, 1953.
Dacier, Anne. *Des causes de la corruption du goust.* Paris, 1714.
D'Alembert, Jean Le Rond. *Preliminary Discourse to the Encyclopedia of Diderot.* Translated by Richard N. Schwab, with the collaboration of Walter E. Rex. Indianapolis: Bobbs-Merrill/Library of Liberal Arts, 1963.
Descartes, René. *Discours de la méthode.* Edited by Etienne Gilson. Paris: Librairie Philosophique J. Vrin, 1989.
———. *Le Monde, L'homme.* Edited by Annie Bitbol-Hespériès and Jean-Pierre Verdet. [Paris]: Seuil, 1996.
———. *Oeuvres.* Edited by Charles Adam and Paul Tannery. Rev. ed. 12 vols. Paris: J. Vrin in conjunction with the Centre National de la Recherche Scientifique, 1964–1976.
———. *Oeuvres philosophiques.* Edited by Ferdinand Alquié. 3 vols. Paris: Garnier, 1963–1973.
———. *The Philosophical Writings of Descartes.* Translated by John Cottingham, Robert Stoothoff, Dugald Murdoch, and [for vol. 3] Anthony Kenny. 3 vols. Cambridge: Cambridge University Press, 1985–1991.
Duff, William. *An Essay on Original Genius; And Its Various Modes of Exertion in Philosophy and the Fine Arts, Particularly in Poetry.* London, 1767.
Encyclopédie ou Dictionnaire raisonné des sciences, des arts et des métiers. 1751–1772. http://www.lib.uchicago.edu/efts/ARTFL/projects/encyc/.
Fontenelle, Bernard le Bovier de. *Nouveaux dialogues des morts.* Edited by Donald Schier. Studies in the Romance Languages and Literatures 55. Chapel Hill: University of North Carolina Press, 1965.
Gerard, Alexander. *An Essay on Genius, 1774.* Edited by Bernhard Fabian. Munich: Wilhelm Fink, 1966.
[Gerstenberg, Heinrich Wilhelm.] *Briefe über Merkwürdigkeiten der Litteratur.* Edited by Alexander von Weilen. In *Deutsche Litteraturdenkmale des 18. und 19. Jahrhunderts,* no. 29/30, edited by Bernhard Seuffert. Stuttgart: G. J. Göschen, 1890.

Glanvill, Joseph. *The Vanity of Dogmatizing: Or Confidence in Opinions. Manifested in a Discourse of the Shortness and Uncertainty of our Knowledge, and Its Causes; with Some Reflexions on Peripateticism: and an Apology for Philosophy.* London, 1661.

Hamann, Johann Georg. "Aesthetica in Nuce: A Rhapsody in Cabbalistic Prose." Translated by Joyce P. Crick. In *German Aesthetic and Literary Criticism: Winckelmann, Lessing, Hamann, Herder, Schiller, Goethe,* edited by H. B. Nisbet, 139–50. Cambridge: Cambridge University Press, 1985.

Herder, Johann Gottfried. "Einleitung in die Fragmente: Über die Mittel zur Erweckung der Genies in Deutschland." In *Über die neuere Deutsche Litteratur: Zwote Sammlung von Fragmenten. Eine Beilage zu den Briefen, die neueste Litteratur betreffend,* 200–206. [Riga, 1767].

———. "Extract from a Correspondence on Ossian and the Songs of Ancient Peoples." Translated by Joyce P. Crick. In *German Aesthetic and Literary Criticism: Winckelmann, Lessing, Hamann, Herder, Schiller, Goethe,* edited by H. B. Nisbet, 154–61. Cambridge: Cambridge University Press, 1985.

———. *Vom Erkennen und Empfinden der menschlichen Seele.* In *Sämmtliche Werke,* edited by Berhard Suphan, 8:207–35. Berlin: Weidmannsche Buchhandlung, 1892.

[Hobbes, Thomas.] "Preface to the Reader Concerning the Vertues of an Heroique Poem." In *The Iliads and Odysses of Homer.* Translated by Tho: Hobbes of Malmsbury. 2nd ed. London, 1677.

———. *Six Lessons to the Professors of the Mathematics.* In *The English Works of Thomas Hobbes of Malmsbury,* edited by William Molesworth, 7:181–356. London: Longman, Brown, Green, and Longman, 1845.

Hutcheson, Francis. *An Inquiry into the Original of our Ideas of Beauty and Virtue.* 4th ed. London, 1738.

Hutton, James. *Theory of the Earth.* In *Transactions of the Royal Society of Edinburgh* 1 (1788): 209–304.

Kant, Immanuel. *Anthropology from a Pragmatic Point of View.* Translated by Mary J. Gregor. The Hague: Martinus Nijhoff, 1974.

———. "Conjectural Beginning of Human History." Translated by Emil Fackenheim. In *Kant on History,* edited by Lewis White Beck, 53–68. New York: Macmillan, 1963.

———. *Critique of Judgment.* Translated by Werner S. Pluhar. Indianapolis: Hackett, 1987.

———. *Critique of Pure Reason.* Translated by Norman Kemp Smith. New York: St. Martin's Press, 1965.

———. *Gesammelte Schriften.* Edited by the Königlich Preußische Akademie der Wissenschaften. Berlin: Georg Reimer, 1902–.

———. *Kritik der Urtheilskraft.* Edited by Wilhelm Windelband. In *Gesammelte Schriften,* edited by the Königlich Preußische Akademie der Wissenschaften, 5:165–485, 512–43. Berlin: Georg Reimer, 1913.

———. *Universal Natural History and Theory of the Heavens.* Translated by Stanley L. Jaki. Edinburgh: Scottish Academic Press, 1981.

La Harpe, Jean-François de. *Cours de littérature ancienne et moderne (Lycée)*. 18 vols. Paris, 1823.

Leibniz, Gottfried Wilhelm. "On the Ultimate Origination of Things. 1697." In *The Monadology and Other Philosophical Writings*, translated and edited by Robert Latta, 337–51. New York: Garland, 1985.

Leroy, [Loys]. *De la vicissitude ou variété des choses en l'univers*. Corpus des Oeuvres de Philosophie en Langue Française. N.p.: Fayard, 1988.

Lessing, Gotthold Ephraim. *Laocoön*. Translated by Edward Allen McCormick. Baltimore: Johns Hopkins University Press, 1984.

Locke, John. *An Essay concerning Human Understanding*. Edited by Peter H. Nidditch. Oxford: Clarendon Press, 1985.

——. *Two Treatises of Government*. Edited by Peter Laslett. Cambridge: Cambridge University Press, 1988.

Marmontel, Jean François. *Eléments de Littérature*. 2 vols. Paris: F. Didot, 1846.

Newton, Isaac. *Mathematical Principles of Natural Philosophy and System of the World*. Translated by Andrew Motte in 1729. Translation revised and edited by Florian Cajori. 2 vols. Berkeley and Los Angeles: University of California Press, 1934.

Pope, Alexander. "An Essay on Criticism." In *Poetry and Prose of Alexander Pope*, edited by Aubrey Williams, 37–57. Boston: Houghton Mifflin, 1969.

——. "[On the Origin of Letters]." In *The Earlier Works, 1711–1720*. Vol. 1 of *The Prose Works of Alexander Pope*, edited by Norman Ault, 1:140–44. Oxford: Basil Blackwell, 1936.

——. "Preface to the Iliad." In *Poetry and Prose of Alexander Pope*, edited by Aubrey Williams, 439–59. Boston: Houghton Mifflin, 1969.

——. "Preface to the Works of Shakespear." In *Poetry and Prose of Alexander Pope*, edited by Aubrey Williams, 460–72. Boston: Houghton Mifflin, 1969.

Rousseau, Jean-Jacques. *The "Confessions" and Correspondence, including the Letters to Malesherbes*. Edited by Christopher Kelly, Roger D. Masters, and Peter G. Stillman. Translated by Christopher Kelly. Vol. 5 of *The Collected Writings of Rousseau*, edited by Roger D. Masters and Christopher Kelly. Hanover, N.H.: Published for Dartmouth College by University Press of New England, 1995.

——. *Discours sur l'origine et les fondements de l'inégalité*. Edited by Jean Starobinski. In *Oeuvres complètes*, 3:109–237, 1285–1389. Bibliothèque de la Pléiade. N.p.: Gallimard, 1964.

——. *Discourse on the Origins of Inequality (Second Discourse); Polemics; and Political Economy*. Edited by Roger D. Masters and Christopher Kelly. Translated by Judith R. Bush, Roger D. Masters, Christopher Kelly, and Terence Marshall. Vol. 3 of *The Collected Writings of Rousseau*, edited by Roger D. Masters and Christopher Kelly. Hanover, N.H.: Published for Dartmouth College by University Press of New England, 1992.

——. *Emile or on Education*. Translated by Allan Bloom. New York: Basic Books, 1979.

——. *Essay on the Origin of Languages* and *Writings Related to Music*. Translated and edited by John T. Scott. In *The Collected Writings of Rousseau*, edited by

Roger D. Masters and Christopher Kelly, 7:289–332 and 566–80. Hanover, N.H.: Published for Dartmouth College by University Press of New England, 1998.

———. *Julie, or the New Heloise: Letters of Two Lovers Who Live in a Small Town at the Foot of the Alps.* Translated and annotated by Philip Stewart and Jean Vaché. Vol. 6 of *The Collected Writings of Rousseau,* edited by Roger D. Masters and Christopher Kelly. Hanover, N.H.: Published for Dartmouth College by University Press of New England, 1997.

———. *Politics and the Arts: Letter to M. d'Alembert on the Theatre.* Translated by Allan Bloom. Glencoe, Ill.: Free Press, 1960.

Smith, Adam. "Consideration Concerning the First Formation of Languages." In vol. 4 of *The Glasgow Edition of the Works and Correspondence of Adam Smith,* edited by J. C. Bryce, general editor, A. S. Skinner, 201–26. Oxford: Oxford University Press, 1983; Indianapolis: Liberty Fund, 1985.

———. *An Inquiry into the Nature and Causes of the Wealth of Nations.* Vol. 2, bks. 1 and 2, of *The Glasgow Edition of the Works and Correspondence of Adam Smith.* General editors, R. H. Campbell and A. S. Skinner, textual editor, W. B. Todd. Oxford: Oxford University Press, 1976; Indianapolis: Liberty Fund, 1981.

———. *Lectures on Rhetoric and Belles Lettres.* Edited by J. C. Bryce. General editor A. S. Skinner. In vol. 4 of *The Glasgow Edition of the Works and Correspondence of Adam Smith,* edited by J. C. Bryce, general editor, A. S. Skinner, 1–200. Oxford: Oxford University Press, 1983; Indianapolis: Liberty Fund, 1985.

———. "Letter to the *Edinburgh Review.*" Edited by J. C. Bryce. In *Essays on Philosophical Subjects.* Vol. 3 of *The Glasgow Edition of the Works and Correspondence of Adam Smith,* edited by W. P. D. Wightman and J. C. Bryce, general editors, D. D. Raphael and A. S. Skinner, 242–54. Oxford: Oxford University Press, 1980; Indianapolis: Liberty Fund, 1982.

Staël, Madame de. *De la littérature considérée dans ses rapports avec les institutions sociales.* Edited by Paul Van Tieghem. Geneva: Droz, 1959.

Sulzer, Johann Georg. *Allgemeine Theorie der schönen Künste in einzeln, nach alphabetischer Ordnung der Kunstwörter . . .* 2nd ed. 4 vols. Leipzig: Weidmann, 1793.

Vico, Giambattista. *The Autobiography.* Translated by Max Harold Fisch and Thomas Goddard Bergin. Ithaca, N.Y.: Cornell University Press, 1975.

———. *The New Science of Giambattista Vico: Unabridged Translation of the Third Edition (1744) with the Addition of "Practic of the New Science."* Translated by Thomas Goddard Bergin and Max Harold Fisch. Ithaca, N.Y.: Cornell University Press, 1984.

———. *On Humanistic Education: [Six Inaugural Orations, 1699–1707].* Translated by Giorgio A. Pinton and Arthur W. Shippee. Ithaca, N.Y.: Cornell University Press, 1993.

———. *On the Most Ancient Wisdom of the Italians: Unearthed from the Origins of the Latin Language, including the Disputation with the "Giornale de' letterati d'Italia."* Translated by L. M. Palmer. Ithaca, N.Y.: Cornell University Press, 1988.

———. *La scienza nuova.* Edited by Paolo Rossi. 2nd ed. Milan: Rizzoli, 1982.

———. *On the Study Methods of Our Time.* Translated by Elio Gianturco. Indianapolis: Bobbs-Merrill, 1965; Ithaca, N.Y.: Cornell University Press, 1990.

Winckelmann, Johann Joachim. "Thoughts on the Imitation of the Painting and Sculpture of the Greeks." Translated by H. B. Nisbet. In *German Aesthetic and Literary Criticism: Winckelmann, Lessing, Hamann, Herder, Schiller, Goethe,* edited by H. B. Nisbet, 32–54. Cambridge: Cambridge University Press, 1985.

Wood, Robert. *An Essay on the Original Genius and Writings of Homer: With a Comparative View of the Ancient and Present State of the Troade.* London, 1775.

Young, Edward. "Conjectures on Original Composition." In *The Great Critics: An Anthology of Literary Criticism,* 3rd ed., edited by James Harry Smith and Edd Winfield Parks, 405–40. New York: W.W. Norton, 1951.

SECONDARY WORKS

Abrams, M. H. *The Mirror and the Lamp: Romantic Theory and the Critical Tradition.* Oxford: Oxford University Press, 1971.

Affeldt, Steven G. "The Voice of Freedom: Rousseau on Forcing to Be Free." *Political Theory* 27 (1999): 299–333.

Alquié, Ferdinand. *La découverte métaphysique de l'homme chez Descartes.* 2nd ed. Paris: Presses Universitaires de France, 1966.

Apel, Karl-Otto. *Die Idee der Sprache in der Tradition des Humanismus von Dante bis Vico.* 2nd ed. Bonn: Bouvier, 1975.

Auerbach, Erich. "Vico and Aesthetic Historism." *Journal of Aesthetics and Art Criticism* 8 (1949): 110–18.

Auroux, Sylvain. *La sémiotique des Encyclopédistes: Essai d'épistémologie historique des sciences du langage.* Paris: Payot, 1979.

Avis, Paul D. L. *Foundations of Modern Historical Thought: From Machiavelli to Vico.* London: Croom Helm, 1986.

Barrell, John. *The Political Theory of Painting from Reynolds to Hazlitt: "The Body of the Public."* New Haven: Yale University Press, 1986.

Bate, Walter Jackson. *The Burden of the Past and the English Poet.* Cambridge, Mass.: Harvard University, Belknap Press, 1970.

———. *From Classic to Romantic: Premises of Taste in Eighteenth-Century England.* New York: Harper and Row, 1961.

Beck, Lewis White. "World Enough, and Time." In *Probability, Time, and Space in Eighteenth-Century Literature,* edited by Paula R. Backscheider, 113–39. New York: AMS Press, 1979.

Becq, Annie. *Genèse de l'esthétique française: De la raison classique à l'imagination créatrice, 1680–1814.* 2 vols. Pisa: Pacini Editore, 1984.

Beyssade, Jean-Marie. *La philosophie première de Descartes: Le temps et la cohérence de la métaphysique.* N.p.: Flammarion, 1979.

Birn, Raymond. "The Profits of Ideas: *Privilèges en librairie* in Eighteenth-Century France." *Eighteenth-Century Studies* 4 (1970–1971): 131–68.

Bitbol-Hespériès, Annie. Introduction to *Le Monde, L'homme,* by René Descartes, iii–liii. [Paris]: Seuil, 1996.

Bohls, Elizabeth A. "Disinterestedness and Denial of the Particular: Locke, Adam Smith, and the Subject of Aesthetics." In *Eighteenth-Century Aesthetics and the Reconstruction of Art,* edited by Paul Mattick Jr., 16–51. Cambridge: Cambridge University Press, 1993.

Boyd, John D. *The Function of Mimesis and Its Decline.* Cambridge, Mass.: Harvard University Press, 1968; New York: Fordham University Press, 1980.

Brittan, Gordon G., Jr. *Kant's Theory of Science.* Princeton, N.J.: Princeton University Press, 1978.

Brodsky, Claudia J. *The Imposition of Form: Studies in Narrative Representation and Knowledge.* Princeton, N.J.: Princeton University Press, 1987.

Brombert, Victor. "Mediating the Work: Or, The Legitimate Aims of Criticism." *PMLA* 105 (1990): 391–97.

Buffière, Felix. *Les mythes d'Homère et la pensée grecque.* Paris: Les Belles Lettres, 1973.

Burke, Peter. *Vico.* Oxford: Oxford University Press, 1986.

Butler, Judith. " 'How Can I Deny that These Hands and This Body Are Mine?' " *Qui Parle* 11 (1997): 1–20.

Butts, Robert E. "Hypothesis and Explanation of Kant's Philosophy of Science." *Archiv für Geschichte der Philosophie* 43 (1961): 153–70.

Cahné, Pierre-Alain. *Un autre Descartes: Le philosophe et son langage.* Paris: J. Vrin, 1980.

Cantelli, Gianfranco. "Myth and Language in Vico." In *Giambattista Vico's Science of Humanity,* edited by Giorgio Tagliacozzo and Donald Phillip Verene, 47–63. Baltimore: Johns Hopkins University Press, 1976.

Caponigri, A. Robert. *Time and Idea: The Theory of History in Giambattista Vico.* Notre Dame: University of Notre Dame Press, 1968.

Cassirer, Ernst. *The Philosophy of the Enlightenment.* Translated by Fritz C. A. Koelln and James P. Pettegrove. Princeton, N.J.: Princeton University Press, 1951.

Cavaillé, Jean-Pierre. *Descartes: La fable du monde.* Paris: Editions de l'Ecole des Hautes Etudes en Sciences Sociales and Librairie Philosophique J. Vrin, 1991.

Caygill, Howard. *Art of Judgement.* Cambridge, Mass.: Basil Blackwell, 1989.

Chédin, O. *Sur l'esthétique de Kant et la théorie critique de la représentation.* Paris: Librairie Philosophique J. Vrin, 1982.

Chouillet, Jacques. "Descartes et le problème de l'origine des langues au 18e siècle." *Dix-huitième Siècle* 4 (1972): 39–60.

Clarke, Desmond M. "Descartes' Philosophy of Science and the Scientific Revolution." In *The Cambridge Companion to Descartes,* edited by John Cottingham, 258–85. Cambridge: Cambridge University Press, 1992.

Clarke, Howard. *Homer's Readers: A Historical Introduction to the "Iliad" and the "Odyssey."* Newark: University of Delaware Press, 1981.

Cohen, Ralph. "Association of Ideas and Poetic Unity." *Philological Quarterly* 36 (1957): 465–74.

Cohen, Ted. "Why Beauty Is a Symbol of Morality." In *Essays in Kant's Aesthetics*, edited by Ted Cohen and Paul Guyer, 221–36. Chicago: University of Chicago Press, 1982.

Collingwood, R. G. *The Idea of History*. Oxford: Clarendon Press, 1946.

Coltharp, Duane. "History and the Primitive: Homer, Blackwell, and the Scottish Enlightenment." *Eighteenth-Century Life* 19 (1995): 57–69.

Courtine, Jean-François, Michel Deguy, Eliane Escoubas, Philippe Lacoue-Labarthe, Jean-François Lyotard, Louis Marin, Jean-Luc Nancy, and Jacob Rogozinski. *Du sublime*. Paris: Belin, 1988.

——. *Of the Sublime: Presence in Question*. Translated by Jeffrey S. Librett. Albany: State University of New York Press, 1993.

Cristofolini, Paolo. *Vico et l'histoire*. Paris: Presses Universitaires de France, 1995.

Croce, Benedetto. *The Philosophy of Giambattista Vico*. Translated by R. G. Collingwood. New York: Russell and Russell, 1964.

Crowther, Paul. *The Kantian Sublime: From Morality to Art*. Oxford: Clarendon Press, 1989.

Daston, Lorraine. *Classical Probability in the Enlightenment*. Princeton, N.J.: Princeton University Press, 1988.

De Bolla, Peter. *The Discourse of the Sublime: Readings in History, Aesthetics, and the Subject*. Oxford: Basil Blackwell, 1989.

DeJean, Joan. *Ancients against Moderns: Culture Wars and the Making of a Fin de Siècle*. Chicago: University of Chicago Press, 1997.

Derrida, Jacques. *The Archeology of the Frivolous: Reading Condillac*. Translated by John P. Leavey Jr. Pittsburgh: Duquesne University Press, 1980.

——. *Of Grammatology*. Translated by Gayatri Chakravorty Spivak. Baltimore: Johns Hopkins University Press, 1976.

——. *The Truth in Painting*. Translated by Geoff Bennington and Ian McLeod. Chicago: University of Chicago Press, 1987.

——. *La vérité en peinture*. Paris: Flammarion, 1978.

Dryer, D. P. *Kant's Solution for Verification in Metaphysics*. London: Allen and Unwin, 1966.

Duchet, Michèle. *Anthropologie et histoire au siècle des Lumières*. Paris: Maspero, 1971.

Dumont, Louis. *From Mandeville to Marx: The Genesis and Triumph of Economic Ideology*. Chicago: University of Chicago Press, 1977.

Eagleton, Terry. *The Ideology of the Aesthetic*. Cambridge, Mass.: Basil Blackwell, 1990.

Ewing, A. C. *Kant's Treatment of Causality*. Routledge & Kegan Paul, 1924; [Hamden, Conn.]: Archon, 1969.

Fichant, Michel. "La géométrisation du regard: Réflexions sur la *Dioptrique* de Descartes." *Philosophie* 34 (Spring 1992): 45–69.

Fisch, Max Harold. Introduction to *The New Science of Giambattista Vico: Unabridged Translation of the Third Edition (1744) with the Addition of "Practic of the New Science."* Translated by Thomas Goddard Bergin and Max Harold Fisch, xix–xlv. Ithaca, N.Y.: Cornell University Press, 1984.

———. Introduction to *The Autobiography*, by Giambattista Vico, translated by
    Max Harold Fisch and Thomas Goddard Bergin, 1–107. 1944; Ithaca, N.Y.:
    Cornell University Press, 1983.
Gammon, Martin. "'Exemplary Originality': Kant on Genius and Imitation."
    Journal of the History of Philosophy 35 (1997): 563–92.
Goetsch, James Robert. *Vico's Axioms: The Geometry of the Human World.*
    New Haven: Yale University Press, 1995.
Gould, Stephen J. *Time's Arrow, Time's Cycle: Myth and Metaphor in the Discov-
    ery of Genealogical Time.* Cambridge, Mass.: Harvard University Press, 1987.
Grafton, Anthony. "Renaissance Readers of Homer's Ancient Readers." In
    Homer's Ancient Readers: The Hermeneutics of Greek Epic's [sic] Earliest Exegetes,
    edited by Robert Lamberton and John J. Keaney, 149–72. Princeton, N.J.:
    Princeton University Press, 1992.
Grafton, Anthony, Glenn W. Most, and James E. G. Zetzel. "Introduction." In
    Prolegomena to Homer, 1795, by F. A. Wolf, translated by Anthony Grafton,
    Glenn W. Most, and James E. G. Zetzel, 3–35. Princeton, N.J.: Princeton
    University Press, 1985.
Greene, John C. *The Death of Adam: Evolution and Its Impact on Western Thought.*
    Ames: Iowa State University Press, 1959.
Guiraud, Pierre. "Etymologie et ethymologia (motivation et rétromotivation)."
    Poétique 3 (1972): 405–13.
Guyer, Paul. *Kant and the Claims of Knowledge.* Cambridge: Cambridge Uni-
    versity Press, 1987.
Hacking, Ian. *The Emergence of Probability: A Philosophical Study of Early Ideas
    about Probability, Induction, and Statistical Inference.* London: Cambridge
    University Press, 1975.
Haddock, B. A. "Vico's 'Discovery of the True Homer': A Case-Study in
    Historical Reconstruction." *Journal of the History of Ideas* 40 (1979): 583–602.
Hahn, Robert. *Kant's Newtonian Revolution in Philosophy.* Carbondale: South-
    ern Illinois University Press for *Journal of the History of Philosophy,* 1988.
Harper, William A., and Ralf Meerbote, eds. *Kant on Causality, Freedom, and
    Objectivity.* Minneapolis: University of Minnesota Press, 1984.
Harries, Karsten. "Metaphor and Transcendence." In *On Metaphor,* edited by
    Sheldon Sacks, 71–88. Chicago: University of Chicago Press, 1979.
Hatzfeld, Adolphe, and Arsène Darmesteter. *Dictionnaire général de la langue
    française du commencement du XVIIe siècle jusqu'à nos jours.* 2 vols. Paris:
    Librairie Ch. Delagrave, [1895–1900].
Hayes, Julie. "Plagiarism and Legitimation in Eighteenth-Century France."
    Eighteenth-Century: Theory and Interpretation 34 (1993): 115–31.
Hepp, Noémi. *Homère en France au XVIIe siècle.* Paris: C. Klincksieck, 1968.
Hintikka, Jaakko. "Kant on the Mathematical Method." In *Kant Studies Today,*
    edited by Lewis White Beck, 117–40. La Salle, Ill.: Open Court, 1969.
Huhn, Thomas. "The Kantian Sublime and the Nostalgia for Violence." *Jour-
    nal of Aesthetics and Art Criticism* 53 (Summer 1995): 269–75.
Huppert, George. "The Renaissance Background of Historicism." *History and
    Theory* 5 (1966): 48–60.

Jackson, Wallace. *The Probable and the Marvelous: Blake, Wordsworth, and the Eighteenth-Century Critical Tradition.* Athens: University of Georgia Press, 1978.

Jaki, Stanley L., trans. and ed. *Universal Natural History and Theory of the Heavens.* By Immanuel Kant. Edinburgh: Scottish Academic Press, 1981.

Jones, Richard Foster. *Ancients and Moderns: A Study of the Rise of the Scientific Movement in Seventeenth-Century England.* 2nd ed. St. Louis: Washington University Press, 1961.

Kallich, Martin. *The Association of Ideas and Critical Theory in Eighteenth-Century England: A History of a Psychological Method in English Criticism.* The Hague: Mouton, 1970.

Kavanagh, Thomas M. *Enlightenment and the Shadows of Chance: The Novel and the Culture of Gambling in Eighteenth-Century France.* Baltimore: Johns Hopkins University Press, 1993.

Kelley, Donald R. "Vico's Road: From Philology to Jurisprudence and Back." In *Giambattista Vico's Science of Humanity,* edited by Giorgio Tagliacozzo and Donald Phillip Verene, 15–29. Baltimore: Johns Hopkins University Press, 1976.

Labio, Catherine. "The Aesthetics of Adam Smith's Labor Theory of Value." *Eighteenth Century: Theory and Interpretation* 38 (1997): 134–49.

———. "Epistolarité et épistémologie: La Fayette, Descartes, Graffigny et Rousseau." *SVEC* (2002) 06: 79–91.

Lacan, Jacques. "The Mirror Stage as Formative of the Function of the I as Revealed in Psychoanalytic Experience." In *Ecrits: A Selection,* translated by Alan Sheridan, 1–7. New York: W. W. Norton, 1977.

Lachterman, David Rapport. *The Ethics of Geometry: A Genealogy of Modernity.* New York: Routledge, 1989.

Lefèvre, Roger. "Condillac, maître du langage." *Revue Internationale de Philosophie* 21 (1967): 393–406.

Létoublon, Françoise, and Catherine Volpilhac-Auger, eds. *Homère en France après la Querelle (1715–1900).* Paris: Honoré Champion, 1999.

Levine, Joseph M. "Giambattista Vico and the Quarrel between the Ancients and the Moderns." *Journal of the History of Ideas* 52 (1991): 55–79.

Lilla, Mark. *G. B. Vico: The Making of an Anti-Modern.* Cambridge, Mass.: Harvard University Press, 1993.

Longuenesse, Béatrice. *Kant and the Capacity to Judge: Sensibility and Discursivity in the Transcendental Analytic of the "Critique of Pure Reason."* Princeton, N.J.: Princeton University Press, 1998.

Lovejoy, Arthur O. "'Nature' as Aesthetic Norm." In *Essays in the History of Ideas,* 69–77. Baltimore: Johns Hopkins University Press, 1948.

Lyons, John O. *The Invention of the Self: The Hinge of Consciousness in the Eighteenth Century.* Carbondale: Southern Illinois University Press, 1978.

Lyotard, Jean-François. *Le différend.* Paris: Minuit, 1983.

———. *The Differend: Phrases in Dispute.* Translated by Georges Van Den Abbeele. Minneapolis: University of Minnesota Press, 1988.

———. *L'enthousiasme: La critique kantienne de l'histoire.* Paris: Galilée, 1986.

——. *Leçons sur l'Analytique du sublime (Kant, "Critique de la faculté de juger," §§23–29)*. N.p.: Galilée, 1991.

——. *Lessons on the Analytic of the Sublime: Kant's "Critique of Judgment," §§23–29*. Translated by Elisabeth Rottenberg. Stanford, Ca.: Stanford University Press, 1994.

Mack, Maynard. *Alexander Pope: A Life*. New York: W.W. Norton; New Haven: Yale University Press, 1985.

Macmillan, R. A. C. *The Crowning Phase of the Critical Philosophy: A Study in Kant's Critique of Judgment*. London: Macmillan, 1912; reprint, New York: Garland, 1976.

Magne, Bernard. *Crise de la littérature française sous Louis XIV: Humanisme et nationalisme*. Thesis presented at the Université de Toulouse le Mirail, May 28, 1974. 2 vols. Lille: Reproduction des Thèses, Université Lille III; Paris: Honoré Champion, 1976.

Mahoney, John L. *The Whole Internal Universe: Imitation and the New Defense of Poetry in British Criticism, 1660–1830*. New York: Fordham University Press, 1985.

Makkreel, Rudolf A. *Imagination and Interpretation in Kant: The Hermeneutical Import of the "Critique of Judgment."* Chicago: University of Chicago Press, 1990.

——. "Imagination and Temporality in Kant's Theory of the Sublime." *Journal of Aesthetics and Art Criticism* 42 (1983/1984): 303–15.

Manuel, Frank. *The Eighteenth Century Confronts the Gods*. Cambridge, Mass.: Harvard University Press, 1959.

Mattick, Paul, Jr. "The Art of Money." In *Eighteenth-Century Aesthetics and the Reconstruction of Art*, 152–77. Cambridge: Cambridge University Press, 1993.

——, ed. *Eighteenth-Century Aesthetics and the Reconstruction of Art*. Cambridge: Cambridge University Press, 1993.

Mazzotta, Giuseppe. *The New Map of the World: The Poetic Philosophy of Giambattista Vico*. Princeton, N.J.: Princeton University Press, 1999.

McFarland, Thomas. *Originality and Imagination*. Baltimore: Johns Hopkins University Press, 1985.

Meerbote, Ralf. "Kant on the Nondeterminate Character of Human Actions." In *Kant on Causality, Freedom, and Objectivity*, edited by William A. Harper and Ralf Meerbote, 138–63. Minneapolis: University of Minnesota Press, 1984.

Meerbote, Ralf, and William A. Harper. Introduction to *Kant on Causality, Freedom, and Objectivity*, edited by William A. Harper and Ralf Meerbote, 3–19. Minneapolis: University of Minnesota Press, 1984.

Meinecke, Friedrich. *Historism: The Rise of a New Historical Outlook*. Translated by J. E. Anderson. London: Routledge and Kegan Paul, 1972.

Meltzer, Françoise. *Hot Property: The Stakes and Claims of Literary Originality*. Chicago: University of Chicago Press, 1994.

Monk, Samuel Holt. *The Sublime: A Study of Critical Theories in XVIII-Century England*. Ann Arbor: University of Michigan Press, 1960.

Morrison, James C. "Vico's Principle of *Verum* Is *Factum* and the Problem of Historicism." *Journal of the History of Ideas* 39 (1978): 579–95.

Mortier, Roland. *L'originalité: Une nouvelle catégorie esthétique au siècle des Lumières*. Histoire des Idées et Critique Littéraire 207. Geneva: Droz, 1982.

Nancy, Jean-Luc. *Ego sum*. Paris: Flammarion, 1979.

The New Palgrave: A Dictionary of Economics. Edited by John Eatwell, Murray Milgate, and Peter Newman. New York: Stockton Press, 1987.

Nicolini, Fausto. *La giovinezza di Giambattista Vico, 1688–1700*. 2nd ed. Bari: Gius. Laterza, 1932.

Patey, Douglas Lane. *Probability and Literary Form: Philosophic Theory and Literary Practice in the Augustan Age*. Cambridge: Cambridge University Press, 1984.

Paxman, David. "Aesthetics as Epistemology, or Knowledge Without Certainty." *Eighteenth-Century Studies* 26 (1992–1993): 285–306.

Perrin, Jean-François. *Le chant de l'origine: La mémoire et le temps dans les "Confessions" de Jean-Jacques Rousseau*. Studies on Voltaire and the Eighteenth Century 339. Oxford: Voltaire Foundation, 1996.

Phillips, Patricia. *The Adventurous Muse: Theories of Originality in English Poetics: 1650–1760*. Acta Universitatis Upsaliensis, Studia Anglistica Upsaliensia 53. Uppsala, 1984; distributed by Almqvist and Wiksell International, Stockholm.

Pluhar, Werner S., trans. and ed. *Critique of Judgment*. By Immanuel Kant. Indianapolis: Hackett, 1987.

——. "How to Render *Zweckmäßigkeit* in Kant's Third Critique." In *Interpreting Kant*, edited by Moltke S. Gram, 85–98. Iowa City: University of Iowa Press, 1982.

Pocock, John G. A. *Ancient Constitution and the Feudal Law: A Study of English Historical Thought in the 17th Century*. A Reissue with a Retrospect. Cambridge: Cambridge University Press, 1987.

Pompa, Leon. *Vico: A Study of the "New Science."* 2nd ed. Cambridge: Cambridge University Press, 1990.

Poovey, Mary. *A History of the Modern Fact: Problems of Knowledge in the Sciences of Wealth and Society*. Chicago: University of Chicago Press, 1998.

Prichard, H. A. *Kant's Theory of Knowledge*. Oxford: Clarendon Press, 1909.

Reill, Peter Hanns. *The German Enlightenment and the Rise of Historicism*. Berkeley and Los Angeles: University of California Press, 1975.

Reiss, Timothy J. "The 'Concevoir' Motif in Descartes." In *La cohérence intérieure: Etudes sur la littérature française du XVIIe siècle présentées en hommage à Judd D. Hubert*, edited by Jacqueline van Baelen and David Lee Rubin, 203–22. Paris: Jean-Michel Place, 1977.

——. *The Discourse of Modernism*. Ithaca: Cornell University Press, 1985.

——. *Knowledge, Discovery, and Imagination in Early Modern Europe: The Rise of Aesthetic Rationalism*. Cambridge: Cambridge University Press, 1997.

——. "Montaigne and the Subject of Polity." In *Literary Theory/Renaissance Texts*, edited by Patricia Parker and David Quint, 115–49. Baltimore: Johns Hopkins University Press, 1986.

——. "Neo-Aristotle and Method: Between Zabarella and Descartes." In *Descartes' Natural Philosophy*, edited by Stephen Gaukroger, John Schuster, and John Sutton, 195–227. London: Routledge, 2000.

Rey, Alain, ed. *Dictionnaire historique de la langue française.* New ed. 2 vols. Paris: Dictionnaires le Robert, 1993.

Ricoeur, Paul. *Temps et récit.* Vol. 1. Paris: Seuil, 1983.

Roger, Jacques. "The Cartesian Model and Its Role in Eighteenth-Century 'Theory of the Earth.'" In *Problems of Cartesianism,* edited by Thomas M. Lennon, John M. Nicholas, and John W. Davis, 95–112. Kingston and Montreal: McGill-Queen's University Press, 1982.

Rogerson, Kenneth F. "The Meaning of Universal Validity in Kant's Aesthetics." *Journal of Aesthetics and Art Criticism* 40 (1982): 301–8.

Rollinson, Philip. *Classical Theories of Allegories and Christian Culture.* Pittsburgh: Duquesne University Press, 1981.

Rossi, Paolo. *The Dark Abyss of Time: The History of the Earth and the History of Nations from Hooke to Vico.* Translated by Lydia G. Cochrane. Chicago: University of Chicago Press, 1984.

Rotenstreich, Nathan. "Vico and Kant." In *Giambattista Vico's Science of Humanity,* edited by Giorgio Tagliacozzo and Donald Phillip Verene, 221–40. Baltimore: Johns Hopkins University Press, 1976.

Rubinoff, Lionel. "Vico and the Verification of Historical Interpretation." *Social Research* 43 (1976): 484–511.

Russo, John Paul. *Alexander Pope: Tradition and Identity.* Cambridge, Mass.: Harvard University Press, 1972.

Saint-Girons, Baldine. *Esthétiques du XVIIIe siècle.* Paris: Philippe Sers, 1990.

Schaeffer, John D. *Sensus Communis: Vico, Rhetoric, and the Limits of Relativism.* Durham, N.C.: Duke University Press, 1990.

Schaper, Eva. *Studies in Kant's Aesthetics.* Edinburgh: Edinburgh University Press, 1979.

Schüssler, Ingeborg. "Causalité et temporalité dans la *Critique de la raison pure* de Kant." *Archives de Philosophie* 44 (1981): 43–61.

Serres, Michel. *Les origines de la géométrie: Tiers livre des fondations.* N.p.: Flammarion, 1993.

Shapiro, Barbara J. *A Culture of Fact: England, 1550–1720.* Ithaca, N.Y.: Cornell University Press, 2000.

———. *Probability and Certainty in Seventeenth-Century England: A Study of the Relationships between Natural Science, Religion, History, Law, and Literature.* Princeton, N.J.: Princeton University Press, 1983.

Simonsuuri, Kirsti. *Homer's Original Genius: Eighteenth-Century Notions of the Early Greek Epic (1688–1798).* Cambridge: Cambridge University Press, 1979.

Smith, Wrynn. "Kant and the General Law of Causality." *Philosophical Studies* 32 (1977): 113–28.

Stam, James H. *Inquiries into the Origin of Language: The Fate of a Question.* New York: Harper and Row, 1976.

Starobinski, Jean. "Rousseau et l'origine des langues." In *Jean-Jacques Rousseau: La transparence et l'obstacle, suivi de sept essais sur Rousseau,* 356–79. Tel 6. Paris: Gallimard, 1971.

———. "Rousseau et la recherche des origines." In *Jean-Jacques Rousseau: La transparence et l'obstacle, suivi de sept essais sur Rousseau,* 319–29. Tel 6. Paris: Gallimard, 1971.

Stone, Harold Samuel. *Vico's Cultural History: The Production and Transmission of Ideas in Naples, 1685–1750.* Leiden: E. J. Brill, 1997.

Strawson, P. F. *The Bounds of Sense: An Essay on Kant's "Critique of Pure Reason."* London: Methuen, 1966.

Struever, Nancy. "Vico, Valla, and the Logic of Humanist Inquiry." In *Giambattista Vico's Science of Humanity,* edited by Giorgio Tagliacozzo and Donald Phillip Verene, 173–85. Baltimore: Johns Hopkins University Press.

Suchting, W. A. "Kant's Second Analogy of Experience." In *Kant Studies Today,* edited by Lewis White Beck, 322–40. La Salle, Ill.: Open Court, 1969.

Tagliacozzo, Giorgio, and Donald Phillip Verene, eds. *Giambattista Vico's Science of Humanity.* Baltimore: Johns Hopkins University Press, 1976.

Thompson, James. *Models of Value: Eighteenth-Century Political Economy and the Novel.* Durham, N.C.: Duke University Press, 1996.

Toulmin, Stephen, and June Goodfield. *The Discovery of Time.* Chicago: University of Chicago Press, 1982.

Van de Pitte, Frederick P. *Kant as Philosophical Anthropologist.* The Hague: Nijhoff, 1971.

Vaughn, Karen Iversen. *John Locke: Economist and Social Scientist.* Chicago: University of Chicago Press, 1980.

Verene, Donald Phillip. *The New Art of Autobiography: An Essay on the "Life of Giambattista Vico Written by Himself."* Oxford: Clarendon Press, 1991.

———. *Vico's Science of Imagination.* Ithaca, N.Y.: Cornell University Press, 1991.

———. "Vico's Science of Imaginative Universals and the Philosophy of Symbolic Forms." In *Giambattista Vico's Science of Humanity,* edited by Giorgio Tagliacozzo and Donald Phillip Verene, 295–317. Baltimore: Johns Hopkins University Press.

Weinsheimer, Joel C. *Eighteenth-Century Hermeneutics: Philosophy of Interpretation in England from Locke to Burke.* New Haven: Yale University Press, 1993.

Whitman, Jon. *Allegory: The Dynamics of an Ancient and Medieval Technique.* Cambridge, Mass.: Harvard University Press, 1987.

Williams, Bernard. "Introductory Essay." In *Meditations on First Philosophy: With Selections from the Objections and Replies,* by René Descartes, translated and edited by John Cottingham. Rev. ed. Cambridge: Cambridge University Press, 1996.

Woodmansee, Martha. "Genius and the Copyright: Economic and Legal Conditions of the Emergence of the 'Author.'" *Eighteenth-Century Studies* 17 (1984): 425–48.

Zagorin, Perez. "Vico's Theory of Knowledge: A Critique." *Philosophical Quarterly* 34 (1984): 15–30.

Zammito, John H. *The Genesis of Kant's "Critique of Judgment."* Chicago: University of Chicago Press, 1992.

INDEX

Addison, Joseph, 80
aesthetics as a form of knowledge, 5–13,
18, 129–30, 166
Affeldt, Steven G., 112n28
agriculture, 3, 121, 123–24, 129
Alembert, Jean Le Rond d', 68, 93
Alquié, Ferdinand, 26n20, 30
Aristotle, 7
association of ideas, 5, 68, 146
Condillac, 96–99
Kant, 13, 154–55, 159, 165
Aubignac, François-Hédelin, abbé d', 39
Auerbach, Erich, 57
Auroux, Sylvain, 61–62
autoarcheology, 6, 9, 48–49, 56–59, 95–96
autogenesis, 62, 86–88, 133. *See also* subject as source of knowledge

Bacon, Francis, 38, 52, 63–65, 117
Batteux, Charles, 10, 67–68, 90n28,
91–93
Baumgarten, Alexander, 4–7, 129
Aesthetica, 4, 6
Meditationes, 4–5
Metaphysica, 4–6
beauty, 4, 80–81, 155, 162–64
Becq, Annie, 8n14, 91n32
Bitbol-Hespériès, Annie, 25, 26n20
Blackwell, Thomas, 39–40
Bodin, Jean, 21–23
body as source of knowledge, 4–6, 34,
60–61, 83, 99
Boileau Despréaux, Nicolas, 74
Brittan, Gordon G., 135, 143, 144n20
Brodsky, Claudia J., 147n23
Brombert, Victor, 1, 173–74

Buffon, Georges Louis Leclerc, comte de,
3, 68, 92–93, 119, 133n4
"Discours sur le style," 92–93
Les époques de la nature, 3, 68
*Histoire naturelle, générale et partic-
ulière,* 3, 68
Burke, Peter, 40n16, 65
Butler, Judith, 25n19
Butts, Robert E., 136, 160

Cahné, Pierre-Alain, 31n33
Caponigri, A. Robert, 47n22
Cartesianism, 8, 34, 50–51, 53, 56, 63, 113
Cassirer, Ernst, 8n14
Castelvetro, Lodovico, 74
causality, 9–10, 19, 57, 94, 136, 139–64, 168
Cavaillé, Jean-Pierre, 23, 34
certainty, 6, 170–71. *See also* Descartes, René:
fiction; geometry; hypotheses
chaos, 17, 29, 60, 134, 138, 152
Chédin, Olivier, 165
childhood, 40, 61, 70, 72
Chouillet, Jacques, 31, 33
Clarke, Desmond M., 18
cogito, 56, 58, 61, 148
Collingwood, R. G., 47n22
conatus, 17, 60, 169
Condillac, Etienne, Bonnot de, 10–11,
66–68, 72, 76, 93–102
Descartes, 95
Locke, 68, 93, 95–97
Rousseau, 66–67, 97n9, 102
creation (God's), 15–19, 24–25, 28–30,
133. *See also* Kant, Immanuel:
Universal Natural History; origins
of the natural world

189

Dacier, Anne, 41–42
D'Alembert, Jean Le Rond, 68, 93
De Bolla, Peter, 122n51
demonstrability. *See* certainty; geometry; hypotheses
Derrida, Jacques, 108n22, 165
Descartes, René
  Discours de la méthode, 3, 16, 18, 23–24, 27–32, 34
  fable (*see* Descartes, René: fiction)
  facts, 8, 18–19, 24, 33
  fiction, 8, 15–18, 23–25, 30–34
  geometry, 15, 17, 21, 28, 33–34
  history, 17, 21–23, 32–33
  hypotheses, 16, 18, 24n18, 33
  Meditations, 19n6, 21, 31n32, 33, 34n40
  Le monde, 8, 15–19, 23–32
  natural philosophy (*see* Descartes, René: *Le monde*)
  origins, limits on the study of, 8, 15–23
  Principles of Philosophy, 16–18
  Rules for the Direction of the Mind, 20–21
  tableau (*see* Descartes, René: vision)
  Vico, 9, 17, 23n17, 34–35, 50–51, 53–54, 56, 63, 144n19
  vision, 8, 18, 26, 31–34
  See also Cartesianism
diachrony. *See* synchrony and diachrony
distance, 33, 68–69. *See also* painting; sight
Duchet, Michèle, 4n2
Duff, William, 10, 67, 81, 86–88, 91–92
Dumont, Louis, 7

Eagleton, Terry, 4, 169
Egypt, 38, 52, 54, 78, 108, 126–27
Eigentümlichkeit, 11, 67, 116–120, 125, 158. *See also* originality
Enlightenment epistemology, 2–13, 32–34, 66–70, 131–34, 150, 167, 173–74
eternity, 131, 137–38
euhemerism, 40, 54

facts, 8, 18–19, 24, 33, 58, 103, 111–12
fiction as source of knowledge, 6, 8, 15–18, 23–25, 30–35
Fisch, Max Harold, 56
Fontenelle, Bernard le Bovier de, 39

Genesis. *See* creation (God's)
genetic epistemology, 1–2, 10, 132, 148, 152–53, 167–73. *See also* Vico, Giambattista: genetic principle
genius, 73, 81–84, 88–89, 92, 115–18
  Kant, 12–13, 147, 154–65
  original genius, 11, 67, 69, 85–88, 114–18, 125–128, 157–61
geometry, 141n14, 169
  Descartes, 15, 17, 21, 28, 33–34
  Vico, 9, 34–35, 47, 50–52, 56–57, 63–65
  See also synchrony and diachrony
Gerard, Alexander, 10, 67, 88–91
Gerstenberg, Heinrich Wilhelm, 11, 115–16
giants, 51–52, 55, 59–63, 169
Gilson, Etienne, 28
Glanvill, Joseph, 94
Gould, Stephen Jay, 141
Gravina, Gian Vincenzo, 39–40
Greece, 126–27. *See also* Vico, Giambattista: "Discovery of the True Homer"

Hamann, Johann Georg, 115, 118
Hepp, Noémi, 36–37
Herder, Johann Gottfried, 11, 117–18
hieroglyphs, 38, 52, 108
historicism, 35, 55, 63–65, 97–102
history, knowability of, 9, 106–8, 111–113
  Descartes, 17, 21–23, 32–33
  Kant, "Conjectural Beginning of Human History," 168–69, 171
  See also historicism; primitivism; Vico, Giambattista: philology and philosophy
Hobbes, Thomas, 40, 50, 64
Homer, 10–12, 74, 77–79, 83–84, 92, 125–29. *See also* Vico, Giambattista: "Discovery of the True Homer"
Hutcheson, Francis, 80–81
Hutton, James, 141
hypotheses, 64, 103–6, 111, 134–37
  Descartes, 16, 18, 24n18, 33
  Kant, "Conjectural Beginning of Human History," 168–69, 171
  See also certainty

ignorance as condition of knowledge, 51–55, 60–62, 95–96, 99, 167–70
imagination, 4–6, 86–87, 89, 96, 155
  and memory, 58, 73, 99–101, 105n16
  See also memory

imitation, 5, 74–76, 81–85, 87–89, 91–93, 114–15, 161. *See also* originality
infinity, 19, 25–26, 131–33, 140
invention, 66, 79, 89, 91–92, 112, 116. *See also* imagination; memory

Johnson, Samuel, 81–82

Kant, Immanuel, 3, 12–13, 131–32
    analogies of experience (*see* Kant, Immanuel: Second Analogy)
    Anthropology, 149, 160–62
    association of ideas, 13, 154–55, 159, 165
    causality, 136, 139–64, 168
    "Conjectural Beginning of Human History," 168–69, 171
    Critique of Judgment, 147–70, 173
    Critique of Practical Reason, 147
    Critique of Pure Reason, 135–36, 140–50, 163, 165, 170, 172–73
    exemplariness, 154–62
    freedom, 130, 146–50, 154–65, 171
    genius, 12–13, 147, 154–65
    mechanistic explanations, 131–34, 137–40, 149–54, 164
    originality, 12–13, 153–62, 166
    permanence, 139–40, 146, 148, 155, 157–58, 165
    purposiveness, 149–54, 162–64, 168
    regress, 136, 149–54, 163, 171–72
    Rousseau, 134, 171
    Second Analogy, 143–47, 151
    serialization, 20n8, 144–47, 171–72
    Universal Natural History, 131–40, 164, 172
    Vico, 134, 139–42, 144n19, 146–48, 167–73
Kelley, Donald R., 34, 51n26, 65
knowledge, human, 5–6, 26, 67, 70, 95, 99, 167–69. *See also* association of ideas; ignorance as condition of knowledge; origins of ideas; subject as source of knowledge

labor, 11, 84, 106–7, 111, 114, 119–25
Lacan, Jacques, 61, 169
Lachterman, David Rapport, 49n21, 63, 65n48
La Harpe, Jean-François de, 114n32
La Motte, Antoine Houdar de, 41–42
language, 71–72, 96–102, 108–113, 162
    and commerce, 75–77, 108

Smith, "Considerations concerning the First Formation of Languages," 76n10, 120, 124
Vico, 48, 57, 60, 109–110
    See also writing
Leibniz, Gottfried Wilhelm von, 147
Le Roy, Loys, 17, 21–23
Lessing, Gotthold Ephraim, 115
Lilla, Mark, 65
Linearity. *See* time, linear
Locke, John, 67–75, 90, 95–97, 120–21, 122n50, 143
    An Essay concerning Human Understanding, 70–73, 75, 95, 132, 143, 172
    "historical method," 3, 9, 67, 70–71, 95, 142
    Two Treatises of Government, 71n4, 121
Lyotard, Jean-François, 151n27, 165

Mack, Maynard, 78
Macmillan, R. A. C., 168
Magne, Bernard, 90n28
Makkreel, Rudolf, 157–58n33, 170
Marmontel, Jean Francois, 114n32
mathematics. *See* geometry
Mazzotta, Giuseppe, 36n2, 51n26
mechanism. *See* Kant, Immanuel: mechanistic explanations
Meinecke, Friedrich, 40n16, 59
memory, 17, 19–21, 71, 96–101, 105, 111–13. *See also* imagination
mind. *See* association of ideas; ignorance as condition of knowledge; origins of ideas; subject as source of knowledge; Vico, Giambattista: "modifications of the human mind"
Mortier, Roland, 113
Mosaic account. *See* origins of the natural world

Nancy, Jean-Luc, 30, 34
natural history. *See* origins of the natural world
nature, 62, 91–94, 103, 106–7, 126, 149–59, 162–64. *See also* Descartes, René: *Le monde*; imitation; Kant, Immanuel: *Universal Natural History*; origins of the natural world; Smith, Adam: labor theory of value
Newton, Isaac, 135–37, 144n20
novelty, 80, 86–87

original genius. *See* genius
originality, 6–7, 10, 37n5, 69, 73–74,
    78–92, 101
    German criticism (1750s–70s),
        113–20
    Kant, 12–13, 153–62, 166
    See also imitation; *Eigentümlichkeit*;
        Wood, Robert
origins, epistemological status of. *See*
    genetic epistemology
origins of ideas, 70–72, 94–99
origins of languages, 71, 96–102,
    109–112. *See also* Smith, Adam:
    "Considerations concerning the
    First Formation of Languages"
origins of the natural world, 12, 15,
    24–25, 31–33, 131–39. *See also* cre-
    ation (God's); Descartes, René, *Le
    monde*; Kant, Immanuel: *Universal
    Natural History*
origins of societies, 100–14. *See also* his-
    toricism; history

painting, 32, 69, 75, 114–15, 125–29
    of language, 77, 100, 108
    See also Descartes, René: vision; dis-
        tance; sight
Pluhar, Werner S., 151n27, 154n29
Pocock, John G. A., 71n4
poetry, 87, 115, 120, 129, 160. *See also*
    Vico, Giambattista: "Discovery of
    the True Homer"; Vico, Giambat-
    tista: poetic wisdom
Pompa, Leon, 59n37, 47n22, 65n48
Pope, Alexander, 72–81, 84, 119, 162
    "Essay on Criticism," 73–75, 77
    "[On the Origin of Letters]," 75–77
    "Preface to the Iliad," 77–79
    "Preface to the Works of Shake-
        spear," 78–80
primal scene, 51–52, 55, 59–63, 169
primitivism, 3, 11, 39–40, 87–88, 120–30
    and originality, 10, 49, 87–88, 161–62
probability. *See* certainty; verisimilitude
property, 82–85, 120–21

Quarrel between the Ancients and the
    Moderns, 38–44, 52–54, 82–83,
    100–1, 115, 162. *See also* Egypt;
    Greece; Homer; imitation

regress, 19
    Kant, 136, 149–54, 163, 171–72

Reiss, Timothy J., 16n1, 19n6, 21n12, 27
Rogerson, Kenneth F., 156
Rossi, Paolo, 29–30, 60n39
Rotenstreich, Nathan, 144n19
Rousseau, Jean-Jacques, 11, 102–14
    Confessions, 113
    Discourse on the Origins of Inequality,
        33, 50, 58, 102–6, 109n24, 124, 134
    Essay on the Origin of Languages,
        60n39, 76, 106–12
    Julie, or the New Heloise, 107
    Letter to M. d'Alembert, 110
    Smith, 120, 123n52, 124
    Vico, 58, 60n39, 107n20, 109–13
Russo, John Paul, 78

Shaftesbury, 3rd Earl of (Anthony Ash-
    ley Cooper), 119–20
Shakespeare, 10, 78–80, 116
sight, 71, 100–4, 111, 129. *See also*
    Descartes, René: vision; distance;
    imagination; painting
Smith, Adam, 11, 66–68, 119–25
    "Considerations concerning the First
        Formation of Languages," 76n10,
        120, 124
    "On Historicall Composition,"
        99n11
    labor theory of value, 11, 119–25
    Lectures on Rhetoric and Belles Lettres,
        99n11, 119–20, 124
    "Letter to the *Edinburgh Review*,"
        124n55
    Rousseau, 120, 123n52, 124
    Vico, 120
    Wealth of Nations, 121–25
Starobinski, Jean, 50n24, 103,
    112nn28–29
Strawson, P. F., 141, 145n21, 172
style, 3, 92–93, 119–20
subject as source of knowledge, 27,
    29n26, 34, 98–99, 106, 112–13. *See
    also* autoarcheology; autogenesis;
    body as source of knowledge;
    ignorance as condition of knowl-
    edge; originality
sublime, 155, 157–59, 162, 165
Sulzer, Johann Georg, 116
synchrony and diachrony, 2–3, 31–34,
    66–68, 70, 95–96, 133–34. *See also*
    geometry; historicism; history;
    Vico, Giambattista: philology and
    philosophy

time, linear, 104–8, 138. *See also* Kant, Immanuel: causality

Verdet, Jean-Pierre, 25
Verene, Donald Phillip, 42, 51n26, 112n29
verisimilitude, 28–30, 32
Vico, Giambattista
  allegory, 37–38, 40–42, 46–47
  Autobiography, 39n10, 58–59
  axioms, 9, 34–35, 47, 50–52, 56–57
  Baumgarten, 6n9
  Descartes, 9, 17, 23n17, 34–35, 53–54, 56, 63, 144n19
  "Discovery of the True Homer," 36–50, 54–55
  genetic principle, 9, 48, 55–56
  geometry, 35, 50, 63–65
  hermeneutics, 9, 44–55, 167–68
  ignorance, 51–55, 60–62, 167–70
  "Inaugural Orations," 36
  Kant, 134, 139–42, 144n19, 146–48, 167–73
  language, 48, 57, 60, 109–110
  "modifications of the human mind," 48–49, 56–59
  New Science, 9, 35–36, 40, 42–65, 112–13, 142, 168–71
  On the Most Ancient Wisdom of the Italians, 36, 53n28, 62, 64, 168
  On the Study Methods of Our Time, 36, 53, 57, 63
  philology and philosophy, 9, 47–50, 64–65
  poetic wisdom, 6n9, 36, 43–50, 63–64
  primal scene, 51–52, 55, 59–63, 169
  Rousseau, 58, 60n39, 107n20, 109–13
  Smith, 120
Virgil, 127–28
vraisemblance, 28–30, 32

Weinsheimer, Joel C., 70
Williams, Bernard, 31n32
Winckelmann, Johann Joachim, 114–15
Wood, Robert, 11–12, 125–29
writing, 75–76, 97, 100, 108, 110
  hieroglyphs, 38, 52, 108
  See also language

Young, Edward, 10–11, 81–88, 114, 116–18

Zabarella, Jacopo, 19n6

Catherine Labio is associate professor of comparative literature and French at Yale University. She has published articles on the history of the novel and the history of ideas in seventeenth- and eighteenth-century Europe and is the editor of *Belgian Memories* (*Yale French Studies* 102). She is working on a book-length project on literature and economics.